T0265501

REINVENTING

— THE —

SUPPLY CHAIN

REINVENTING

—— THE ——

SUPPLY CHAIN

A 21ST-CENTURY
COVENANT WITH AMERICA

JACK BUFFINGTON

Georgetown University Press / Washington, DC

Library of Congress Cataloging-in-Publication Data

Names: Buffington, Jack, author.
Title: Reinventing the supply chain : a 21st-century covenant with America / Jack Buffington.
Description: Washington, DC : Georgetown University Press, 2023. |
Includes bibliographical references and index.
Identifiers: LCCN 2022005423 (print) | LCCN 2022005424 (ebook) |
ISBN 9781647122997 (hardcover) | ISBN 9781647123000 (ebook)
Subjects: LCSH: Business logistics. | Business logistics—United States.
Classification: LCC HD38.5 .B84 2023 (print) | LCC HD38.5 (ebook)
| DDC 658.500973—dc23/eng/20220509
LC record available at https://lccn.loc.gov/2022005423
LC ebook record available at https://lccn.loc.gov/2022005424

∞ This paper meets the requirements of ANSI/NISO Z39.48-1992 (Permanence of Paper).

24 23   9 8 7 6 5 4 3 2 First printing

Printed in the United States of America

Cover design by Faceout Studio, Paul Nielsen
Interior design by Paul Hotvedt

CONTENTS

INTRODUCTION

The global supply chain is something most consumers take for granted. We order something today, and almost magically it arrives at our doorstep from a local distribution center the next day, with free shipping. However, we do not understand the raw materials and energy required to make and ship the product or the source country of origin. It was only when the coronavirus pandemic disrupted the global supply chain system in the spring of 2020 that consumers began to pay attention to the weaknesses in the system. Even business leaders and supply chain executives, who may be experts in their industries or sectors, sometimes lack a global perspective on the system. *Reinventing the Supply Chain* takes a "wide-angle lens" approach to tell the story of how our modern supply chains work, how they deliver goods to us seamlessly and inexpensively, why the global supply chain network needs to evolve continuously to be effective, and what changes we need to make for a better future.

When we take the time to think about it, we can appreciate how these global supply chains, in aggregate, constitute some of the most important inventions in human history. In 1990, 5.2 billion people inhabited the earth, with 1.9 billion, or approximately 36 percent, living in poverty, mainly in Asia and Africa. By 2019 the world population had grown by 45 percent to 7.5 billion; at the same time, there was a reduction in the number of people living in extreme poverty, down to 600 million. During this period extreme poverty in the world fell from 36.2 percent to 8.6 percent, with 60 percent of the improvement happening in China alone.[1] However, the system that has delivered some of the most significant accomplishments in human history is also insufficient to meet the economic and societal needs of the 21st century. Recent examples include an inability to provide life-saving medicine, supplies, and technologies during the global COVID-19 pandemic and a failure to manage natural resources, address significant socioeconomic inequality across the planet and within communities, and ameliorate the growing environmental crisis of climate change.

What forecaster from the 20th century would have predicted such a remarkable reduction in poverty, numbering in the hundreds of millions if not a billion, within the last few decades? Could this same clairvoyant have predicted the frequency and severity of today's unprecedented challenges in the environment, pandemics, increasing reliance and dependence on technologies, global conflicts, and other seemingly far-fetched scenarios? The global supply chain drives a massive logistics system, a $9.8 trillion business enterprise that can ship material or products anywhere in the world.[2] One of the world's largest ocean shipping companies, Maersk, headquartered in Denmark, owns 737 ships, many as large as a skyscraper on its side, and has an annual global capacity of 4.3 million containers, owning 17 percent of the world market share.[3] These massively scaled delivery mechanisms hide in plain sight until disruptions impact our daily lives, as evident through the global shipping crisis. Because these supply chains have struggled to manage the current state of volatilities, the field is quickly becoming a board-level topic for companies, with 93 percent aspiring to make their systems more resilient to challenges and responsive to future events like what we have faced during the pandemic.[4] Supply chain professionals are more relevant than ever; ten years ago the topic of supply chain management came up in corporate earnings calls slightly more than 30 percent of the time; in 2021 this number rose to almost 70 percent, and continues to grow.[5]

How can such apparent contradictions of success and failure exist within the same system? When I answer this question, I reply that while supply chain management is a problem-solving field, we focus solely on how the problem is defined, which can often lead to solving one problem while inadvertently creating another. This paradox can be a maddening juxtaposition, for why is it rational to produce nearly all the world's personal protective equipment in a few factories in the world to increase economies of scale while at the same time not being able to support the health and safety needs for material during a global pandemic? The war between Russia and Ukraine has led to similar challenges related to food, energy, and other critical commodities within the global economy. The answer is that our supply chains are optimized to meet private market objectives rather than consider the resiliency needed to ensure the public good in a time of crisis. For example, when a lack of demand exists in ranching and agriculture, it becomes financially optimal to pour milk down the drain, turn crops over in the fields, and euthanize cattle at the ranch rather than providing these foodstuffs to the world hungry. Wasting food may be ethically wrong, but market efficiency delivers a scalable, efficient system that provides the highest service levels and lowest cost at the most significant volumes to consumers, leading to higher profitability.

Deindustrialization and Its Fallouts

Before the COVID-19 pandemic, these supply chains showed their inherent weaknesses in handling the complexities of a growing and technologically advanced marketplace. The pandemic was more of a tipping point than a root cause of the problem.

The pandemic's impact on the global economy has undoubtedly been devastating, with the global gross domestic product initially falling by approximately 7–8 percent, an unprecedented result for over a century, if not longer.[6] It is convenient for the media to jump on the bandwagon in blaming the pandemic for what's happening, concluding that these supply chain weaknesses are only a temporary setback that will run its course once the virus is under control. I will show that this point of view lacks a deeper understanding of the supply chain's fundamental weaknesses that have existed for decades. These weaknesses stem from a lack of a corresponding strategy in the United States to address the problems resulting from deindustrialization, a process that has left too many Americans behind. As a kid growing up in Baltimore, Maryland, in the 1970s and 1980s, I could not tell you what a supply chain was, but I knew of its impact on my relatives who lost their stable, middle-class, blue-collar jobs and lifestyles working at the Bethlehem Steel mill at Sparrows Point and other local factories. What happened in Baltimore played out in various cities across the nation. As recently as 1980, Flint, Michigan, had the highest median income for workers under thirty-five.[7]

Deindustrialization in America and elsewhere may be one of the worst-kept secrets, often ignored yet appearing in the ugliest manners, unaddressed and fermenting over decades. Despite the title of Thomas Friedman's acclaimed, bestselling 2005 book *The World Is Flat*, it is not: instead, the world is a spiky place, nation by nation and even community by community, with global supply chains choosing winners and losers and unintentionally leaving others behind. We think of this as a uniquely American problem. But it is also the case in Germany, France, the United Kingdom, and even China, a nation of 1.4 billion that still has hundreds of millions living in poverty. Once-prosperous crown jewels of America's industrial yesteryear have morphed into boneyards of steel and textile mills and automobile factories—infamous museums to the global supply chain. In China, factories and even entire cities have been abandoned. Deindustrialization has become an international problem.

The challenge in today's 21st-century supply chain competition must involve leadership in technology to achieve a fast-paced, innovation-driven engine to solve problems and an emphasis on training, education, and achieving societal and environmental balance within communities. Supply chains must incentivize across public and private sector objectives rather than an out-of-balance path toward one and away from the other. The evidence demonstrates that a short-term view of profit and growth required of publicly traded companies that often focus on markets through consumer obsession and maximization of shareholder value is not sustainable. In my career, I have worked in manufacturing and supply chain for a company that paid its hourly employees a stable wage to support a middle-class lifestyle while returning adequate profits to its shareholders. This strategy was in no way contradictory to meeting market objectives, and I was responsible for meeting financial targets while at the same time treating our workers with respect and admiration. When I did not hit my financial targets, I was responsible for following a structured, problem-solving exercise to address the issues and develop solutions rather than focusing on the symptoms that might have been easier to remedy through stopgap measures like outsourcing to lower-paid workers. Indeed, I sometimes had to make short-term, short-sighted decisions that focused more on quarterly earnings and stock market performance than the company's longer-term viability and its employees. A problem-solving supply chain system must focus on all stakeholders, including shareholders, workers, suppliers, and the community. Supply chains must meet these objectives by being rebalanced to better meet the needs in the long term for all stakeholders.

Today's short-term financial markets and their impact on supply chains focus on benefiting the shareholder above all, asserting that everything else will naturally fall into place if its needs are met. Theoretically, this makes sense, but the benefits are skewed primarily to shareholders and consumers, leading to waste, inefficiency, and other stakeholders viewed as externalities, as unimportant. These shortcomings spurred the noted supply chain quality expert W. Edwards Deming to assert that US manufacturing methods led to America being "the most underdeveloped country in the world."[8] Deming's 1984 statement was not meant to suggest that the US economy was poorer or less advanced than other nations but rather that unintended waste of natural and human resources was occurring through this myopic focus on short-term and less rational objectives. Deming was an engineer who intended to measure quality principles and reduce waste, especially the underutilization of the talents of the American workforce. He saw the danger of obsessing over quarterly profits, which led to the eventual commoditization of labor markets to the lowest-cost country rather than focusing on value, quality fundamentals, process improvements, and waste reduction. When US automakers declined Deming's offer to apply these quality principles during the 1950s and 1960s, he worked with Japanese companies instead, directly fostering the renaissance of its industries—most notably through the development of the Toyota Production System, known as the standard-bearer of best practices today. When Deming returned to America, he spoke of the crisis that had been (and still is) festering for decades, resulting in the redeployment of capital investment away from the United States to more innovative and lower-cost nations. Sadly, Deming's message was ignored and is primarily dismissed today. Too many businesses focus more on abstract financial formulas than on commonsense, structured problem solving. In business and business school, structured problem solving has become a lost art, overtaken by unstructured brainstorming, creativity, and overcomplexity.

Process controls, statistical analysis, industrial engineering, and quality circles were techniques that built the United States into an industrial power in the early 20th century and led to its industrial superiority during World War II. After the end of the war, America was the only economic superpower standing while the rest of the developed world was mainly in disarray; in 1960, the United States accounted for 40 percent of the world's gross domestic product; today its share is slightly less than 16 percent.[9] Accounting for less than 5 percent of the world's population, the United States is still disproportionately wealthy but no longer has the same dominant world position in manufacturing capacity and techniques. It was this lack of discipline—a need to focus on reducing waste and improving quality—that Deming discussed with the Ford Motor Company in 1981 when he returned from Japan. The average hourly wage in the United States since the 1960s has risen around 2–3 percent per year but from a purchasing power standpoint has been flat, showing no growth at all.[10] Segmenting the aggregate data into worker groups shows the differences: from 1980 to 2020, hourly worker's wages for the top 5 percent grew by 63.2 percent, by 15.1 percent for the 50th percentile, and only 3.3 percent for the bottom 10 percent of the workforce.[11] These data show the effects of deindustrialization on the middle-class, blue-collar workforce and its loss in purchasing power since the 20th century after a devastating blow to their wages and lifestyle.

A significant fallout from deindustrialization has impacted the US education system. The United States continues to lose momentum in the standing of its educational system compared to other nations, particularly in the crucial areas of science, technology, engineering, and math (STEM) that will be increasingly important, especially in manufacturing and supply chain. Yet in the United States, federal spending on education, infrastructure, and scientific research fell from approximately 2.5 percent of gross domestic product in 1980 to 1.5 percent today.[12] Recently there has been a conscious effort to increase spending in education, but there is a need to improve competitiveness in strategy for these increases in funding to succeed. Out of seventy-one nations, the United States ranks 38th in math and 24th in science in K–12 education, according to the Programme for International Student Assessment.[13] The United States dominates in higher education, housing fifteen of the top twenty universities in a 2022 *US News and World Report* ranking, but is falling behind in its K–12 educational system, especially in urban and rural communities.[14] A growing digital divide is evidence that an increase in spending without a pivot in strategy will lead to a lack of progress, something that had been the case since the deindustrialization of the US economy.

Over the past decades, a remarkable convergence has occurred of Western knowledge and Asian manufacturing muscle to fuel the hyperglobalization of the supply chain system.[15] Yet developing nations like China are more interested in becoming an equal partner or even the global leader rather than serving only as a source of low-cost labor in manufacturing cheap goods. After the impact of the COVID-19 pandemic, there is potential for seismic shifts in the global economy to serve as a wake-up call in the United States to properly understand the global supply chain rather than assume that America is solely a knowledge-based economy and that industry no longer matters. Our ancestors would be shocked and probably even horrified if they knew how little today's American consumer understands and is involved in producing and distributing life's staples such as food, medicine, shelter, clothing, and other purchases that we take for granted. This convenience is mainly a blessing but also a curse. Without directly participating in the production of most of our clothing, medicine, and electronics, Americans are becoming disconnected from the design and engineering of the future of the 21st-century supply chain. As has been the case for decades, supply chain leaders are rewarded by focusing primarily on the needs and desires of the customer, even at the expense of the worker. Americans must examine whether it remains viable to be so disconnected from their supply chains, believing that industry is not relevant to a nation in a postindustrial society.

Becoming more conscious of the supply chain system offers many benefits to Americans, not just as consumers but as workers and citizens, including mitigating the impact of economic activity on the planet. It seems illogical that the same supply chain system capable of producing 1.5 billion plastic water bottles in a day to provide clean, safe drinking water to distressed communities also enables 32 percent of all plastic packaging to flow into the ocean, creating an environmental catastrophe.[16] It shouldn't seem plausible that a company like Amazon can use predictive analytics to know what its Prime customers want before they order, but that same supply chain system cannot plan and execute an effective health care supply chain during the grip of a global pandemic. In the current outdated model, Americans are forced to choose between outsourcing pharmaceutical production to overseas factories that may not be effectively regulated to produce generic drugs or risk not being able to afford these medications, putting their lives at risk in possibly either case. The most significant challenge we face in this direction is not whether these changes are technically viable (because innovation will find the answers) but instead whether we view it as a priority to enable these systems to work more effectively in balance. The most critical question is whether Americans can sacrifice and focus on systemic change for a longer-term future.

Fear of a Global Planet

According to a recent Pew study, Americans find it challenging to define the impact of globalization on their daily lives. Many blue-collar workers feel swept up, a phenomenon where there are clear winners and losers outside of a person's span of control.[17] It is difficult to disagree with this sentiment, given that just a little over half (53 percent) of what Americans consume is made in the United States, and the total imported rises significantly when the components of an end product are calculated.[18] For example, as of 2020, Proctor & Gamble had 382 suppliers in China alone, accounting for 9,000 materials in over 17,000 products.[19] From the 1960s to today, global supply chains have grown from 37 percent to 50 percent of total trade, and are a much higher percentage when raw materials and components are factored into the equation.[20]

Because these global supply chains are so complex, and most citizens are too busy in their personal and professional lives to take the time to learn about them, most people lack more than a passing understanding of the subject. Yet when any effort to track the flow of goods is undertaken, it is challenging. During the pandemic, I tasked undergraduate and graduate students to document the material flow of these supply chain systems for specific critical products, such as pharmaceuticals and personal protective equipment, to help them understand the global flow of these goods. Despite decent data sources, persistent efforts, and legitimate contacts in industry, their understanding of these products' origins and material flow was limited at best. The sourcing of raw materials, components, and finished goods is so complex and fluid that most manufacturers and suppliers do not know the origin of material beyond their supplier relationships in the supply chain. The difficulty in tracking materials is a significant problem for governmental agencies responsible for protecting citizens, such as the US Food and Drug Administration for America's pharmaceutical supply. If the national regulatory bodies responsible for safety cannot track the material flow of the global supply chain with their resources and responsibilities, how can average Americans feel safe with the food they eat, the medicine they take, and other intimate encounters with globalization? As the scale and scope of goods imported to the United States continue to grow without a good way to track them to the end consumer, these questions are worth asking. Global ocean shipping has a capacity of 20 million standard shipping containers that transact 200 million times a year, with over 2 million containers entering the United States every month and growing.[21] The massive scale of these global transactions is impossible to control, including for safety and homeland security. Another example of the scale and scope of materials that flow around the world is the approximately 380 million tons of plastic that permeate in a variety of forms and product types and a worldwide growth rate of roughly 8 percent, with an 8 percent recycling rate that is barely keeping pace, from a material flow standpoint.[22] A near-infinite number of permutations of plastic—starting as raw materials, converting to polymers, and ultimately finished products—is imported and exported around the world in a manner that isn't regulated and is impossible to manage from a sustainability standpoint. The lack of sufficient controls in the global supply chain related to plastic is a primary reason why 6 million tons escape into the ocean every year. By the year 2050 there will be more plastic in the sea than fish.[23] A lack of global control and management of plastic has led to an increase in synthetic materials on our bodies and other close encounters that cannot be investigated. These are just a few significant examples of how these global supply chains have become so large and complex that they are beyond any nation's or regulatory body's ability to control. Since these systems are often multinational, there are questions of whether governance would be possible across a global model.

The Achilles's heel of the supply chain was on full display in 2020 in the health care meltdown that happened across the planet when nations could not source enough masks, gowns, and cleaning supplies to fight the emerging COVID-19 pandemic. A 2020 study led by an organization called Get Us PPE surveyed 978 hospital facilities and found critical protective gear like N95 masks, surgical masks, gloves, disinfecting wipes, and other items to be sometimes entirely out of stock or often with less than one week of inventory in the middle of the health crisis; even two years after the start of the pandemic, approximately 70 percent of hospitals have fewer than seven days of inventory of critical materials.[24] The meltdown was a failure point from a health and safety standpoint and a financial hardship, with suppliers raising prices at a time when hospitals had lost their most profitable source of revenue—elective surgery—due to the pandemic. These economic hardships led to the forced furloughing of critical staff, further exacerbating the crisis. A spiraling out of control of the health care and hospital supply chain is an example of the impact of the pandemic as the tipping point, but it was not the root cause of the problem. Instead, the industry's lack of structured problem solving focused on data and analytics prevents the supply chain from functioning as needed for hospitals to provide critical aspects of patient care.

Another interesting dynamic of today's global supply chain is the burden imposed on America's unappreciated workforce, such as nurses, bus drivers, truck drivers, delivery drivers, retail employees, manufacturing and warehouse workers, and teachers compared to the rest of the population, especially during the COVID-19 pandemic. When many white-collar workers could shelter in place and work in their homes through Zoom teleconferences, these essential workers had to keep the nation operating, almost always at a lower pay scale than those who were safely at home. Finding workers for these essential roles is difficult, if not impossible, even as wages and benefits escalate to higher levels. Labor challenges involving our most essential workers are symptoms of the lack of structured problem solving focusing on the workforce, not just the consumer, in a supply chain system. Back in the golden age of manufacturing, workers' rights were promoted as a critical element of morale and productivity, as shown in the Toyota Production System, developed by its legendary leader Sakichi Toyoda. A focus on worker morale, safety, and empowerment was a function of the overall calculus rather than the commoditization of the employee through a global supply chain of low wages. Yet, during the 1960s and into the 1970s and 1980s, the trend moved away from quality circles and industrial engineering; instead, the focus was on inducing consumption through understanding the human psyche (psychology and marketing), humanism in the management discipline, and shareholder wealth via the stock market. It was not until I worked for a company in manufacturing that I was taught the principles of Deming, the Toyota Production System, and others, which begin with a focus on the safety and morale of its workforce. I learned that as much as I thought I was fearful of a global planet before, I had misunderstood where the problems lie and how to fix them by doing things the right way and including the workforce as part of the process. I realized that globalization was the symptom of a much more significant problem that could only be solved through these supply chain principles.

Supply Chain Super-Lubricants and Glue

Contrary to popular misconception, supply chain management is more of a technical field than a general business field. In reality, it is a STEM field more so than marketing, management, or finance. Its origins arose due to the discovery, processing, and use of fossil fuels, which led to the Second Industrial Revolution. Before the Second Industrial Revolution, the energy source to create economic progress was restricted almost entirely to human- and animal-driven activities rather than fossil fuels. Nate Hagens, an economist who has studied the role of oil in economic activity, determined that one barrel of oil has about 5.8 million British thermal units (BTUs) of energy, giving the barrel of oil an equivalence of 7,733 hours of energy output of a trained athlete. At an average hourly rate of $24/hour, the athlete's work would cost about $188,000, while the oil is conservatively priced at $100 a barrel, making the cost of the athlete completing the work 1,880 times that of the oil.[25] Likewise, gasoline has a power density five thousand times greater than wood and two hundred times more efficient than concentrated solar energy. There is a clear cause and effect for how the discovery and processing of fossil fuels in the middle of the 19th century enabled economic growth to take off through these supply chains. It was this super-lubricant that empowered economic growth, reduced global poverty, and created a modern way of life, notwithstanding that overreliance on it has put our planet in jeopardy.

Further innovations driven by the STEM fields would enable supply chains by creating new materials for new products. According to the US Energy Information Association, approximately 7 percent of fossil fuels account for noncombustion in products, such as plastics, asphalt, fertilizers, and additives such as coal tar for skin treatment products.[26] These petroleum-based products are everywhere in our lives, including pharmaceuticals, cosmetics, textiles, medical prosthetics, and even human consumables such as toothpaste and chewing gum. Without question, this era of economic enlightenment has only been possible through this super-lubricant of the Second Industrial Revolution, fossil fuels. By deploying capital in supply chains and with the advancements in STEM, fossil fuel development transitioned our economic activity from animal to machine driven and developed materials to reshape our organic world to a synthetic one.

Before supply chains there were only markets, which were limited, largely manual and unstructured processes of numerous one-off relationships. The key parties in this model were often powerful mercantilists who owned the land and resources, hoarding capital for their benefit rather than using it for a more significant percentage of the population. In *The Wealth of Nations* economist Adam Smith advocated for capitalism, an open system rather than the closed system of mercantilism, to unleash the capital and multiply its benefit to society. Smith viewed capital as a lightning rod for economic growth rather than an impediment when hoarded by the wealthy and powerful. Achieving economic growth required new structures and organizations to liberate markets from mercantilists who acted like feudal lords receiving their land rents from the masses. Henry Ford's Model T factory at River Rouge, Michigan, was an early example. Ford's factory required new people and process structures to scale the volume of automotive production to a high level of quality, standardization, and timely process. Through a streamlining and rationalization of the inbound and outbound logistics and the manufacturing assembly process, Ford revolutionized the mass production process in America, leading to a balanced supply chain of public and private benefit through a superior approach to management. The use of standards and processes was a game changer in the industrial era, leading to an exponential growth pattern for manufacturing, the reduction of lead times for logistics, and the enablement of the American workforce.

These industrial engineering–led systems were transformations through effective use of people, processes, and technologies to balance supply and demand in a marketplace, a concept founded in the STEM fields. Most historical accounts of the Second Industrial Revolution focus on energy, capital, and technology as the most crucial factors for industrial growth but fail to mention the importance of organization, information, and management in this era. A professional working class separate from the owners, known as management, would operate these work processes and capital structures, such as a railroad, to optimize the benefits across the stakeholders. With oil as the catalyst and organization and systems as the glue, a new covenant was created to enable businesses to flourish in a manner that was more balanced across production and consumption, seeking to optimize the two as best as possible across all stakeholders—owners, workers, and citizens. Balance was always an aspiration before the Industrial Revolution, as there was always more demand than supply. A balance of supply and demand would then become possible as production capacity increased due to available energy, emerging technology, and a well-organized workforce. To effectively bring together supply and demand in this new model, organization and information were essential; it was the glue to bind the interests of the public and private sectors, where both would succeed by benefiting the other. The supply chain glue worked for the most part as workers' rights were improving (but not greatly), production capacity was soaring, and shareholders and consumers were benefitting. A focus on structure and process has been perhaps the least understood element of the economic success that has taken shape over the past century.

Nobody should confuse Henry Ford's manufacturing and supply chain efforts as serving some higher-level purpose for the people. Neither should it matter because this new covenant succeeded in offering higher wages and benefits to create a more substantial middle class. At the same time, the owners made more money. Improvements in industrial engineering and supply chain management let Ford cut the cost of a car from $950 in 1909 to $295 in 1923 while offering employees a wage of $5 a day for an eight-hour shift versus the earlier standard of $2.25 for a nine-hour shift. By providing his workers a higher, more stable labor wage, Ford improved the quality of its cars and the productivity of its workers, leading to an exponential increase in cars sold from 79,000 in 1912 to 1.3 million in 1921. During Henry Ford's era, pay of $2.25 a day was a good wage, but the work on an assembly line was difficult and led to an enormous amount of turnover; 52,000 workers were hired over the course of a year to run an operation that needed only 14,000.[27] Employee turnover is very costly in terms of training expense, downtime, and quality issues, so increasing wages to increase productivity and quality is cost-beneficial. Ford became an innovator not necessarily for his love and respect for his employees but instead for using rational, empirical methods to develop people, processes, and technologies to achieve greater sustainability in his business through the use of organization and information. In the process, he and other captains of industry delivered significant benefits to society, unintended or not. It was in their individual best interests because they were the owners of the businesses, in contrast to today's public stock ownership model that bifurcates the owner from the investor.

The term "organization" meant something different in the early 20th century than it does today. Then, its purpose was to foster balance, rationality, and structured processes to solve problems within a growing industrial model. It was an organization of work processes using statistical techniques perfected by engineers such as W. Edwards Deming to achieve remarkable breakthroughs in production efficiency during World War II. Peter Drucker notes that while "organization" is today a standard term, it was essentially not used until after World War II, when it became a distinct species.[28] The goal for the organization in a business is to optimize capital, labor, and technology to balance supply and demand, not in the structural, bureaucratic sense that it is often used today. The organization was necessary to standardize processes to achieve efficiencies in an industrial setting since prior production consisted mainly of individual artisans who produced based on skill versus process. An individualized artisan model was no longer possible, given the factory's pace, mechanization, and the scale required. A highly skilled worker performing production tasks at a slower pace and low volume was no match for a moderately skilled factory worker completing compartmentalized and repeatable processes alongside a mechanical industrial production line at greater efficiency and scale.

In 1911 Frederick Taylor's scientific management theory sought to improve the efficiency of the end-to-end operation, resulting in a system that benefited the worker by offering a higher wage through increasing efficiency and reducing waste. The labor unions protested, viciously attacking Taylor and his techniques, calling them inhumane and alleging that his system treated the workers like machines. It was not an entirely untrue statement, given that the goal was for the workforce to coexist with mechanization rather than to work separate and distinct from it. Until his dying day, Taylor held steadfast to his belief that the goal of his methods was to increase the salaries of the worker. His writings show that he was not a tool of the owners, whom he called "hogs" and who attacked him personally, calling him a troublemaker and a socialist.[29] The term "organization" to Taylor focused on efficiency, not authority; it was to consider ultimate decision-making not the role of an owner but the *one best way* of working to increase wages and profits. Taylor believed that work should be analyzed, organized, and documented into formal structured processes for management and the workers.

In contrast to Taylor's view, the craft guilds of the era advocated for artisan work and craft monopolies. Members were restricted to certain families and sworn to secrecy, unable to document work processes. The net result of Taylor's efforts led to the most significant improvement in benefits to blue-collar workers in history: the labor manager or employment manager role, one who handled recruitment, queries, training, and grievances at these large factories, evidence of process and humanism in the supply chain.[30] Too often today, documented work procedures are dismissed as draconian and disempowering, an assessment that often leads managers to adopt symptomatic fixes to address efficiency issues, such as outsourcing to lower-cost labor markets and the misapplication of automation to replace labor. Today this concept of scientific management is a lost art, and America's supply chain is imbalanced between supply and demand, leading to a spiky model of globalization.

Moving Forward

If supply chains are correctly designed and used, they can work for the betterment of private and public interests rather than for one or the other. At their best, they provide a multiplier effect through supply and demand, as was the case with Henry Ford's Model T production, which enabled innovation that benefited both the workers and management. At their worst, supply chains have delivered a zero-sum mentality across the planet of spiky globalization, leading to the deindustrialization of inner cities and rural towns that has left entire communities behind and has commoditized the role of work in the production process. The supply chain was the originator of the American Dream, led by an industrial engineering and industrial psychology approach; a balance of structured, rational methods; STEM thinking; and effective human resources management. While not perfect, supply chains can be the driver of a form of capitalism superior to other socioeconomic systems such as mercantilism, socialism, and communism. The system that can deliver fresh fish from Alaska to your favorite restaurant is the same system that should address the inequalities in society and the damage to the environment. Through their role, supply chains can enable capitalism and act as a check and balance when it spins out of control.

Can the American Dream exist once again in the 21st century? Do Americans still aspire to regain a sense of balance as an industrial nation and society? It will require significant economic and societal changes, led by supply chains. The starting point in this path forward is the subject of chapter 1, which explains how America lost the supply chain, the starting point for how the nation moved away from an industrial-based economy. Chapter 2 discusses the distractions and diversions encountered as America became deindustrialized. Implementing a strategy focused on structured problem solving—the next step, explained in chapter 3—is to develop a supply chain strategy that emphasizes the value chain. Chapter 4 explores the future of manufacturing within this new system, including people, processes, and technology, to form a model that balances economic growth and the sustainability of society and the environment. Chapter 5 posits the development of a networked, community-based supply chain that creates a flatter world of opportunity rather than a flattened one of winners and losers. Chapter 6 explores the "storeless store" of peer-to-peer retail, and chapter 7 advances a platform for this global supply chain transformation.

If the weakening of the supply chain system in the 21st century can bring anything positive to our lives, let it be this: a recognition that how capitalism is deployed by supply chains needs to be reformed to meet the challenges of the future, not to put an end to free enterprise and industrialization but rather to save capitalism from itself. Perhaps there's now an opportunity to achieve a joint alignment between the prosperous and the less fortunate. In the 19th century, Karl Marx argued that capitalism would, in the end, destroy itself through the overproduction of products that the people would not be able to afford, using the example of how production has and will exceed demand if left unchecked. It may be difficult to argue with Marx's prophecy given the current overproduction of some goods and waste, but that is more likely an error of a "wrong use" of capitalism, as Gandhi noted. Capitalism's disorders are legion, including corruption, overconsumption, and mercantilism. Still, it also happens to be the optimal economic system in the world today, if done properly, and supply chain management can play a vital role in improving it for the benefit of multiple stakeholders. Now is the time to see clearly past the ideologies and divisions to focus on good people, processes, and technologies that can bring hope for the rest of the 21st century.

CHAPTER 1

HOW AMERICA LOST SUPPLY CHAIN LEADERSHIP

A Primer

Understanding how America lost supply chain leadership must start with understanding how America invented and became the superpower of the field in the first place. After the end of the US Civil War, the young nation's focus was on westward expansion and the use of science, technology, engineering, and math (STEM) that led to some of history's most significant technological innovations, such as steel, oil, electricity, and automobiles. Despite the upcoming challenges of the Great Depression and two world wars, America was the greatest show on earth. It was a nation in the right place and destined to win the supply chain at the right time. Although the United States was fortunate to be spared much of the world wars' death and destruction, Americans paid a hefty price during World War II, with over four hundred thousand killed. Afterward, the young nation faced the difficult challenges of leading the free world as the only industrial superpower and, most importantly, of transforming the domestic economy at home. Indisputably, the Allies' victory over the Axis powers in World War II was due to America being an "arsenal of democracy" built from its manufacturing and supply chain superiority. In the aftermath of the war, with millions around the world dead or homeless and much of the European infrastructure flattened, America's industrial base was fully intact; the United States' public infrastructure—its national railroad network, ocean ports, and world-class factories in jewel cities such as Baltimore, Maryland, and Flint, Michigan, with trained people and processes—led the nation in being the sole industrial superpower of the world.

American innovation and efficiency during the war remain legendary today: Operation Overlord, the code name for the Normandy D-Day invasion, had a planning cycle that commenced two years prior and sent 17 million tons of military and other equipment (including 400,000 liters of blood plasma) to be staged in Britain in preparation for 130,000 soldiers to land through 6,900 ships.[1] Historians talk of the Nazi's success with their war machine, but the reality is much different: the Germans built 1,347 tanks compared to the Americans' 49,000 tanks.[2] The Nazis knew that they were losing the *Materialschlact*, or "battle of materials," as they called it, to the Americans and their superior industrial base.

In grade school, I learned that America was the only standing economic power in the world after World War II, which would lead to prosperity for a majority of the population. The truth was much different: America's leaders were already grappling with how to pivot an economy built to fight a massive world war that was no longer happening. Without sufficient demand for production, would the end of World War II lead to America's next Great Depression due to an imbalance between supply and demand? There would no longer be a need for so many tanks, guns, and battleships, and the government spending associated with fighting the war could not be sustained, leading to an economic cliff of sorts. To add to this challenge, between 1944 and 1947 the military released over 20 million people (nearly 14 percent of its total population) from the armed forces and related employment, and non–military employment only increased by 4 million, leaving millions of servicemen and servicewomen potentially without work.[3] The generally accepted notion among economists was that another Great Depression would be next, with unemployment ranging from 7 to 10 million.[4] Nobel Laureate Gunnar Myrdal predicted that the economic turmoil would be so severe that it would generate an "epidemic of violence."[5] The United States was potentially a large and prosperous nation yet it was essentially turned inward, with over 90 percent of its income coming from within its borders and few opportunities abroad.[6]

To avoid the calamity of the next Great Depression, Uncle Sam had to make a Faustian bargain to prevent an economic collapse. In 1944 government spending accounted for 55 percent of the gross domestic product (GDP), but this dropped to 13.75 percent—a 75 percent decrease—by 1947.[7] President Truman made a difficult but necessary decision to replace a government-directed command-and-control war-time economy with a new consumer economy, modifying the supply chain accordingly from guns to butter. After decades of sacrifice on the part of the Americans, it was time to unleash the American consumer like never before: to purchase automobiles, household appliances, and other staples after decades of pent-up demand. The war machine was to be transitioned to a consumer-based model to balance peacetime supply and demand. Transitioning to a consumer-based economy was a logical policy choice, but there was a price to eventually be paid. As is the case today, a consumer-based economy would lead to an overreliance on consumption out of balance with production. Yet in the 1950s a greater reliance on personal consumption was healthy for the economy and its supply chain, through a multiplier effect of greater demand that led to higher production. Growing manufacturing capacity was beneficial for employees and workers as long as it fostered productivity and efficiency; if this goal for balance ceased, this supply chain covenant would be lost, and the economy would become overreliant on consumption, as it exists today in the United States.

Consumer Society

After World War II, the US economy was the largest globally, with no other nation even close, and the United States accounted for a significant percentage of overall manufacturing production capacity for the entire world. These were the so-called golden years of America; between 1950 and 1960, the GDP increased by 41 percent, and the social welfare state experienced growth that led to decades of compassionate capitalism.[8] A newly minted model of a consumer-based supply chain was repurposed to meet the requirements of a new lifestyle beyond the needs and desires of any society in history. This lifestyle included a suburban life of furniture, electric appliances, and other definitions of conspicuous consumption for most, but not all, in the community. My grandmother lived during the two world wars and the Great Depression, and this new economy gave her a life that she could have never imagined as a daughter of a blue-collar immigrant from Poland. Between 1945 and 1949 Americans purchased 20 million refrigerators, 21.4 million cars, and 5.5 million stoves.[9] For those from my grandmother's generation, these initial expenditures were more liberating than wasteful, although some purchases, such as the family television set, were bashfully viewed as an embarrassment of riches. This time epitomizes the American Dream, when a combination of hard work, a consumer economy, and a public-private partnership that was fair to the American worker because it was profitable for businesses to do so coexisted. Of course, segments of the population were prevented from participating in the American Dream, and the legacy of these social policies remains with us today. But for many, like my grandmother, the new consumer-based economy was the most significant economic miracle of balanced capitalism in history.

Maybe the American Dream survives today through the immigrants who continue to enter the United States seeking a better life. But today's American Dream is not the same fixture of the culture as it was during the early 20th century. To my grandmother, it was an experience earned from the government (her words, not mine) after a long, extended period of sacrifice across the decades of World War I, the Great Depression, and World War II. Growing up in Baltimore during the 1970s and 1980s, I had this American Dream too, but it was different; my American Dream was personified through sacrifice and hard work but expected as an American birthright perpetuated through consumer markets. Because nothing good lasts forever, the multiplier effect of the American Dream was lost during this era. At the same time, business leaders, labor unions, government agencies, advertisers, and others forged a new campaign to create a paradigm shift in which Americans would come to see that mass consumption wasn't a personal indulgence but rather a civic obligation.[10] During my and my parents' generations, the change was made from consumption as a civic duty of patriotism to an intentional shift toward a demand-driven economy of consumption and self-indulgence. Such a shift required a movement from the rational and balanced to the psychological through a new professional service sector called marketing that transformed from seemingly harmless "public relations" to full-fledged campaigns and programs. These professionals would position the consumer base to believe that owning one television set or automobile was fine, but owning two or a newer model reflected an individual's self-worth. Rather than an appeal to consumption as loyalty and patriotism (and, thus, to increased production), this new position was an acknowledgment that Americans are the chosen people who deserve anything they want, with conspicuous consumption becoming a positive, not negative, reflection on the person's character. The use of marketing and psychology to redefine the American citizen from a saver to a consumer worked; the American public bought into the practice of conspicuous consumption.

This new model of American capitalism asked citizens to become ravenous consumers who were unleashed and no longer repairing old pantyhose and buying war bonds to sacrifice for the troops at the front. It was, in the words of philosopher Isaiah Berlin, the concept of negative liberty, the ultimate expression of liberty unencumbered by any barriers or obstacles from government or elsewhere.[11] The opposite of this concept is positive liberty, where workers are discouraged from consuming in order to sacrifice for the nation's collective well-being. During the Cold War, positive liberty was embodied, rather unsuccessfully, by governments such as the Soviet Union and the People's Republic of China, who employed state-sponsored controlled economies. America's marketing and product design model appealed to consumers' emotions, increasing economic development while allowing for the expression of individual liberty. Many have argued that America's consumer-based model of capitalism helped it win the Cold War through an experience of negative liberties.

The Demand Chain

This concept of a demand chain is an ideological system focused on consumption that creates a power shift from a production-based, back-end supply chain focused on capacity and efficiency to one based on consumer demand. In the process, the keys to the car, so to speak, are taken from the industrial engineers, quality control specialists, and logisticians and handed to those focused on understanding and shaping consumer behavior. Doing so changes the nature of how the supply chain in the United States evolves by elevating the role of the consumer in society over all of the other stakeholders, a system of imbalance. Marketing and psychology professionals dove deeply into the human mind to poke at the consumer's instinctual irrational element. Sigmund Freud's theory of id led to the manufacturing of demand to keep the economic growth rolling. Once the demand chain was codified through the economy, there was no longer any requirement for a multiplier effect, and citizens were no longer asked to consume as a matter of patriotism to enable manufacturing growth. Instead, consumer markets became instinctual, emotional engines to achieve economic growth by manipulating feelings of self-worth.

Those in the supply chain profession understand this model: a product becomes an embodiment of financial markets and marketing principles, such as the four Ps of marketing: product, price, placement, and promotion. A transformation to a front-end focused business model from a balanced front- and back-end supply chain focus led to the need to understand and define the consumer rather than the market: the former is a function of desires and image while the latter solves problems across all stakeholders. In a balanced view of markets from the past, markets mainly were delivery mechanisms to solve problems since the demand was almost always greater than supply capacity. The noted 18th-century economist Thomas Malthus pointed to this in his treatise "An Essay on the Principle of Population," stating that food production could not keep pace with population growth. Malthus's economic theory was prevalent since the beginning of economic time but by the 20th century had changed. Production in the United States was now more significant than the public's demand for the product. As production capacity grew, such as in Henry Ford's Model T scenario, a covenant that drove higher demand was deployed to ensure that production efficiency led to more significant benefits to the workers as well as consumers.

In the new model of a demand-driven economy, separate from the supply chain covenant of the past, the focus is not on multiplication but on the consumer as a sole means to an end via marketing methods and does not emphasize supply/demand balance. Instead, demand is created by "engineering consent," a term used by Sigmund Freud's nephew, one of the fathers of modern marketing, Edward Bernays.[12] As an immigrant to America who was inspired by his uncle's psychoanalytical theories, Bernays focused on the irrational nature of the human mind to drive consumer demand; with a background in journalism, he was far from an engineer. His 1928 book, *Propaganda*, suggests that it is possible to manipulate human intentions without understanding the human mind.[13]

Bernays's methods in "public relations," as marketing was then called, seemed to be the quick hit necessary for demand creation, or as he called it, "engineering consent," an easier path to growth than achieving a balance between supply and demand. One campaign that Bernays championed was to increase sales of Dixie cups by evoking fear in consumers who used reusable cups for drinking water. Bernays was unapologetic regarding using his uncle's knowledge of the human mind. In *Propaganda* Bernays notes, "So the question naturally arose: If we understand the mechanism and motives of the group mind, is it not possible to control and regiment the masses according to our will without their knowing about it?"[14] This new technique of public relations became a dangerous proposition. Far from the days of a focus on supply to meet demand or the balance between supply and demand on behalf of the worker, it transformed into a demand chain, driving consumer growth by focusing on any weakness or element of human psychology possible, including manipulation of the consumer. In this model, an automobile was no longer a product of Henry Ford's Model T multiplier effect between supply and demand but rather an extension of one's self-worth in society, reflecting an individual's personality. And it wasn't just in the realization that a Chevrolet was not adequate when your neighbor drove a Cadillac but also in the desire for a new car—the id overpowering the ego and superego for the company's sake, enabled by marketing. It was about self-esteem, sex appeal, other psychological motives, as well as the market's needs. While speaking to a group of public relations executives, Herbert Hoover remarked that they had created desire by transforming people "into constantly moving happiness machines."[15]

Focused on the culture war, the Cold War ideology of negative liberties, freedom of the individual, and compassionate capitalism—the principles that drove production growth and efficiencies in the past, such as Deming's quality principles and Taylor's scientific management theory—were no longer in fashion as a driving force. Stemming from good intentions but spiraling out of control, sophisticated marketing tools led to demand induction beyond a natural point, becoming increasingly dependent on creating more demand every year. These techniques would stretch the distance so wide between supply and demand that any synergy between them was no longer seen as feasible or viable. Ultimately, this led to the next tool in the tool belt for marketing to commoditize the product to increase demand through lower cost, pushing the supply chain overseas and spilling hundreds of millions of low-cost workers into the labor market. It would only be a matter of time before a dress shopper would buy despite a closet already full of dresses and would even purchase fast fashion, wearing something once before discarding it. In the end, Uncle Sam's bargain with the devil led to the disassembly of the most extraordinary supply chain transformation in the history of the world. But, as is the case with anyone who takes the devil up on his Faustian bargain, the allure of the promise outshines the payment to be made, and ultimately there comes the time when the devil must be paid his due.

Supply Chain to Demand Chain

Through this progression from a supply-driven to a demand-driven system, the US supply chain became a de facto delivery mechanism for today's unbelievable service levels of high-quality goods at low prices, including free shipping. Even before World War II, there were early movements toward a demand-driven approach that focused on product marketing and sales rather than on quality and production. In 1924 legendary General Motors head Alfred P. Sloan Jr. proposed quicker design cycles for its cars to convince consumers to purchase this year's model. In 1932 New York real estate developer Bernard London developed a "planned obsolescence" concept to end the Great Depression, announced in an article appropriately titled "Ending the Depression through Planned Obsolescence."[16] In this article, London notes that while factories were ready to ramp up production, they were limited by a lack of consumer demand. He proposed that products should have a planned end-of-life date: "The original span of life of a commodity would be determined by competent engineers, economists, and mathematicians, specialists in their fields, on behalf of the Government."[17] This concept of modifying production away from quality and toward greater consumption was antithetical to the ideas of industrial engineering and structured problem-solving but became relevant in this new financial capitalism model. Waste became considered the ultimate means to an end of the supply chain rather than its enemy, which supply chain professionals were taught but often did not practice. Planned obsolescence became widely popular as marketers realized that consumers wouldn't make new purchases without being goaded. It became a focus on product sales and stock market gains rather than long-term sustainability, productivity, and quality that began to win the day.

In just one generation, the supply chain built on STEM principles, industrial engineering, balance toward stakeholders, and structured problem-solving transitioned to more of a front-end business model that used psychology and quick-hit marketing and finance imperatives to transform the American consumer and culture. Americans changed from frugal penny-pinchers to conspicuous consumers who became oblivious to waste and other collateral damages. As Bernays noted, through marketing campaigns to engineer consent, life cycles were shortened through planned obsolescence, including through single-use items, such as plastic products consisting of 50 percent of the annual 380 million tons of plastic produced worldwide. Eventually, the public began to take notice of the egregious nature of a demand chain fostered by psychology, marketing, and waste. In Vance Packard's 1960s book *The Waste Makers*, he addresses this problem of consumers' overbuying, induced by advertising and business mechanisms that pressure and manipulate. Packard begins by redefining the term "consumerism" from a positive expression of individual freedom and support for industry to a negative expression highlighting selfishness, materialism, and waste.[18] Supply chains became foundational for what is worst in our culture and society rather than an emblem of the legends of history, in the Normandy invasion and Henry Ford's Model T. In his famous article "Price Competition in 1955," Victor Lebow notes, "Our enormously productive economy demands that we make consumption our way of life, that we convert the buying and use of goods into rituals, that we seek our spiritual satisfactions, our ego satisfactions, in consumption."[19]

Data from the Bureau of Economic Analysis found that today's US economy is 70 percent consumption-based versus well below 50 percent before the 1970s. In contrast to an earlier era when demand increase led to a rise in production, today's consumption does very little as a multiplier effect when products are made in other nations. In his 2013 book *The Unwinding*, George Packer narrates the decline of significant American institutions that led to an "unwinding" of American society. According to Packer, there was a "contract" in America in which individuals were ensured a secure place in society if they worked hard and were good citizens. The truth is, however, that with this unwinding, a void was filled with less charitable factors, such as an economy that commoditized products and labor.[20] With the industrial economy going off the rails because of this demand chain, economist Milton Friedman noted in a 1970 essay that "corporate shareholder wealth is all that matters."[21] Friedman contends that a corporation has no social responsibility to any entity, public or private, other than its shareholders, a perspective that can be viewed differently in a predominately global economy. In 1976, through the use of overly complex and abstract economic equations, professor Michael Jensen and Dean William Meckling of the University of Rochester published a paper titled "Theory of the Firm" that provided quantitative evidence for why corporations should only focus on shareholders rather than other stakeholders involved in the supply chain and public interest.[22] Rather than supporting longer-term strategic capital projects focused on production, financial markets became a means to an end by rewarding CEOs who enabled short-term profits to increase stock prices. No CEO embodied this formula better than Jack Welch, the CEO of General Electric between 1981 and 2001, considered the most successful corporate leader of this era for his ability to increase shareholder value and hit his quarterly numbers to make Wall Street happy.[23] Much like product marketing schemes built on leveraging the irrational nature of the individual, financial security markets took on a similar philosophy, driven by forces beyond the corporate managers who must obey them to keep their jobs.[24] During Welch's reign, GE's stock price hit an all-time high of $480 a share in 2000.

In his famous 1942 book *The General Theory of Employment, Interest and Money*, John Maynard Keynes writes that "when the capital development of a country becomes the by-product of the activities of a casino, the job is likely ill done."[25] Legendary investment pioneer John Bogle, credited with creating the first index fund, challenged Wall Street's speculative culture, favoring long-term investing and low transaction fees over short-term transactions made for the benefit of the investment firm. Bogle created the Vanguard Group, a firm with over $5 trillion in assets today, based on his senior thesis at Princeton. In his book *The Battle for the Soul of Capitalism*, Bogle notes that managerial capitalism and a bottom-line society are capitalism's mutations where executives are rewarded for pumping up the perception of short-term stock prices.[26] Bogle calls this process "financial engineering," not actual engineering based on math and science but a distorted technique of ginning up market prices to meet or exceed analyst expectations within public accounting rules. Even the term "engineering" was reengineered away from STEM principles to Bernays's engineering consent in marketing and Wall Street's financial engineering.

Thinking for a Living

In 1960 the US economy accounted for 40 percent of total global output, but today it is approximately 24 percent.[27] As a policy focus, America has become bored with production, only feigning interest in the manufacturing sector and supply chain. At the same time, other nations have caught up to the United States; in 1950 the Japanese had a negative net worth, were devoid of natural resources, and could only compete through quality principles.[28] Compared to Japan, America's hourly output was half of Japan's from 1973 to 1989 because Japan invested twice as much in capital investment during the same period.[29] This focus and support of a new demand chain model led to a natural progression away from blue-collar production fields to white-collar office roles centered around marketing, finance, and other service industries. While American manufacturers were outsourcing production to lower-cost nations, labor unions led boycotts asking consumers to "Buy American" as a patriotic gesture. For the most part, policymakers seemed content with a demand chain economy and other nations doing the "hard work" of production while American managers did the white-collar "thinking." To those who understood supply chains and manufacturing, this was concerning. Deming's 1986 book *Out of the Crisis* provides a tedious yet thorough mathematical analysis of the failures of short-termism to US manufacturing instead of focusing on his famous "14 Points for Management."

Conveniences of a global economy, both in supply and demand, are optimal for short-term benefit gain rather than an empirical and detailed analytical approach to manufacturing that requires significant effort to achieve efficiencies. Moreover, the advent of computer technology during the 1970s and 1980s improved the viability of convenient globalization and a further sway away from industrial engineering and structured problem-solving that was no longer fashionable through New Age thought leaders. One such futurist was Alvin Toffler, who wrote *The Third Wave* in 1980 to describe this transition to a new economy.[30] According to Toffler, the first wave of human civilization was agriculture; the second wave, the Industrial Revolution; and the third wave, the information-based computer revolution. Toffler describes this as a "postindustrial society," implying that manufacturing is no longer a requirement for the American economy. American thought leaders of the 1970s and 1980s validated the deindustrialization of US factories, believing that we have reached a postindustrial economy and society. Toffler's theories are in stark contrast to Deming's evidence that quality principles are required to take root in US manufacturers to prevent its losses to overseas operations. The futurists and management thinkers of the time were the overlords, and Deming's principles were then viewed as a relic from a nostalgic era of yesteryear. According to these new thinkers, the world was becoming "flat"; according to the theory of comparative economics, nations should focus on what they are good at and let others do the rest. Americans should become the world's knowledge workers, the thinking went, allowing the developing world to manufacture our goods.

Theoretically, it made sense, but practically, it ignored the realities of one-third of the nation who relied on the industrial sector for their livelihood and were now left on the outside looking in at this "postindustrial" society. It also ignored the eventuality of a planet of 8 billion, leading to a near-infinite source of low-cost production workers, rendering American blue-collar workers obsolete.

During the 1980s it was not only Deming who highlighted the issues of the American manufacturing sector; Peter Drucker, often known as the father of modern management, was invited by General Motors to conduct a two-year observational analysis of all the company's structures, organization, and employees. His resulting book, *Concept of the Corporation*, identified the qualitative structural problems of the organization relating to customers, dealers, and employees.[31] Drucker's methods primarily focused on what he classified as the "organizational development" of human capital, leadership, and the white-collar worker versus Deming's main focus on labor, the factory worker, and manager as well as productivity improvements through industrial engineering. Drucker's and Deming's views of productivity and efficiency were the same even though one was primarily from the factory floor and the other from the executive suite. Drucker's focus was on the emerging role in corporations of the "knowledge worker," a white-collar employee such as a computer programmer, architect, lawyer, accountant, or academic—someone who, in the words of Thomas Davenport, "thinks for a living."[32] Peter Drucker saw knowledge as an asset increasingly more important than financial assets, land, or labor. Therefore, increasing the knowledge worker's productivity is the most important contribution management needs to make.[33] According to Drucker, the future of manufacturing is on the knowledge worker, and his forecast has been proven correct, as I discuss through the remainder of the book. Bridging Drucker's and Deming's perspectives of how to save manufacturing is the best hope for American industry in a world of 3 billion factory workers and with 200 million unemployed and growing. Deming is correct about the foundation for productivity, and Drucker is correct regarding the importance of information in the new economy, but their strategies have been misinterpreted by many corporate executives who believe the easiest, short-term plan is to outsource factory production and focus on the white-collar knowledge worker. In my 2007 book *An Easy Out*, I explain that these quick-hit fixes concentrate on symptoms, the "easy outs" versus the "difficult ins" of the hard work that leads to a more balanced economy across all population segments.[34]

Like other MBA students in the early nineties, I was fascinated by the futurists who emphasized the importance of the knowledge worker in this new economy. I fell for the belief that manufacturing could be sent overseas and all Americans could become so-called knowledge workers. Back then we could not have conceived what would happen next in an age of advanced computerization and the internet that flows electrons freely across the world, in near-infinite volumes of data. In the late 1980s and early 1990s it seemed feasible, yet simplistic, that a more significant percentage of Americans, if retrained after deindustrialization, could become knowledge workers, with white-collar professionals in America doing all of the thinking, and developing nations around the world doing all of the producing. However, a contention that manufacturing production is no longer core to a national economic strategy seems short-sighted and more dictated by financial markets than empirical logic. And yet, upon the closer review provided by thinkers such as Deming and Drucker, the flaws in this thinking are too obvious, and the question that needs to be asked and answered in more detail is exactly who benefits in this new postindustrial economy and who does not.

The American public never received a detailed and complete explanation of dein-dustrialization during the 1970s–1990s. Yet policymakers in government and busi-ness often speak of the benefits of "free and open global markets," bringing back the Cold War storyline of negative liberties and the purpose of individual freedoms af-forded to us as consumers. Unfortunately, the more detailed calculus is left out, never mentioning how entire inner cities and rural towns have been hollowed out, never re-covering from deindustrialization. Moreover, management thinkers and industrial engineers from the past, such as Frederick Taylor, W. Edwards Deming, and Peter Drucker, are long forgotten as economic policy has focused on demand growth rather than supply and demand in balance. "Free and open global markets" can be good for workers and consumers around the world but is difficult to balance within a local or even national economy. Still, corporations and policymakers should subscribe to a theory of the difficult work of improving efficiency and productivity before making such "easy out" decisions. And no one has articulated yet to the American blue-collar worker of the past—not the corporations, government, or labor unions—why they have not subscribed to this theory or why this is not an aim today.

Flat or Flattened Supply Chain?

The verdict was clear: the world was officially flat at the end of the 20th century, Thomas Friedman declared it so in 2005.[35] Theoretically, his thesis makes sense: First, free trade has improved the fate of the planet in aggregate, reducing the num-ber of people in poverty every year. Second, technology such as the internet has enabled more outstanding communication and coordination than ever across the planet. Trade liberalization with the two empires in the East—China and India—and China's entrance to the World Trade Organization (WTO) in 2001 took down some of the limits from the past. Third, turning hundreds of millions of factory workers into middle-class consumers would be the rising tide for all boats, leading to greater peace and stabilization. And fourth, Americans no longer wanted to get their hands dirty in making goods that could be produced cheaper in other nations. Walmart and other large US companies were ready to unleash this flat-world model through the innovation of its supply chain system.

Compared to the small corner store or even the chain department store that ushers their products through a three-tier distribution system, with manufacturers who sell to distributors who sell to the stores, Walmart has used the power of its scale and inventory management systems to "cut out the middleman." Computerized inventory management control was a rational innovation of Walmart that partnered people, processes, and technologies to excel in a broader range of product offerings at a lower price—and this was just the start. Using its direct relationship with manufacturers, Walmart pressures suppliers to continually provide the lowest price, most significant volume, best quality, and seamless integration with its stores. Large consumer product manufacturers, such as Proctor & Gamble, Kimberly-Clark, and Coca-Cola, can meet these supplier commitments, but smaller companies cannot keep up, leading to supplier consolidation and outsourcing to lower-cost providers in poorer countries. Through these more efficient, higher-scale relationships with larger suppliers, Walmart places extreme pressure on its retail competition, both large national retail chains and every tiny corner store across the United States.

After the trade liberalization of China in the WTO, Walmart was ready to take the next step and arrange direct relationships with Chinese manufacturers to further lower prices, increase shareholder value to investors, and wow its customers. In 2013 China's imports via Walmart totaled $49.1 billion and accounted for 15 percent of the United States' trade deficit since its entry into the WTO.[36] These decisions decimated manufacturing employment in the United States, marking the second phase of deindustrialization, which impacted 314,500 well-paying blue-collar jobs.[37] For the consumer, this was pure joy: rather than having to go to different department stores in the city, strip mall stores in suburbia, or rural corner stores without much selection, consumers can go to Walmart for the highest selection of 100,000-plus unique items at the lowest price available anywhere, all in one place. Walmart's early mantra— "Always Low Prices. Always"—resonated not only with the consumer but also Wall Street due to exploding revenue and profits from this transformational retail model.

Beyond Walmart's cutting-edge information technology systems to manage inventory and connect with its suppliers, the company benefits through advancements in international logistics. Marc Levinson's remarkable book *The Box: How the Shipping Container Made the World Smaller and the World Economy Bigger* explains how a confluence of regulators, unions, shipping companies, ports, engineers, and innovators shaped and created today's remarkably efficient international logistics supply chain, including standardized containers and procedures and a network of shippers (ship, rail, and truck), warehouses, and retailers. It started with Malcolm McLean, who kicked off modern containerization in 1956 when he launched a converted tanker that he called a "trailership" from Newark to Houston.[38] In the 1990s the largest container ships had space for five thousand containers, and now they can hold over twenty thousand, a sign of how global supply chains have grown.[39] This new formula for a free trade model of a flat supply chain enables companies to offer more degrees of freedom than ever because of these supply chain innovations. For example, it is no longer cost-effective for a domestic US company to make a bicycle with a manufacturing labor rate of $20 or $30 an hour if the same product can be produced in China at $1 or $2 an hour and marginal shipping costs. The field of supply chain management became a competitive advantage for businesses because of this innovation in logistics. Demand could be driven not just through marketing and psychology but through innovations in the supply chain that slash ordinary products' prices. Supply chain innovation not only perpetuates the existing consumerism and focus on short-term profits, it also unleashes globalization, but in an imbalanced manner across the world and within nations. American consumers have continued to aspire to become white-collar knowledge workers and so have acquiesced to China taking the role of the world's factory as long as American purchasing power improves. As a result, the world has become flat and has been flattened simultaneously.

It was not a surprise to Asia that it would return as a prominent player in the global economy; after all, the continent had the same per capita income as the Europeans until 1500, but this changed by the end of the Mao regime in the mid-1970s, with the West's per capita income at that time fourteen times higher.[40] Kishore Mahbubani, a Singaporean academic who advises the West on its strategy toward the East, tells us that since the economic "awakening" of Asia in the 1990s and 2000s, the West has fallen asleep.[41] The United States, in particular, distracted by wars in the Middle East, found itself increasingly disassociated within the global supply chain, with the balance tipping toward the East. Mahbubani makes an excellent case that the problem isn't the global supply chain but rather America's inability to understand it. Mahbubani writes that America's lack of a coherent supply chain strategy, along with its belief that a nation could succeed through outsourcing production and relegating its attention only to knowledge work, has been its failure; Mahbubani strikes a similar chord to Deming, America's quality and supply chain expert of the past. Globalization means many things, and for the past twenty years it has been a distraction to America, providing an opportunity for the East to catch up.

The World Is Spiky

In a study conducted at George Mason University, the world was measured as more spiky than flat. The study found the world's economy to be disproportionately concentrated in terms of sheer economic horsepower and cutting-edge innovation.[42] In addition, the study found that vast segments of the world are being left out due to a lack of talent and resources, as has always been the case. Still, population segments within high prosperity nations are no longer focused on manufacturing and industry, which was previously not the case. This concept of a spiky world isn't new, said Korean economist Ha-Joon Chang in his 2007 book *Bad Samaritans: The Myth of Free Trade and the Secret History of Capitalism*. Chang notes that nations, particularly in the East but now in the West as well, have been required to change their economic policies as table stakes to get a piece of the supply chain pie that might be different from what is best for society. Through his study of history and economic data, Chang shows a general clash between free-market principles and democracy, calling these supply chain systems "bad Samaritans" for their applications represented as capitalism and free markets. Chang is not against free trade, but he argues against how it is administrated through the global supply chains in today's capitalist model, a perspective similar to Gandhi's proposal that capitalism is not evil but rather misapplied. Chang's book, based on relevant data and analysis, supports that globalization has been good and bad and proposes that we must better balance its objectives and results to improve its outcomes.[43] Contrary to what many in the United States—especially former factory workers—may believe, globalization has not been entirely a win for Asia; addressing the financialization of the global supply chain system seems to be in the best interests of the entire world.

Starting with the Faustian bargain after World War II, the US economy morphed into a demand chain, concerned primarily with consumer sentiment to grow markets and with less emphasis on the production element of the supply chain system. The business case for the demand chain was built on sales, marketing, and psychological methods and was fostered through outdated classical economic theories used in the present as a rationale for a cheeky the "world is flat" view of globalization. In 2022 no public policy expert has entirely rationalized a business case for a knowledge economy as a suitable replacement for industry lost by deindustrialization, which has resulted in an increase in income inequality. For seventy years, America's transition to a consumer-based economy has accelerated a spiky model of economic growth not only around the world but also within our nation. In his 2020 book *The Tyranny of Merit: What's Become of the Common Good*, Harvard professor Michael Sandel notes that the current era of an "age of merit" as a response to deindustrialization has hung the Western working class out to dry with its thesis that the failure of the working class to raise their incomes is their own fault.[44] Fermenting deep within the roots of America's working class, a blue-collar segment of the population is feeling betrayal, not just that the system is rigged against them but, more important, that this "meritocracy argument" humiliates them through no fault of their own. This concept that "anyone can go to college" may be accurate in individual cases. But it is inaccurate to state that the knowledge economy also means equal access for those from a blue-collar comparable with those of a white-collar background. During the deindustrialization of the 1980s, Peter Drucker noted that knowledge had become the economy's foundation and capital, the quickest and easiest way to secure a job, but that did not necessarily translate into a strategy that provided equal access to all Americans to reach this high threshold.[45] A high school–educated American from my father's era could have expected to eventually earn at least $30 an hour (in today's earnings) in a full-time manufacturing job with benefits; that employment offered a much better lifestyle than can be had by a person today with the same education, who now earns only $15–$20 an hour without benefits or company stability. Every blue-collar manufacturing job lost puts at risk those higher-paying engineering, management, and information technology jobs associated with the factory. A report from the Manufacturing Institute shows that every dollars' worth of manufactured goods creates $1.34 of value elsewhere in the economy, the most significant multiplier of any sector.[46] These facts are indisputable, but the problem is not that some manufacturing jobs should not have left the United States but rather that suitable alternatives were promised but not delivered to those families impacted by deindustrialization and outsourcing.

Beyond the most painful chapters of US history, including the treatment of African Americans and Native Americans and other infamous policies impacting social groups, there may be no other circumstance that affected the fate of such a large chunk of the population than the deindustrialization of the manufacturing sector that transpired in the second half of the 20th century and continues today. As an action, deindustrialization is undoubtedly less intentional than slavery and massacres. Still, deindustrialization has been unquestionably a breaking of the multiplier effect of balancing the benefits of supply and demand that tipped the balance of power, including moving away from free-market principles that it asserts to support and enabling the oligopolistic behavior of some of the largest manufacturers, the same who lobbied the government for protection against competitors and antitrust despite having market shares as high as 90 percent.[47] Not only the owners of industry but also the powerful trade unions played a role in America's deindustrialization, with large institutions acting outside the best interests of the American worker for short-sighted gains. The original intentions of the labor unions were significant and important for the well-being and safety of the American worker. Trade unions became more defined by an out-of-balance focus on worker wages and organizational interests than on productivity and efficiency results, with the worker most impacted in the end. By concentrating on securing jobs first rather than on productivity and efficiency, unions often ignored the importance of the company's competitiveness by protecting poor performance for security and stabilization. A focus on job stability alone rather than productivity and performance to enable employment led to a stagnant operating performance bested by upstart nations such as Japan and low-cost, low-regulated nations such as China and Mexico. A lack of innovation, competition, and motivation around supporting and improving the manufacturing sector has led to a decline in manufacturing employment, from its high in the Rust Belt at over 50 percent of jobs to roughly 30 percent by 2000, and since falling.[48] Almost on cue, what happened next was, as predicted by one-time presidential candidate Ross Perot, "the great sucking sound of jobs leaving the United States" as the natural progression, driven by trade agreements such as the North Atlantic Free Trade Agreement (NAFTA). These failures were not justified by structured problem-solving and industrial engineering principles for managing manufacturing and supply chain operations. Almost thirty years after the NAFTA deal, estimates show a minor improvement in America's GDP of 0.5 percent.[49] NAFTA has led to an increase of 200,000 largely white-collar jobs related to import/export that pay 15–20 percent more than the jobs that were lost; however, the auto manufacturing sector alone has lost 350,000 jobs since 1994.[50] What the math shows is essential, but more important is what it does not show: the lost opportunities to optimize existing operations within existing companies. As I explain in my book *An Easy Out*, the "difficult in" before outsourcing and offshoring production facilities is to conduct a complete root cause analysis to learn why the operation isn't competitive; then, if it makes sense to outsource, do so. Instead, an "easy out" approach creates sleight-of-hand trade policies manufactured by politicians, and corporate leaders make supply chain decisions based on convenience rather than rational, mathematical analysis conducted by industrial engineers—the type of analysis that is being done more in China than the United States today.

Off to Hell?

If there ever was a Faustian bargain in the economics of selling one's soul to the devil, it is what America is facing today regarding its role in the global supply chain. For all the proper reasons, the United States had a right to be worried about the economic stability of the country after decades of the brutal wars of World War I and World War II and the Great Depression that wreaked havoc over the nation. It made sense to transform and unleash the industrial might into a more consumer-based economy. Still, it may have been a deal with the devil, when a decision to shift from a supply chain to a demand chain fostered not growth through a balance between supply and demand but rather overconsumption driven by marketing principles founded in psychology. To paraphrase the famous words of Federal Reserve Chair William McChesney Martin Jr., in October 1955, there was a need for the chaperone to remove the punch bowl when the party was warming up, but instead, the bowl kept getting filled.[51] This 20th-century policy shift would lead to an economy that not only fostered waste to enable growth, eventually impacting our environment, but also seeped into and permeated our culture, turning us into wanton consumers without balance in other areas of our lives, as is evident today. Not only this, but we lacked the *desire* to balance supply and demand, ultimately leading to an "easy out" model where we saw ourselves as the knowledge workers with less need for supply and manufacturing roles in our economy. This is a clear image of how good intentions paved this road to hell.

Are we destined to continue down this path to hell, having signed a contract with the devil with a drop of our blood, or is there hope to reform and move to a different approach? Perhaps the events surrounding the pandemic beginning in 2020 and Russia's invasion of Ukraine in 2022 can point us toward a new path to restore the purpose of the supply chain with more of a value chain than a demand chain. It is essential to understand how and why America lost supply chain leadership so we can understand where we need to go, which is the basis of this chapter. Contrary to political hyperbole that the pundits often espouse, what happened was not an intentional strategy by politicians from either party to sell out blue-collar Americans from their earlier way of life but rather was a legitimate strategy that addressed the post–World War II and Cold War realities which have since spiraled out of control. For the remainder of the book, I discuss strategies for how we might pull ourselves off our current path and onto a 21st-century supply chain system. As we assess this global supply chain that has spun out of control, we see the results from the COVID-19 pandemic and its impact on the world economy as a precursor for things to come—not as it relates to a biological virus but rather to the lack of resiliency in our supply chain today that is more harmful to us than we initially understood. The problem extends beyond the missing personal protective equipment, cleaning supplies, and toilet paper and includes those Americans who have been left behind for decades. If we can understand what has happened over the past seventy-five years, we can understand how important this field of supply chain management has been to our economic history—or not, in its absence—to understand its role in the 21st century as a driver of innovation and progress. The supply chain need not continue as a back-end deliverer of front-end demand chain–driven growth, a national economy driven by consumption and not production and consumption. As I discuss in the next chapter, we need to notice what our competitors (e.g., China) are doing to learn how to proceed. When we understand what has happened, we have a chance not simply to win against economic competitors such as China but, more importantly, to provide economic opportunity and equality to a significant percentage of our population through a means that has worked in the past, the industrial sector. In doing so, we can stop our path toward hell and reclaim our soul from the devil's grasp.

CHAPTER 2

FALLOUTS FROM DEINDUSTRIALIZATION

A Strategy for a Distracted and Divided Nation

Washington Post foreign affairs columnist David Ignatius wrote in 2020 that the United States is a very divided and distracted nation, enshrining selfishness as it turns inward, letting international order be on autopilot, allowing chaos on the world stage, and abdicating its role as a leader in geopolitical matters.[1] Should the United States resume its traditional global leadership role, as Ignatius advocates, or should it focus more on its pressing domestic challenges, such as the COVID-19 pandemic and its implications, economic issues such as inflation, social justice issues, protests and ancillary acts of violence, record forest fires, other climate catastrophes, and a drug addiction epidemic? Even in the light of a significant world event such as Russia's invasion of Ukraine, most Americans want the prioritization to tilt mainly toward domestic issues with a focus on the world stage as well. America has less than 5 percent of the world's population but uses approximately 80 percent of opioids and has 22 percent of the world's incarcerated.[2] In a November 2021 poll, 73 percent of Americans wanted the government to focus on jobs and economic growth, and despite international conflict, this remains the case today.[3]

China's approach seems to be more focused on domestic issues; at the 2021 Central Economic Work Conference in China in December, its leaders emphasized the importance of domestic economic stability as its top focus, prioritizing these issues over global matters.[4] At the same time that China has been focused on its domestic policy and growth, the United States lost its supply chain dominance due to its lack of focus on the industrial sector, an imbalance between production and consumption, and a lack of investment in education, particularly in the STEM fields. Coming out of World War II, America's lead in manufacturing production was historic. At the same time, the United States focused on restoring economic stability in the free world through the Marshall Plan, the postwar reconstruction effort. As a result, nations such as Germany and Japan became competitors through their innovative public-private partnerships in production. The postwar American economy was strong as manufacturing employment continued to rise into the late seventies and productivity had grown continuously, albeit increasingly at lower employment levels. Moreover, every president since John Kennedy has publicly emphasized the importance of manufacturing to the US economy. In reality, American capitalism has prioritized production allocation as a motive for price, profit, and market growth, with other factors as externalities.

Rather than manufacturing and supply chain sectors, the economic focus was on nonindustrial sectors such as finance, banking, marketing, and retail. Even today the capital markets justify this approach, as measured by the stock market. From January 1960 to today, the Standard & Poor's stock index grew from nearly zero to over 4,500, evidence of the benefit to financial markets in a consumption-based approach.[5] With the nation still in the grip of a COVID-19 pandemic and global war, the stock market continues to shine like the sun as an economic bellwether, flashing record-breaking results decade after decade. In November 2020 the Dow Jones Industrials surpassed 30,000; more than a year later, amid historic levels of inflation, it was over 34,000. Despite these benefits to the wealthy and middle-class Americans with investments and retirement accounts, 14.4 percent of American children don't have enough to eat. Among Blacks and Hispanics, it's 22 percent.[6] Using a calculus based on balance, not just the stock market, the health of the US economy looks much different. An approach primarily focused on consumption has led to a model of excess and absence rather than balance. To use a term coined by economist John Maynard Keynes, it is a strategy of economic growth based on an understanding of human behavior guided by "animal spirits" rather than rationality.

This out-of-balance, emotionally market-driven culture has led to a loss of younger Americans' confidence in the US economy. A recent study found that 51 percent of eighteen- to twenty-nine-year-old Americans have a favorable impression of socialism due to their distaste for the present form of capitalism.[7] Capitalism as an economic system has existed since the 18th century and, when properly applied, is the best system. However, its methods and tools are outdated relative to the dynamic nature of a 21st-century global economy, leading to a loss of confidence in it. For example, the Phillips curve is a theory demonstrating an inverse relationship between inflation and unemployment that originated in 1958 from a paper written by New Zealand economist William Phillips. Sixty-four years later, an eternity in today's fast-paced supply chain system, the Phillips curve is an outdated concept, if it was ever relevant. For example, in the 1970s the United States experienced "stagflation," the combination of a stagnating economy and high inflation. In recent years, however, the United States has had an economy of low inflation and low unemployment and, now, high inflation and low unemployment. In the past, economists would develop theories that represented their limited data sets; today the data sets are infinitely more extensive, and theories such as the Phillips curve are no longer relevant as a tool to study the economy. In the past and even in the present, government economists have developed strategies based on force-fitted data sets to abstract theories that have proven to be simplistic and inaccurate. The legacy of these failed theories and strategies resides in America's inner cities and rural communities.

A Tale of Many Cities

Those most impacted by the ineffectiveness of prevailing economic policies have been the Rust Belt communities that have been forgotten for decades. The story begins in my hometown of Baltimore, Maryland, proud owner of the moniker "Charm City," a tagline sold as a fresh coat of paint to cover the scars from deindustrialization that began in the 1970s and 1980s. Since its origin, Baltimore has been essential to America, the home of the "Star-Spangled Banner," the city near the Mason-Dixon line that separated the North and South that was critical during the slave migration, and a harbor location that led to a vital role in the nation's supply chain development, including the first commercial railroad, the Baltimore & Ohio (B&O) Railroad. Its geographic location in the mid-Atlantic region is ideal, with its Inner Harbor and Patapsco River that flow into the Chesapeake Bay and to the ocean, making it a major port city, and it is proximate to the nation's capitals of government and finance, Washington, DC, and New York City, respectively. Baltimore was a strategic cog for America's Industrial Revolution, including the development of the Sparrow's Point region that housed Bethlehem Steel, the world's largest steel mill by the middle of the 20th century. Through industrial strength came culture as well, with the city's millionaire philanthropists who built music institutes (George Peabody), art galleries (Henry Walters), and universities and hospitals (Johns Hopkins). In many ways, Baltimore has been a progressive city, a melting pot of white European immigrants and African Americans, demonstrating cultural growth and harmony, even as the city has not escaped the scourge of systemic racism that afflicts so many American cities.

Although the steel industry was dying a slow death that lasted over decades, the bottom dropped out in the late seventies and the early eighties; by 1982 US steel production dropped to 43 percent of capacity, with Baltimore's Bethlehem Steel's workforce dropping from 17,500 to 3,100.[8] Eventually, Bethlehem Steel filed for bankruptcy in 2005 and, in 2008, sold to a Russian company for a steeply discounted price, an outcome that seemed preordained. McCormick & Company was founded in Baltimore in 1889 and today remains the world's largest spice maker but is now headquartered farther north in Sparks, a suburb twenty miles north of the city. Employment migrated to the city's suburbs and other nations, as did a suburban flight that led to 10,000 people leaving the city in the 1950s and 35,000 in the 1960s.[9] From this suburban and even global flight from Baltimore, much of what remained was the industry of last resort, the illegal drug trade. Without legitimate alternatives to manufacturing available to the community, the city crumbled; a 1993 study by the Abell Foundation found that 62,000, or one in twelve, people in Baltimore had acquired a substance dependency.[10] Baltimore, once a model for the American Dream, is defined by despair, de facto segregation, failing schools, and unrepaired infrastructure. These tragedies are symptoms of the city's deindustrialization, the exit of the supply chain without a suitable replacement strategy.

Another Rust Belt city with a similar story is Flint, Michigan, known as "Vehicle City," once the automotive capital of the United States and the world. When automobile manufacturing was on the rise at the start of the 20th century, a local entrepreneur named William Durant founded General Motors (GM) in Flint in 1908 and opened the largest GM factory globally and the world's largest auto body manufacturing site. In the early 20th century, GM in Flint was responsible for 12 percent of the US car market with a workforce increasing from 49,000 to 85,000 workers, requiring the newly arriving to sleep in tents and other makeshift shelters.[11] Through its leadership in the auto industry, Flint's population ascended from 13,000 in 1900 to 156,492 in 1937.[12] Even before deindustrialization there were challenges, such as the massive Flint sit-down strike of 1935 at the most important single GM location that led to corresponding changes to labor terms and an increase in unionization; unions grew from 30,000 to 500,000 members by the next year and pay increased by 300 percent.[13] Flint also played a vital role in the US World War II effort through retrofitting from car production to tank production for the sake of the war effort. Arts and culture thrived, leading to contributions such as the Flint Cultural Center, which houses the Sloan Museum, the Flint Institute of the Arts, and the Flint Institute of Music.

As in Baltimore, paradise would eventually be lost for Flint. Before World War II, GM formed a strategy to migrate from the city limits of Flint into the suburbs. Between 1940 and 1960, GM built eight industrial complexes in surrounding suburbs, leading to migration out of the city and closures of locations such as the famous Fisher Body Flint Plant #1, which shut its doors in the 1980s, and the crushing blow of the Buick City factory that eliminated 2,900 jobs.[14] Vehicle City went from 80,000 employees in the 1960s to fewer than 7,000 in 2008—and had $30 million in debt; the city's population fell from 190,000 in the 1970s to less than 100,000 in 2013.[15] As recently as 1980, Flint had the highest median income for workers under thirty-five, but that was before GM almost entirely left town.[16]

Fallouts from this deindustrialization crisis included a decrease in police officers, where, as of 2013, the city of Flint employed 1 police officer for every 830 citizens versus New York's 1 officer for every 235 citizens.[17] Given this fiscal crisis, in 2011 Michigan governor Rick Snyder declared a state of financial emergency in the city, giving the state government emergency management control. He began to cut the city budget despite 40 percent of its residents living below the poverty line.[18] One emergency action taken reduced municipal costs by switching the city's water source from

Lake Huron (via Detroit) to the Flint River, but for decades GM never remediated the damage its manufacturing operations caused to the river. A 1963 Department of the Interior study found the damage to the Flint River came from two sources: GM industrial plants and the city wastewater facilities.[19] Another study in 1974 found acceptable levels of contaminants upstream but potent toxins and bacteria levels downstream near the water source.[20] Without adequately analyzing the river's health before making the move, the state government made the switch without remediation of the environmental damage, which would have been significantly less costly than addressing the problem as it stands today. Governor Snyder and President Barack Obama declared states of emergency two years after tens of thousands of citizens were exposed to an unsafe water source. Today Flint's public water has been tested as safe for years, but many of its residents are wary given a lack of trust in its government. How is it possible that a city of approximately one hundred thousand American citizens did not have access to clean water? Flint's water problems stem from a lack of a strategy after its deindustrialization. This void existed between its industrial past and the lack of alternatives to manufacturing when GM left the city.

But it is not just the inner cities that are the boneyards of the deindustrialization of forgotten America; approximately one in five Americans live in an area classified as rural America that used to be a strategic linchpin in America's manufacturing network. For at least the last twenty-five years, much of rural America has been in a relentless economic decline and, thus, a downward spiral of unemployment, depopulation, and drug abuse.[21] In 2020 drugs killed over 70,000 Americans a year, significantly more than car crashes and guns (each ~39,000), AIDS at its height (~42,000), or the Vietnam War in its entirety (~58,000).[22] In 2021 the number of drug deaths increased significantly, with over 100,000 Americans dying, a number surpassed only by heart disease, cancer, and COVID-19.[23] Typically when we think of drug overdoses, we think of our inner cities, but the data show that the problem is becoming more significant in our rural communities as well. According to the National Center for Health Statistics, drug overdoses rose precipitously in both urban and rural areas: from 1999 through 2019, the rate of overdose deaths rose from 6.4 to 22.0 per 100,000 in urban communities and 4.0 to 19.6 per 100,000 in rural counties.[24]

The landscapes of these communities may look more rustic and pristine than the inner cities, but beyond this veneer there exists a storyline of solid commonalities. These locations were home to cornerstone factories built by the towns that processed food from the fields or from livestock, milled textiles, fished from lakes and oceans, and mined for minerals and energy. Rural towns were located near farms, ranches, forests, oil fields, oceans, rivers, and other strategic locations where transportation lines could keep these communities vibrant. When these manufacturing and supply chain activities left, so did the jobs, and younger generations left for areas of more significant opportunity, as had happened in the inner cities. While much of the attention related to the malaise focuses on the inner cities (and rightly so), not enough attention is paid to the utter collapse of these rural communities. These rural communities share with the inner cities a lack of economic opportunity that becomes fertile soil for despair, leading to a near fivefold growth in drug overdoses in less than twenty years. These communities have been on the outside of American economic policy looking in, a spark that has fueled angry politics, protests, criminal activity, and death.

Supply Chain Math

These cities and towns are evidence of failures in American economic policy in the latter half of the 20th century. Since World War II, America's focus has been on marketing, consumption, and the financial markets, with manufacturing an afterthought and left to developing nations. A recent study shows that a 1 percent market share move of production to a low-wage country leads to a 3.1 percent reduction in producer prices that keeps inflation low and spending high, at least when supply chains are operating properly.[25] From a macroeconomic standpoint, this has proven valuable to consumers, shareholders, and white-collar workers but unattentive to the collateral damages to our inner cities and rural towns. For example, through information technology and shipping containerization, a shoe's manufacturing labor cost is $1–3 an hour in an Asian factory versus over $20 an hour in a US factory.[26] Company investors and executives love an outsourced model because it increases revenue and profits, raising share prices and bonuses. Consumers also love it because they purchase comparable-quality products at lower prices. Low-cost nations, from a labor, tax, and environmental regulatory stance, become viable through two-hundred-thousand-ton cargo ships that carry twenty-thousand-plus containers. This has led to what we in the industry call "long-tailed supply chains," the ultimate embodiment of globalization. Even as shipping costs are four times higher than historical averages, the long-tailed solutions are economically optimal (for consumers and shareholders, for example) to on-sourcing back to the United States.[27] Consider an average of ten thousand pairs of jeans in a twenty-foot container: the cost to ship across the ocean has increased to $1 a pair versus $0.15 a pair earlier, which is not a material cost increase on a $70 piece of clothing. The media has made a big deal over this so-called supply chain crisis, but the calculus still favors these global systems. Any calls for the reshoring of supply chains have their work ahead of them to make the math work favorably.

Even those adversely influenced by this supply chain math are unaware of its impact on their communities, given the failure of today's economists, policy analysts, and politicians to curtail the loss of manufacturing jobs. Between 2000 and 2010 the United States lost 5.8 million jobs primarily due to a perfect storm combination of trade liberalization (China's entrance into the WTO), technological innovations in the supply chain and the internet, and the emergence of retailers with effective supply chain strategies such as Walmart.[28] Despite the devastating impact on US manufacturing through deindustrialization, with its percentage of total employment falling from over 25 percent in the 1960s to less than 10 percent today, manufacturing output as a percent of the entire economy has remained relatively flat for the same period, around 12 percent of GDP.[29] Manufacturing has remained a viable contributor to the US economy, but more as an advanced technology contributor in white-collar jobs and capital investment than a mainstay for blue-collar employment and prosperity. According to a study conducted by the Economic Policy Institute, 3.6 million of the 5 million jobs lost at the start of the 21st century were due to trade deficits, not productivity.[30] Therefore, productivity driven by technology did what was intended for the financial markets. The term "creative destruction" was coined in 1942 by Joseph Schumpeter to describe when innovation replaces an old model with a new one. In contrast, poor economic theory and strategy that disregard traditional blue-collar manufacturing without proposing or producing a suitable replacement happened as well. The theory used conventional economic principles that developed starting with Adam Smith 236 years ago, which could not have even conceived of a global supply chain model with instantaneous virtual technology; powerful, agile robots that are gaining functions of intelligence; and a worldwide surplus of 200 million factory workers always willing to work for less. Traditional economic models and public policy should have been revised to better understand these realities and pair the need for consumption and financial markets with mainstream worker well-being.

Sam Walton understood this supply chain math and leveraged it to grow the world's largest retailer. Walton started his business in 1962 and by the mid-1970s had 125 stores with annual sales of over $300 million. By the late 1980s Walmart began to innovate using information technology systems to track and manage inventory, gaining a competitive advantage in the retail landscape and growing to over $30 billion in 1990, becoming the most profitable retailer in the United States. Walmart leveraged China as the world's factory and marketed it through lower prices built on these imported products. In 2006 Walmart was responsible for $27 billion in imports from China and 11 percent of the US trade deficit with China alone between 2001 and 2006, accounting by itself for a job loss of 200,000 in the United States.[31] Walmart's model was precisely what the consumer wanted: lowest prices, always. There were some public outcries regarding Walmart's treatment of its employees. Still, lower-waged workers were part of the financial calculus to operate a one-hundred-thousand-square-foot supercenter with products at the most affordable prices in the market. If Walmart did not offer the consumer and the financial markets continuous improvement, another innovator would step in, such as Amazon, which started as an online bookstore in 1995. Today Amazon sells practically everything, tens of millions of unique stock items versus the one hundred thousand or so found at a Walmart Supercenter. Amazon's Prime model for its 100 million customers worldwide is brilliant and simple: offer free shipping and gain understanding of customer ordering patterns while earning a small membership fee and optimizing inventory levels, shipping costs, and worker productivity—resulting in rapid sales growth and lower profit margins. This model obsesses over the customer while commoditizing all other factors that leave Amazon's competition unable to keep pace, with every year more companies unable to stay in business. Customers find it convenient and affordable to shop at Amazon, with tens of millions of items eligible for free two-day or next-day shipping, a potentially unsustainable model in the future, given the variable costs in the expeditious shipping of a package.[32] Today's retail battle between Walmart and Amazon is a ruthless creative destruction exercise with no end in sight. Walmart seeks to catch up to Amazon and has spent over $11 billion on e-commerce in the last two years.[33] Amazon's investments are exceptional, with 40 percent of its procurement automated, soon to be 80 percent, leading to cost savings of 3–10 percent.[34] But by aiming to delight consumers with tighter fulfillment windows, wider selection, and lower costs, an increasingly widening disconnect continues to take shape between us as workers and as shoppers in this hypercompetitive model.

When Amazon was little more than an online bookstore, few could imagine it would be able to defeat Walmart's customer experience of "always low prices." The founder of Amazon, Jeff Bezos, has called his approach to retail "a customer obsession," an apt description given the imbalanced distribution of benefits to the customer versus other stakeholders. For example, suppose the average Amazon associate makes $15 an hour. Even if Amazon provides an increase in pay to $20 an hour, with the productivity required for package sortation being 1,800 packages an hour, the distribution costs per worker are practically nothing.[35] Furthermore, to achieve productivity targets, Amazon route drivers must straddle the line between safety and speed, potentially putting people in danger to deliver your parcel in a next-day shipping model. Finally, the impact of the Amazon model on the environment is often discussed but infrequently measured in any level of detail, such as the incremental use of fuel and packaging material to make home-delivery drop shipments versus conventional retail at a storefront. With every improvement gained by Amazon, an increasing number of retailers and logistics companies are seeking to keep up in this hypercompetitive omnichannel market of the demand chain through a customer obsession and these pronounced collateral damages.

Over thirty years ago I was taught in business school that creative destruction in the marketplace leads to advancements that benefit the worker, consumer, and shareholder. However, today's calculus increasingly favors the consumer and investor and disfavors workers and citizens. Today's economic models are woefully inadequate to find an optimal solution. It reminds me of the alleged conversation between a union official and Henry Ford II regarding whether Ford's new robots would be able to buy the cars that used to be purchased by the factory workers. As Amazon continues to delight consumers with faster, more convenient, and lower-cost ways of buying products, the question is who will be buying products from them once robots and AI bots are running the entire supply chain? And does this consumption model only succeed when it continues to require us to buy more stuff?

The Sleeping Giant Awakens

Before the COVID-19 pandemic, there had been three big economic shocks in the 21st century: the integration of China into the world economy, the 2008 financial crisis, and the digital economy.[36] Of these three, a financial crisis should not have been a great surprise, as there have been twelve since the Great Depression up to the 2008 crisis, an average of one every six to seven years, not counting what's been happening since the pandemic began in 2020. Likewise, the advent of a digital economy should not have been a surprise either, considering that widespread use of the World Wide Web began in the early 1990s, with e-commerce in full swing within the decade. Finally, the emergence of China into the global economy itself is not a massive surprise; however, its rapid growth has been the most remarkable economic transcendence in human civilization. Measured in terms of GDP, the United States has the world's largest economy ($24.88, versus China at $19.41 trillion), but in terms of purchasing power parity, China's economy is larger than that of the United States, producing $25.3 trillion in 2018, with the European Union second, at $22 trillion, and the United States only third, at $20.5 trillion.[37] Over the past two decades since China's accession to the WTO in 2001, China has been focused on manufacturing and market growth while America has been distracted by various competing objectives. *Washington Post* columnist David Ignatius may question America's so-called selfishness in turning inward versus retaining its traditional leadership role in global geopolitics. Still, there are few such calls in China where it seems as if the entire nation is focused on economic stabilization to achieve self-reliance. China's so-called cake theory debates whether the priority should be to make a bigger cake or share the existing one more fairly.[38]

Production accounts for 27 percent of China's economy and 20 percent of the world's output versus the United States at 12 percent and 18 percent, respectively.[39] Initially, the focus of China's manufacturing strategy was remedial, focusing on low-cost toys and textiles. China has eventually dominated other industries, such as solar panels, wind turbines, commercial drones, and smartphones. America has lost crucial sectors such as aluminum production, leading to its smelters falling from two dozen at the start of the century to just five today.[40] Worldwide consumer retail, critical automotive parts for car manufacturers worldwide, and advanced manufacturing for the newest industries, particularly in sustainable energy, minerals, metals, and even food, such as seafood, are a part of a complex global supply chain that relies heavily on one nation, China. Large consumer product companies source a significant amount of their supply chain from China, including Steve Madden (73 percent), Best Buy (60 percent), and Wayfair (50 percent).[41] The automotive sector continues to be dominated by US, EU, Japanese, and Korean manufacturers as brand names. Still, China has become a hub in the supply chain for a significant number of components.

China's entrance to the world stage was perfect timing for what was happening across Western economies less focused on manufacturing, on transformational retailers like Walmart, and on technological advancements in shipping containers and the internet. Yet few American economists, policy analysts, and politicians focused on a need for manufacturing production and resiliency, as discussed in this book. Once the pandemic made its mark, media headlines announced China's growing role as one of the world's largest producers of finished pharmaceutical products and active pharmaceutical ingredients, or APIs, the most critical component in the medication. The global supply chain systems are so complex and dynamic that it is challenging even for government regulators to track and trace material flows to protect the American consumer. For example, the US Food and Drug Adminstration (FDA) cannot adequately track and trace the origin of finished drugs and APIs flowing from foreign factories to ensure those medications meet the safety requirements according to US law. According to FDA estimates, 28 percent of API world production occurs in the United States, followed by 26 percent in the European Union, 18 percent in India, and 13 percent in China, but these numbers are difficult to validate, as many ingredients require different sources of production.[42] Developing nations have become critical in the pharmaceutical supply chain in the production of generic (off-patent) medication and the supply distribution of vital drugs to poorer regions of the world, such as anti-HIV and malaria drugs that have drastically improved health in these communities. The United States remains the largest pharmaceutical manufacturer in the world. Still, you will see a different story if you peel back the data a bit and look closer: China has come to dominate critical aspects of the supply chain, such as 95 percent of the US ibuprofen, 91 percent of hydrocortisone, 70 percent of acetaminophen, 40–45 percent of penicillin, 40 percent of heparin, and 80 percent of antibiotics.[43] Much of China and India's growth in the US drug business is in generic drugs that constitute approximately 90 percent of the drugs sold in the United States. This trend has led to questions about the safety of drugs from these developing nations when there are insufficient inspectors assigned to these operations to ensure that proper regulations are followed. A 2016 Government Accountability Office report found only twenty-nine inspectors assigned to audit three thousand foreign facilities. This number fell with job cuts in the FDA; now only 1 percent of foreign drugs produced for the United States is checked for safety protocols before entering the country.[44] According to a former inspector for the FDA, Massoud Motamed, inspectors struggle with tracking these foreign drug manufacturers who hide production and safety issues, leaving them to rely solely on the word of the facility managers.[45] The pharmaceutical industry must strike a balance between having adequate capital to fund lifesaving drugs, such as the enormous success in developing multiple COVID-19 vaccines in less than a year, and making medicines affordable for patients, not just in the United States but around the world.

In the global pharmaceutical supply chain, the rights to produce off-patent drugs are often sold to lower-cost manufacturers, often in developing nations where labor costs are much lower. For example, Novartis, a Swiss multinational pharmaceutical corporation, agreed to sell three hundred generic drug formulas to India's Aurobindo Pharma once it was no longer financially viable for Novartis to make the drugs, a frequent practice in the industry, which is improperly tracked and traced.[46] In stable times, such as before the COVID-19 pandemic, few consumers gave much thought to the origin of their medications and the safety procedures enacted. But when these supply chains were disrupted in the early 2020s, there were over one hundred drugs that were in short supply in US hospitals, leading to a significant crisis.

The woefully inadequate supply of personal protective equipment also highlighted American dependence on China because a majority of the world's face masks are produced in China, with 10 million masks a day produced before the pandemic and, after quickly ramping production into crisis mode, accelerating to 116 million a day.[47] American manufacturer 3M stepped in to address a worldwide shortage of personal protective equipment in hospitals in 2020 but was limited in its ability to help, providing only 70 million a month, a number that is far below the goal needed to maintain the US strategic stockpile of 500 million total, based on daily consumption.[48] In the onset of the COVID-19 pandemic, mask suppliers were charging up to six dollars a mask, approximately six times the list price, given the imbalance between supply and demand.[49] It was also a time when hospitals were under severe financial stress, having to cancel profitable elective surgeries to free up capacity to fight the pandemic. A combination of the pandemic and the inadequacies of the global supply chain weakened our hospital systems just when we needed them the most.

During these serious challenges related to COVID-19 and global conflict, nations must continue to focus on the natural resources required to power their economies. Even during significant COVID-19 lockdowns, China seems primarily focused on its future strategies, including the need for the mineral supply chain to grow by 87,000 percent just for the batteries required for electric vehicles.[50] The supply chain fulfillment of lithium, nickel, cobalt, graphite, and critical rare earth metals such as neodymium and dysprosium are the essential raw materials for the digital economy, a global competition that China intends to win. Solar panels and wind turbines require a similar bill of materials to create a sustainable energy strategy. It is no surprise that China is the leader in this space as well. For the United States to be competitive in these future technologies, it must develop a strategy of cooperation between the private and public sectors to extend its supply chains, which will require independence from China for a substantial supply of raw materials. Today China controls 80 percent of the world's rare earth supply chain, while the United States relies on Chinese imports for 50 percent of its supply of rare earth minerals and is 100 percent dependent on China for a smaller list of fourteen to eighteen minerals deemed critical for our national defense.[51] It's certainly true that a global supply chain driven by Chinese imports of essential raw materials puts the US high-tech industry and innovation engine in a precarious situation related to the flow of these vital materials for the future.

There is an interesting comparison to be made between China's strategy and that of the United States regarding the public and private sectors. In China, there are legitimate questions regarding the role of the government in industry, such as its crackdown on the Ant Group's CEO, Jack Ma, after his criticism of the Communist Party's control over the banking sector. Amid the Chinese government's crackdown on tech companies, CEOs and founders of its largest companies, such as JD.com, ByteDance, Pinduoduo, and Alibaba, have stepped down from their roles.[52] A 1993 Chinese law requires both domestic and foreign companies operating in China to adhere to the practices of the Communist Party, and recent actions have shown a great sphere of control over private sector activity. In comparison to China, which embodies a private enterprise economy under Communist Party control, the US government provides scant control over private industry activity in the interest of the public sector in favor of market liberalization. For example, rare earth mineral production in the United States rose by 44 percent in 2019. Still, these raw materials were sent overseas for processing, sparking further concern regarding the viability of the US supply chain from an end-to-end perspective.[53] China defines its practices as "capitalism with Chinese characteristics," and the United States defines its practices as "advancing free, global markets," both with benefits and disadvantages. America's strategy shows a growing vulnerability to national defense and supply resilience; today the United States ranks nineteenth in the world in commercial shipbuilding due to a lack of a public-private partnership, which threatens its national defense security.[54] In advanced computing, the United States remains the world leader in designing and fabricating electronic hardware, but this advantage is shifting to Asia—as expected, given the public-private partnerships that have been formed most notably in Taiwan and China. In a supply chain, benefits start in design. As manufacturing capacity shifts from the West to the East, so do engineering and product development efforts, leading to synergies developing into supply chain world dominance.[55] This path is consistent with 5G networks and batteries, a grim prospect for America's future as it stands today. Even the US military has some dangerous dependencies on the Chinese supply chain for satellites, missiles, and drones.

China is not satisfied with being the world's manufacturer of clothing, toys, and other commodities to support an economy of over 1 billion citizens. In 2015 China diversified its strategy from low-end, commodity-based manufacturing to more sophisticated, advanced manufacturing in critical industries such as semiconductors, pharmaceuticals, aerospace, automotive, robotics, and artificial intelligence. The nation is willing to invest in these industries to become less dependent on other countries—notably, less dependent on US semiconductor manufacturers in the electronics industry. China's model of capitalism is an interwoven strategy between government and industry to invest in the growing, critical sectors of the future. This model of "capitalism with Chinese characteristics" has been challenged in the WTO by the United States and its allies as state-controlled and state-sponsored, creating an unfair advantage compared to its competitors. From a Chinese perspective, its intentions are not to control global supply chains and markets per se but rather to ensure market stability and independence from US companies. For example, China is concerned about its dependence on US companies regarding the design and production of critical semiconductors, including concerns regarding back doors built into hardware that can be exploited, akin to American concerns for Huawei's 5G network. In 2019 a messy debate between the United States and China regarding using Huawei's 5G network centered on security concerns in the same way that China has expressed fears about reliance on American microchips. To circumvent these trade wars, China is moving forward to develop its domestic semiconductor industry, which grew from $7.9 billion in 2004 to $653.2 billion in 2019. The three-millimeter transistor developed as an industry benchmark, which has led to further growth.[56] When understanding this critical competition for semiconductor dominance in the future, it is also essential to know that in 2019 Taiwan accounted for 92 percent of high-end semiconductor production, demonstrating how this tiny island nation is a flashpoint between the two economic superpowers.[57]

As it stands today in its semiconductor supply chain, China is on track to meet its domestic design objectives by its goal of 2025. Moreover, China's strategy in these global rifts seems to be focused on reducing its interdependence on Western markets through its public-private partnership model, concentrating on domestic policy. In contrast, the United States is more focused on a geopolitical trade war and petitioning its case to the WTO rather than on developing concrete and achievable domestic strategies devoid of politics and special interests. In contrast, Taiwan and Korea have strategies to succeed through government-sponsored research funding and significant subsidies to offset the costs of land acquisitions and factory fabrication.[58] The United States uses 20th-century tactics that will fall short to win in a 21st-century competition.

In the past two decades, while there has been outright neglect of the long-forgotten blue-collar worker in America, China has focused on pulling hundreds of millions of its citizens out of extreme poverty. In 2018 China's per capita income was $9,800 in real terms, comparable to that of the United States in 1962 when America was at the midpoint of its manufacturing boom.[59] China's progression as an economy is impressive from any point of view. Of course, any progress would have been relatively easy to achieve given that its starting point was Mao's Great Leap Forward in the middle of the 20th century, which relegated many in the population to starve to death as poor farmers. As a result of China's economic growth, China's official poverty rate is similar to Western standards, at 0.6 percent, when using the developing world standard of $2 a day. The number of poor is much higher when using the standard of upper-middle-income nations of $5.50 a day—then it becomes 600 million, or 43 percent.[60] For China, the good news is there are fewer in extreme poverty, and income inequality in China is better than it was a decade ago. The bad news for China is its inequality rating, measured by the Gini index, which is higher than that of most advanced nations, including the United States.[61] In China, 45 percent of the country's disposable income is taken by the top 20 percent, and the top 1 percent of the population owns 30 percent of the wealth.[62]

Compared to the simplistic notions often portrayed in the media, China's progression as a world economic power is complicated. China itself has also been hit hard by deindustrialization, with its workforce having fallen by 12.5 million workers in the most recent five-year span.[63] The reality is that China faces domestic economic challenges equal to, if not more significant than, that of the United States, including concerning the global supply chain, which is a ruthless system driven by the financialization of markets that hold no loyalties to anyone other than its shareholders. No matter how much China seeks a balanced, even protected economic system from these challenges, it will have difficulties overcoming these obstacles for a nation of 1.4 billion, especially through a system that lacks social, political, and economic liberties. Americans need to understand better what's happening in China to develop an effective strategy to compete; a more strategic approach related to the global supply chain for the United States can put it in an enviable position in comparison.

Define, Measure, and Analyze the Problem

This chapter began with a grim picture of the American economy due to the impact of deindustrialization that began shortly after World War II. The net fallouts from this include rampant drug abuse and addiction, growing income inequality between white-collar and blue-collar workers, a lingering exacerbation of racial disparities, and challenges in the public education system, to name but a few of the most prominent problems. And yet, as ominous as these challenges may appear, they are arguably less severe than the challenges facing China, the world's other economic superpower. Given this, there can be great hope for the United States if a suitable strategy is put forth in the 21st century. Americans are self-confident, sometimes overconfident, due to their track record of success in a relatively short period. Contrast this to China, the Middle Kingdom, a three-thousand-year-old culture with the experience and bruises to understand the wisdom of a longer-term strategy. Since the 1980s China has been the fastest-growing economy in the world, transforming from an isolated socialist state of failed programs such as its Great Leap Forward to a manufacturing superpower due to its optimized supply chain strategy. This transformation was only possible through realizing the inherent weaknesses in its present system that Deng Xiaoping addressed after the disastrous impact of Mao's Cultural Revolution and the power struggle that occurred in its aftermath, including the Gang of Four debacle. Deng's vision was called the Four Modernizations—in agriculture, industry, national defense, and science and technology. Even though these reforms were conceived in 1963 during Chairman Mao's Great Leap Forward and Cultural Revolution, they were not launched until 1978 by Deng. But the nation found a way to escape this devastating past to launch the most significant economic miracle in history. If anything, China's experience should provide hope that similar healing can occur in these uncertain times in the United States; for the first time in history, most younger Americans do not believe they will do as well economically as their parents. In a 2019 study conducted by the mobile application Even, only 24.1 percent of Americans thought they had achieved their version of the American Dream, while 24.5 percent said it's attainable but not accomplished yet, and more than 50 percent were not hopeful at all.[64]

Differences in politics and culture notwithstanding, I wonder whether America will take notice and learn from one of its main competitors, from both its strengths and weaknesses. The first step for China to escape a debilitating economic structure and ideology was to realize that it had a problem that needed to be solved. The second step was to focus on fixing its domestic issues, albeit through an autocratic government. Today there is much discussion about the symptoms of economic malaise and social unrest in America but no acknowledgment and acceptance of the root cause of the problem, which is needed for institutional reform. Rather than pandering to politics, experts with experience fixing and building things, such as those from the STEM fields, must develop detailed, rational plans and make a covenant with the American public, which needs to sacrifice its habit of overconsumption of cheap goods for the betterment of future generations and for our nation's growth and well-being. After a seventy-year overconsumption binge, can Americans build for the future? Developing a national supply chain strategy can be a movement in the right direction; America's commitment to sacrifice and the common good hasn't been tested since World War II.

A starting point in developing a national supply chain strategy is stating the problem clearly: The United States has an outdated 20th-century approach to supply chain focused primarily on front-end sales and marketing, instant consumer gratification, and quarterly financial earnings for stock market performance. America's obsolete model has led to the demand chain, one that seeks optimization through an imbalance of supply and demand, discussed so far in this book. From an apparent problem, the statement comes to a straightforward solution: to build future prosperity through a balanced 21st-century supply chain system. No longer should business leaders and policymakers kick the problem down the road by not addressing these imbalances within society and the environment, and between the public and private sectors. Today consumer spending accounts for over $13 trillion, or 70 percent of the US economy in terms of its GDP, up significantly since the 1970s, when it was around 60 percent of the economy.[65] In comparison, less than 40 percent of China's GDP is consumption, with production being about 40 percent, an even balance. These data points show the differences between an American economy that is overwhelmingly focused on consumption as a method of growing the economy but only in the short-term, which mortgages the future.

In contrast, China's economy is more balanced between production and consumption, with the great challenge of reducing the income inequality that has left 600 million Chinese citizens—just under two times the entire population of the United States—in poverty. Moreover, a more balanced economy between production and consumption is viable from a longer-term perspective as well as during today's volatile times. For example, during the early years of the COVID-19 pandemic, America's economic dependence on consumption was on full display as the bottom fell out due to outbreaks and lockdowns that limited activities, requiring government stimulus spending to keep the economy going.

The second most prominent element of the US economy, after consumer spending, is business investment of 18 percent, or approximately $3.5 trillion, according to 2019 Bureau of Economic Analysis data.[66] This includes capital investment in supply chains, manufacturing, information technology, commercial and residential real estate, and business inventory changes. Because the US economy remains the largest globally, it is logical that capital investment is a major element but is significantly smaller than consumption, indicating a problematic short-term lack of strategy. Regarding the government, America's public spending as a percentage of GDP isn't much greater than China's (17 percent versus 14 percent). Yet the role of government in these two nations is vastly different. Finally, it is telling that China's net import percentage is close to 40 percent of its economy while the United States has a deficit of 13 percent, with imports running at 18 percent and exports at 5 percent. This statistic explains why so many cargo ships have been waiting offshore the Los Angeles and Long Beach ports versus US cargo leaving the port, heading for Asia. These data show a clear difference that Americans should heed to understand our need for a new supply chain and production strategy moving forward.

US wage data has shown positive growth in only ten of the last forty years, and with a rising level of wage inequality.[67] According to an Economic Policy Institute study, the median hourly wage in the United States is $19.33 an hour, which translates into approximately $40,000 a year for full-time work. The American factory wage is four times higher than China's but significantly lower than that of the traditional blue-collar manufacturing role of yesteryear when adjusted for inflation; back then, a worker expected an adjusted hourly wage of $30.00 an hour and with overtime could earn between $75,000 and $90,000, a decent middle-class income. These statistics demonstrate the challenges of deindustrialization: today's American factory workers remain prosperous in the eyes of most of the world but not compared to their fathers and grandfathers. These data are the inescapable truths about how out-of-balance globalization has affected the US middle class.

From this clear data, the question is, will America continue down this path or face its realities? A rising bifurcation between the haves and have-nots in American society is not just an economic concern but a societal one as well, with its effects permeating in increasingly dangerous, unsettling ways. Moreover, the fault lines have been exposed across different population segmentation, such as race, gender, age, geography, and education level, as solid indicators of the haves and have-nots in society.

The 21st-Century US Supply Chain Strategy

In May 2015 the Chinese government developed a national strategy called Made in China 2025 to increase its domestic production of critical materials, components, and products to 40 percent by 2020 and 70 percent by 2025.[68] Rather than making these announcements with great fanfare, the Chinese government chose not to draw much attention to these goals, calling them "aspirational and unofficial." Other nations are similarly developing a manufacturing strategy for the future, including Germany's Industry 4.0 development plan. But no prominent policymakers have developed any such approach for the United States. Besides policy papers written by nongovernmental organizations and think tanks with few details, scant attention has focused on this root cause problem; instead, the focus is on symptoms and quick-hit, politically pleasing messages. As I discuss in this chapter, I am in no way suggesting that America adopt a Chinese approach to government. However, there are things we can learn from the Chinese, such as more rational and less political strategies developed by engineers and scientists, who view matters from a longer-term perspective for the betterment of society.

In contrast, American policymakers are often public policy analysts and lawyers (and even celebrities) with a mindset focused on legislation, policy, and even public relations and electability, a less empirical approach, albeit one that is sometimes unavoidable to an extent in any democracy. For example, American political leaders have focused more on establishing trade wars and petitioning the WTO, which looks good to the electorate, and on formalizing strategies to appeal to short-term public opinion rather than long-term results. As a result, despite the evidence that trade wars and disputes are rarely successful in today's complex and interconnected global system and are even harmful, these strategies are only red meat for the masses.

China's other crown jewel in its strategy is its Belt and Road Initiative (BRI), which extends its supply chain through Central and West Asia, Africa, and even into South America and other areas while avoiding much of the West. As an alternative to an overreliance on its largest trading partner, America, which China finds increasingly adversarial, China's logical strategy is to create its sphere of influence, which reduces its dependency on the Western-dominated conventional supply chain model. China's BRI is breathtaking in recreating a main global supply chain that excludes the world's other economic superpower. Inaugurated in 2013 by Chairman Xi Jinping, the system, with China as the hub, stretches through eastern Asia to Europe, much like the original Silk Road from the dawn of the Roman civilization. The United States has raised some valid concerns regarding the BRI, including that it would lead to a "debt trap" phenomenon when nations cannot pay back their loans, giving the Chinese influence and ownership over strategic assets abroad. However, many of the regions being developed in the BRI have notoriously been outside the scope of the existing supply chain logistics routes, such as central Asia and Africa, which account for only 6.2 percent of global trade.[69] By creating a Chinese-centric supply chain infrastructure of ports, roads, rail lines, pipelines, and border crossings, the goal is to achieve Asian connectivity within the supply chain versus a Western-dominated model based on multinational corporations based in the West. Furthermore, by establishing a global supply chain system that spans approximately two-thirds of the world's population, China seeks to insulate itself from Western influence.

For the sake of economic self-reliance and stability, the United States should develop a strategy that seeks balanced and sustainable growth. This supply chain system wouldn't over-rely on a private sector model that migrates production worldwide based on a cost-only focused approach. Much like China's BRI, an American strategy should invest as well in infrastructure but in a different model: according to a 2016 McKinsey study, $2.5 trillion is spent annually around the world on infrastructure capital projects, yet the needs are at least $3.3 trillion annually to support the current level of economic growth, with 60 percent of the investment occurring in developing nations.[70] It is well known that the countries that invest in their infrastructure will win in a global supply chain, as China has demonstrated through its investment in its roads, bridges, trains, ports, electrical grids, 5G networks, and health care and innovation laboratories.[71] Since 1978 no nation in the world has enjoyed the level of investment, both public and private, that China has; in constant 1978 prices, China's investment in transportation infrastructure was 609.11 billion RMB in 2008, seventy-six times greater than in 1978.[72]

In contrast, in real terms, infrastructure funding in the United States has fallen from $450.4 billion in 2007 to $440.5 billion in 2017 but is expected to increase.[73] While most of China's infrastructure spending has also led to a growth in foreign direct investment due to cutting-edge ports and manufacturing capabilities, much of America's infrastructure investment is to repair crumbling roads and public utility systems rather than building bridges for the 21st century and beyond. The last report card from the American Society of Civil Engineers gave the United States a D+ for the state of its infrastructure, the same grade it gave in 2013. For each of the sectors, the report card score was disappointing: airports (D), bridges (C+), dams (D), drinking water (D), energy (D+), hazardous waste (D+), inland waterways (D), levees (D), parks and recreations (D+), ports (C+), rail (B), roads (D), schools (D+), solid waste (C+), transit (D-), and wastewater (D+). In comparison to China, which has developed a nationwide strategy, most US projects aren't funded by the federal government (only 27 percent), with the rest from state bonds (27 percent), user fees, and other (38 percent), according to the State Budget Officers 2019 State Expenditure Report.[74]

For decades many politicians have made a case for a 21st-century infrastructure investment strategy, and there is hope for the future with the Infrastructure Investment and Jobs Act enacted by the US Congress in June 2021. However, transitioning to a 21st-century economy will require more than just federal spending; it will require a conscious strategy with a new economic approach that includes trade-offs between the short and long terms and a new calculus based more on rationality and less on politics. The remainder of the book presents solutions that can be part of this new model to establish a 21st-century economy and society that can compete on the global stage on behalf of American citizens. This will require changes and sacrifices that are not usually included in how we think about strategy today.

Before the Industrial Revolution, markets were in place to solve problems because the demand for goods and services was always more significant than the supply. For the 21st century, we need a strategy to return to the basics of markets to solve problems rather than a prioritization to only increase shareholder value and sell products through any means necessary. When supply chains were first implemented, America employed problem-solving tools such as Six Sigma, industrial engineering, quality and waste reduction programs, and lean manufacturing. W. Edwards Deming focused on productivity toward solving problems for the private and public good, a technique that the Japanese learned with enthusiasm. Today markets and supply chains can be systems for good, as is demonstrated by the millions, if not billions, of people pulled from extreme poverty through innovation and structured problem solving. If we redefine our markets in these terms, there is no reason why our supply chains cannot become vehicles for good on behalf of our brothers and sisters from affected communities, lifting them out of despair. A 21st-century supply chain in the United States can create a model of design, sourcing, manufacturing, and logistics based in the United States to generate an improved multiplier between supply and demand, reduce the impact on the environment, and strengthen our national defense in times of crisis. These are all possible with the right strategy for the future.

Some of the most incredible feats ever achieved in this nation have been a function of supply chain management. The railroads that united our continent into a country, the military logistics required to achieve the near-impossible at Normandy Beach on D-Day, and landing the first man on the moon in 1969 are triumphs of the supply chain. These achievements used structured problem-solving techniques to define the problem/opportunity, gather endless streams of information/data to understand the problem/opportunity, and then analyze what was collected to determine the proper solution. We developed rational answers to massive issues and opportunities using analytical engineering techniques, not marketing, social science, or politics. And the same should apply to today. This chapter argues for an economic redirection to develop the 21st-century supply chain system of the future like China is on the path of creating through its transformational strategies. This redirection could be accomplished through another Manhattan Project or Marshall Plan, a research and development project completed by the most renowned scientists and industrial engineers across the nation and with our allies. In times of great need, anything is possible when Americans follow the right processes. Right now, under the threat of the COVID-19 virus, scientists from around the world are collaborating to find therapies, tracking systems, and vaccines to get the virus under control. The same thing can happen in the United States for the supply chain, with the federal government putting together a team of the most knowledgeable in supply chain logistics to develop a world-class strategy for the 21st century.

CHAPTER 3

NEW ECONOMICS

From Supply Chain to Value Chain

According to a Pew Research Center poll of thirteen European nations, the assessment of America's response to the COVID-19 pandemic in 2020 was not good: respondents gave a 74 percent favorability rating to its own nation's handling of the crisis, 64 percent to the World Health Organization, 57 percent to the European Union, 37 percent to China, and the lowest score—just 15 percent—to the United States.[1] According to a University of Chicago poll, Americans share a similar sentiment with those in other nations, with 56 percent holding the US government accountable, 47 percent blaming other countries, and 39 percent blaming the World Health Organization.[2] In Gallup's most recent study, the total percentage of Americans who have either "very little" to "no" confidence in the respective institution is as follows: Congress (14 percent and 46 percent, respectively), big business (29 percent and 36 percent, respectively), public schools (11 percent and 22 percent, respectively), the president (16 percent and 37 percent, respectively); the medical system (4 percent and 17 percent, respectively), and banks (10 percent and 19 percent, respectively).[3] Culturally, Americans are known for placing greater faith in our communities, families, and the individual than in large institutions like government and big business. However, in times of crisis, such as World War I and II and the Great Depression, these institutions had come through to earn the public's trust. Seventy-seven percent of Americans trusted the federal government in 1964, with the results nosediving downward to 25 percent in 1979, roughly where they have settled today.[4] I remember as a kid when my grandmother told me the story of how Franklin Delano Roosevelt promised to "put a chicken in every pot" during the Great Depression. Fifty years from now, I doubt my daughters will be reminiscing fondly with their grandchildren about the government's handling of the COVID-19 pandemic in the 2020s.

After World War II, American society was generally more unified than today, even despite systematic racism, and was centered around traditional Judeo-Christian values, family structures, and even political beliefs. During this era, greater commonalities existed in culture and politics, with the 1950s known for conformity, civility, bipartisanship, community, and government consensus—at least relative to today's politics. However, this was only true in some settings—witness Senator Joseph McCarthy's Hollywood blacklist and the violent suppression of the struggle to de-segregate schools and expand voting access in the South. In many cases, politicians were rewarded for compromise and getting things done and for civil discourse that re-spected the primary culture and shared values. Unfortunately, not all groups in society were equally represented by the government, so this definition of consensus and unity applied to some and was inequitable to others. Nevertheless, for those who benefited, the economy was driven through a multiplier effect that balanced economic gains that, for the most part, led to political and economic stability. However, later in the 1960s, this tenuous harmony began to decouple through poor policy, the effects of deindustrialization, and even critical efforts by those underrepresented to gain equal rights and opportunities—efforts that others resented. Rather than as a rallying point focusing on consensus, bipartisanship, and unity, the political calculus seemed to call for "conquering by dividing," winning elections and customer loyalty by segmenting populations. This is an important marketing technique that applies as much to elec-tions as it does to running a global supply chain: the use of marketing segmentation to classify individuals into more focused groups to present more effective campaigns to increase revenue and profitability. Likewise, politicians developed strategies to win elections by segmenting populations based on race, socioeconomic status, religious af-filiation, and geography. Starting in the 1960s and 1970s America's institutions have won through segmenting versus uniting, leading to today's distrust. Likewise, within the supply chain, companies have segmented the role of the worker and the consumer to focus on achieving improved results by optimizing one at the expense of the other. As I note earlier in this book, this strategy is different from the early supply chain that led to the multiplier effect between the consumer and worker.

Since this era, the data clearly show the deterioration in economic prosperity be-tween the blue- and white-collar classes, segmentation of politics, and distrust in institutions. Americans are more segmented based on religion, race, geography, and education, which leads to tribalism in politics. From one perspective, this cultural discourse is expressed as a caste system in the United States that restricts the op-portunity for some groups in the population compared to others. In her book titled *Caste*, Isabel Wilkerson argues that America's institutions have codified long-standing divisions that persist even today.[5] From another perspective, writes David Horowitz in *The Enemy Within*, the threat to America is that of an anti-American, totalitarian posture that fights traditional American values.[6] Studies have found that this politi-cal polarization stemming from and exploited by marketing segmentation arises less from apparent differences between groups and more so as the result of an intentional effort to use these techniques to win voters and elections.[7] According to a model de-veloped by Northwestern University researchers in 2020, polarization and extremism are successful political strategies to attract voters from the middle.[8] Political polarization has been a theme across democratically governed nations for many of the same reasons in the United States. According to a study conducted by Brown and Stanford University researchers, America's political polarization has grown faster than other developed world democracies due to racial divisions, twenty-four-hour cable news media, and the limitations within the US two-party system.[9] Starting in the 1960s and reaching a boiling point today, the fractures are significant roadblocks that could prevent a necessary manufacturing and supply chain strategy for the 21st century.

A Common Objective

America must have a shared vision for the 21st century that can unite us through a common objective. Even though it was not applied equally, the 20th-century concept of a multiplier effect was a unifying platform enabled by government and business to benefit the community and individual. In contrast to a market segmentation concept that maximizes financial results through driving prices down and often lowering wages, the multiplier effect optimizes market value for workers and consumers. As a result, the covenant was destroyed through the deindustrialization process, and the balance of power shifted from the individual and community to the large institution, ultimately through large global supply chains. Industry and politicians benefit through a "conquer and divide" mentality, even though both parties find these practices unsavory. The benefit of a unifying multiplier effect in GDP in the 1960s was a consistent growth rate of nearly 4.7 percent per annum, demonstrating relative (and limited) fairness through consistency. However, the growth rate fell to around 3.2 percent per annum, with higher variation from year to year in the 1970s. Then in the 1990s the growth rate continued to fall, with an average of 2 percent with high deviation, all according to Bureau of Labor Statistics data.[10] Economies and supply chains do not like volatility, and as demonstrated in the data, volatility driven through private and public policy from US institutions had a negative effect. There was a clear relationship between a loss of unity and shared purpose through a multiplier effect to lower economic growth and trust in America's institutions since the 1960s. Moving forward, a new and improved multiplier effect for the 21st century, focused on communities and individuals rather than larger institutions, could serve as a unifying strategy.

Segmentation broke citizens down as workers versus consumers, which led to spiky economic growth, as shown in a deeper look into the numbers. Compared to this strategy, Sweden (where I studied for my PhD) has a more inclusive and balanced well-being and growth system. The Swedish word *lagom* translates into English as "enough," or literally "enough is as good as a feast." In Sweden, culture and institutions have enabled economic growth through shared social values focused on balance, as shown through the lower rate of poverty and inequality and higher innovation ranking than in the United States. Rather than a strategy of segmentation and a zero-sum game, institutions in Sweden achieve greater trust from the population through balance and values and not through segmenting groups for political and marketing purposes.

Change can only happen through a common objective among the American public if fostered through its institutions. For example, from 1948 to 1979, US productivity improved by 108 percent and compensation by 93.2 percent, but between 1979 and 2018 these numbers were 69.6 percent and 11.6 percent, respectively.[11] Again, look at the official positions taken by political and business institutions. You will see agreement from both parties and large corporations that these economic imbalances need to be addressed, but from different ideological perspectives. A divergence between productivity and labor wages is a loss of value due to a poor economic strategy and is perpetuated through advances in technology and a commoditized global supply chain. For decades, conventional econometric models have ignored these simple principles of value as a term that did not fit neatly into an equation due to a lack of available data. In addition, many multinational corporations have lost their focus on the long-term strategic plans that W. Edwards Deming championed in the 1960s and 1970s and that China's leaders focus on today. The more convenient strategy relative to short-term quarterly financial performance is defined by the "easy out" versus the "difficult in," discussed in earlier chapters.

Without a culture for shared norms, trust, and competency, the term "value" changed in its purpose away from empirical industrial engineering toward more convenient options that segmented the population into winners and losers, such as offshoring and technology to achieve short-term benefits driven by capital markets. Moreover, global supply chains made it easy for technology and labor to become commodities that lent themselves to short-term measures of profitability that are preferred by financial markets. Due to the short-termism of the financial markets in the United States, there has been less incentive to undergo a strategy of the "difficult in" with a surging stock market, regardless of its impact on income inequality. From 1979 to 2018, the top level of wages increased 63.2 percent; the middle range, by 15.1 percent; and the lower range, by 3.3 percent.[12] According to a Congressional Research Service report from 2019, actual wage trends have shown a dramatic bifurcation from 1980 to the present regarding median wages by educational class. There are steady hourly wage increases for those with a bachelor's degree ($25.95 to $28.37) and an advanced degree ($29.66 to $36.71), but the data show a decrease for those with some college ($22.46 to $19.80), a high school diploma ($19.51 to $17.00), and no high school diploma ($16.88 to $13.50).[13] While the middle range of income has remained flat from 1971 to 2016, dwindling slightly over time from 61 percent to

52 percent of the population, the lower and higher ranges have grown somewhat, 25 percent to 29 percent and 14 percent to 19 percent, respectively.[14] These data indicate a failure of economic and supply chain strategy to become a more unifying strategy for the nation as a whole.

A New American Dream?

Ten years ago, Senior Fellow of the American Enterprise Institute Mark J. Perry penned an article that embodied US public policy: Americans should be happy with the decline of manufacturing. Perry's central premise is that America's growing GDP and declining prices of purchased products are a sign of progress.[15] But, of course, this perspective focuses only on one stakeholder of the supply chain—the consumer. Yet Perry's position begins to break down when understanding a definition of rationality within a global supply chain that provides value to consumers through low prices and American public policy, as is shown above in labor rates within economic classes. A global supply chain strategy that is best for the consumer might infer, unintentionally or not, that America's blue-collar workers achieved a rarefied upper-middle-class status only as an anomaly due to the circumstances of the post–World War II global economy rather than as a function of an effective American policy. Throughout the economic history of capitalism, it was the middle class—or bourgeoisie, composed of merchants and other self-employed professionals—who, according to Marx, controlled the means of production. America was the first society where the middle class consisted of those involved in, not owning or managing, the production process. The so-called American Dream of the past was not necessarily about the elite wealthy of executives, celebrities, and heirs of wealth or about the professional class of college-educated; rather, it was about the middle-class, blue-collar workers who succeeded through participating in manufacturing and supply chain.

The question is, what should be the future strategy for America's middle class—that of the white-collar knowledge worker and a well-paid, secure, blue-collar manufacturing worker? Before deindustrialization, America and other Western democracies had a healthy segment of blue-collar workers composed of the middle class, craftsmen, and manufacturing workers who did not have a college education. Tied to this segment were the working class and working poor, the nonskilled who aspired to enter the middle class through blue-collar production work. The failure of deindustrialization was a lack of understanding of the supply chain and manufacturing value proposition to these middle and working classes of blue-collar workers. While some children of blue-collar workers and immigrants did go to college, a large part of the population could not or did not, instead expecting an American Dream defined by blue-collar work like that of their parents. Concurrently, politicians promised a restoration of manufacturing and well-paid jobs, with no need for college. Unintentionally or not, this lack of a strategy led to the bifurcation of the white- and blue-collar classes, with their fates heading in opposite directions. Through market segmentation, opportunistic politicians and business leaders leveraged these separate paths to make further promises never fulfilled.

A 21st-century American Dream can neither be a restoration of manufacturing's past nor the transition of all Americans to white-collar knowledge work. First, the math is not on the side of repairing manufacturing's former role in American prosperity within the existing system. Labor rates in the United States are increasing while workers' wages in the developing world remain very low. Today's demand-driven supply chain does not support the wages of a middle-class lifestyle in the United States for factory workers. With three billion factory workers on the planet and another two hundred million waiting to join the ranks, there is an endless source of factory workers and robots for industry to hire costing around $1–$2 an hour on a planet with a poverty level set by the United Nations as $1.90 a day.[16] In the United States, a highly developed nation, the official poverty threshold is approximately $26,000 a year, or roughly $13–$15 an hour for full-time work, an untenable status in America but significantly higher than the global minimum labor rate. As labor rates for unskilled workers are pushing upward to $20 an hour, a semiskilled factory worker will require $25–$40 an hour, which isn't a feasible calculus in today's demand-driven supply chain. The math is inescapably straightforward: the old days of manufacturing will never return. But it will also never be viable for all Americans to become traditional white-collar workers, defined today as those who perform professional, managerial, or administrative work and are not required to do physical labor.

The United States should neither neglect the supply chain's production element nor concentrate solely on consumption. In contrast to Perry's assessment that offshoring the production of goods creates a healthier economy, the data tell a different story. As measured in GDP, global economic growth has averaged between 2–3 percent over the recent decade (before the pandemic), with developing nations having higher growth rates than developed nations.[17] In the global economy, the United States has a lot to lose, with 25 percent of the world's GDP total but less than 5 percent of the world's population. While the official numbers may tell us otherwise, there has been an apparent loss in economic value within the US economy that must be addressed across all population segments.

It is time for a new economic path that achieves growth through value, which cannot be wholly defined in terms of stock market indices; for example, at the same time that the Dow Jones Industrial Average hit record-breaking numbers in 2020, the poverty rate in the United States also grew to 11.4 percent, the first increase in five years.[18]

For a variety of reasons, from the ability to earn a living wage to self-sufficiency as a nation, manufacturing and production still matter, even to the economies and societies of advanced nations.

Like the conditions that prompted Adam Smith to write *The Wealth of Nations*, today our financial markets view competition primarily in terms of economies of scale and market concentration. For example, in 2018 the Apple iPhone carried 62 percent of the smartphone market, three credit card companies owned 95 percent of the credit market, Google was 60 percent of the browser market, three companies provided 78 percent of the mobile networks, and four airlines represented 69 percent of air travel, a clear signal of the concentration of corporate dominance.[19] Market concentration in the United States has grown in recent decades. Between 1985 and 2017 the number of mergers increased from 2,308 to 15,361 annually, representing 75 percent of industries.[20] These mergers and acquisitions led to levels of market concentration that would have been viewed as violating antitrust laws in the past. Those who are winning in this model are clear regarding the rules of the game; in the words of American billionaire entrepreneur and venture capitalist in the tech industry Peter Thiel, "competition is for losers"; monopoly is the goal.[21] Rather than prosecuting these so-called entrepreneurs for taking advantage of the system, we need to change the rules of the game. Value, defined as the concentration of market, has proven detrimental to the interests of the common good.

The Value of Nothing

Much of the concentrated power emerging in today's Big Tech companies is what I call the value of nothing. These nonmarket activities happen much differently from traditional value transactions, where a consumer pays for a product or service. The Big Tech companies are the primary drivers in this paradigm shift in price, cost, and value. Companies like Google and Meta have market capitalization values reaching close to or over $1 trillion. How can trillion-dollar companies have such high stock market valuations when they frequently require no traditional payment from consumers for their services? How can Amazon, another company worth nearly $1.5 trillion, make money by shipping products for free for Prime members? This 21st-century model, built on a new value proposition and used consistently by Big Tech, serves a different purpose in a market setting and could become the basis of a valuable new American Dream model for individuals and communities. This model could become the foundation of a 21st-century supply chain model.

This model focuses on benefits to individuals and communities as a utility, with the process—not the product or service—monetized. The process is through modern technology tools to improve communication and transaction capability across different mediums, such as peer to peer, community to community, and myriad other arrangements. In this new economy, according to David Byrne of the Federal Reserve and Carol Corrado of the Conference Board, smartphones and broadband connections should be classified as investments and not expenditures due to their ability to harvest benefits for the provider beyond a traditional payment.[22] This same philosophy can enable market value to communities and individuals through broadband and other technologies that encourage localized and entrepreneurial development. This concept of a nonmarket transaction has created some of the most valuable companies in the world defined by market capitalization; as of September 2020, only three of the top ten are not technology companies (Saudi Aramco, Berkshire Hathaway, and Johnson & Johnson), while the other seven are (Microsoft, Apple, Amazon, Alphabet, Meta, Alibaba, and Tencent), an astonishing transformation in less than a decade.[23] This concept of the "value of nothing" can change the nature of transactions and, thus, value across today's supply chain systems beyond the benefit of Big Tech. It could lead to the redefinition of today's conventional approach to finance and economics that has commoditized our definition of value, leading to the problems discussed in this book. This approach can restore a greater balance between institutions, communities, and individuals in markets and society. This new model could create a shared vision for the future and lead to greater trust and commonality between America's institutions, communities, and individuals.

When we think about this new economy of the future, we must look beyond the technology that often gets the attention, such as artificial intelligence, automation, and Big Data. Instead, we must think through how these tools can lead to an improved definition of the value proposition from our model today that focuses on price and profit, with everything else discarded as an externality. Technologies in use today are often a more advanced way of perpetuating an imbalanced economy. Widely available data provided as a utility benefit could liberalize and democratize transactions to a level playing field for individual entrepreneurs. Using a peer-to-peer approach as an alternative to (not a replacement for) large, institutionalized global supply chains, individuals as both producers and consumers can use data in a completely different approach as a value proposition. A new peer-to-peer model could correct a problem of today's markets described by a character in the 19th-century Oscar Wilde play *Lady Windermere's Fan*, who said, "a cynic is someone who knows the price of everything and the value of nothing."[24] An economy that scales as a function of the price leads to nonmarket transactions that commoditize everything, reducing the value of everything other than what benefits the consumer and shareholder—which has led to today's lack of balance between production and consumption.

If used differently, as a public utility rather than solely by Big Tech companies, a value of nothing model can create virtual communities that could liberate information that could pose an opportunity for today's demand chains to transform into tomorrow's value chain. Rather than creating stock market value by pushing more products and services to consumers through automation and lower labor costs in faraway countries, communities and individuals can create their own community market-based economies as an alternative. With the cost of technology continuing to fall, enabling users to have unlimited free access as is the case with Facebook, Snapchat, and TikTok, a public sector investment in technology infrastructure for a utility purpose could yield enormous opportunities for multiplying benefits across communities. Today consumers are commoditized through their phones and data, with companies like Meta and Google profiting from this so-called free use. But, as is so aptly presented in Netflix's 2020 documentary drama *The Social Dilemma*, these new technologies are designed to be addicting for the benefit of the service provider. They are used to exploit the user, much as Edward Bernays's marketing and advertising ideas were used to increase consumer demand. And it isn't just on social media but also within our supply chains: the behemoths Amazon and Walmart are providing nonmarket value to consumers, such as free shipping, leading to more purchases. What if these emerging technologies enabled individuals and communities to unlock new markets and value propositions to society? It would change the nature of supply chains that would naturally balance supply and demand within communities rather than across a spiky globalization scheme solely by large multinational corporations. What if these new processes were to become the keys to unlocking a new economic model of the supply chain to create this desperately needed disruption for change—a model where innovation is enabled for the public benefit within a private enterprise capitalism model? It could be a unifying strategy across these politicized market segments that do not trust its institutions or each other.

Economics: The Dead Science

New methods to measure a value proposition are necessary to address these challenges of discourse and division in America and to replace today's outdated method that measures the price of everything and the value of nothing. The field of economics has been under scrutiny almost since its origins, often for a good reason, with Thomas Carlyle labeling economics "the dismal science." For example, in the 19th-century Thomas Malthus predicted that food production could not keep pace with population growth, leading to worldwide starvation. In the end, Malthus's theory was wrong because of the lack of data and tools to forecast what was about to happen at the end of the century through the Industrial Revolution. Malthus is just one of the many economists who did not possess the tools to keep pace with the market possibilities, innovations, and human dynamics. Although general theories, introduced in such works as Adam Smith's *The Wealth of Nations* and John Maynard Keynes's *General*

Theory of Employment, Interest and Money, are heuristically valuable, they have been insufficient in precision due to a lack of data and analytical techniques and tools to keep pace with accelerating growth.

As a graduate student, I struggled with the relevancy of economics that was forced to use ridiculously abstract and overly complex econometric models, simplistic assumptions, and the phrase *ceteris parabus* (defined as "all other factors as constant or irrelevant"). These tools are insufficient for the complexities of the global supply chain–driven economy of today. Today companies like Amazon and Walmart use data science and analytics tools to understand and respond to the markets, gathering and analyzing near-infinite amounts of data. In contrast to today's most valuable companies moving in this direction, public institutional economics is stuck in the 20th century, still creating and interpreting abstract models that do more harm than good in establishing trust in America's institutions with the public. US agencies such as the Bureau of Labor Statistics and the Bureau of Economic Analysis continue to publish economic analysis not much differently from how the reporting had been done after World War II, despite seismic shifts in the speed and nature of data within the US and global economies. Whether concerning the great recession of 2008, the influence of China, e-commerce, global supply chains, or the most recent impact of the COVID-19 pandemic, conventional neoclassical economists have performed poorly in describing, diagnosing, and predicting the economy. And yet, rather than reforming their practices to conduct a structured problem-solving exercise to leverage advances in data and analytics, the econometricians, economists, and policymakers seem to be doubling down and repeating these outdated procedures, expecting an improvement in the accuracy of their results. As a result, today's leading companies are moving forward with new processes and technologies to advance their interests while those institutions responsible for advocating for the public good are stuck in neutral.

The solution to understanding the complex and dynamic 21st-century economy and supply chains is to take a page from Amazon, Walmart, Google, Meta, Alibaba, and others with a movement toward structured problem solving, data science, and sophisticated analytics technologies.

America's public and private institutions must develop a strategy focused on data and analysis to keep up with the escalating complexities of today's markets. Free applications—or, more correctly, those posing as free—are growing in ubiquity, complexity, and scale and are creating a virtual supply chain that needs fewer employees to develop marketing campaigns because the applications' users are providing free marketing content to the application. These Big Tech platforms are anything but our hope for a future value chain; instead, they are $1 trillion-plus market behemoths, companies with shareholders who expect a growing return on investment in developing the next innovation. At their worst, companies like Meta can use these analytical tools to addict their users (note the term "users"), which leads to higher profits for the company. At their best, the Big Tech platforms are a value proposition that users accept to communicate to friends and family about life events. These non-market-value applications are beyond national borders and a government's ability to control, which often leads to no regulation or some form of censorship. When social media is used by the government, in partnership with Big Tech or the government on its own, there is the potential for these social media applications to take the form of "surveillance capitalism." Therefore, personal data can become an unbridled source of revenue and used by Big Tech and governments to assert some form of control over its users. Is this new commerce and supply chain platform the ultimate expression of a free market, or is the prophecy of George Orwell's *1984* realized? Or perhaps is it just the demand chain on steroids, a further weakening of the fabric for a value chain?

Today, with production capacity in the world far exceeding demand and data/information a relatively free, infinite commodity, demand is constantly being chased to the point where applications become free just to track it. In Marshall's day, the term "value" was replaced with "price" because the latter could be measured and thus calculated while the former could not. This has led to markets understanding the price of everything and the value of nothing. The fundamental principles of financial and economic measurement are being lapped by the acceleration of market innovations, leading to a disconnect between the old and new economy, with 100 million Americans left on the outside of an emerging 21st-century economy, among billions of others worldwide.

What does any of this have to do with the future supply chain? First, it helps to explain how today's methods of measuring economic well-being do not resonate with an increasingly disenchanted public. Therefore, an economist using econometrics and the stock market to measure and benchmark the financial performance of the US economy is like an astronaut trying to ride a bike to the moon—a model for measurement that is unreliable, invalid, and even dangerous because it defines value by commoditizing it through a price. This also includes relying solely on using GDP, the most widely accepted term of measurement for the health of the US economy, or the financial system measured by the Dow Jones Industrial Average, to describe the state of our economy. Consider that the Dow surpassed 30,000 for the first time just before Thanksgiving 2020, right when the United States hit a record number of coronavirus cases in the nation. The stock market is not only an incomplete measurement but also easily manipulated for the benefit of stock traders and hedge funds, as was evident in the GameStop fiasco in January 2021. These outdated economic and financial tenets, the drivers of this 20th-century supply chain system, impede understanding of the 21st-century definition of value needed to address the present-day crisis. An erroneous assumption that economics is more science and math than psychology because economists develop quantitative equations has birthed the concept of financial capitalism. A commoditization of everything within a supply chain is related to price. Karl Marx called this a "transformation problem" by translating value into the price—hardly a controversial statement as Adam Smith, the father of capitalism, said it as well. We live in a surreal state where reality is much different from what we perceive it to be, leading to hopelessness and anxiety.

None of these claims that I'm making are new, not by a longshot. I address many of them in my 2006 book *An Easy Out*, stating that corporations make clear, suboptimal decisions based on financial valuation tools that lead to taking the shorter term "easy out" path. In 2008, months before the financial crisis, I spoke to an audience in Midtown Manhattan, blocks from Wall Street. I recorded on *Book TV* the upcoming challenges the American economy would face while many in the audience bristled at these notions.[25] At the time there were few acute indications from Dow Jones and GDP indicators of a potential problem, but this had more to do with the weaknesses of the measurements than the actuality of the real problem; just a few months after this event the stock market would have its most significant one-day crash in history (until 2020), dropping 777 points. My warning to the audience was scarcely prescient: as a corporate leader, I understood from working in various fields such as accounting, finance, financial services, management consulting, information technology, manufacturing, supply chain, and academia that the corporations and the stock market measurements have displaced an understanding of value, disconnecting it from a longer-term sustainability definition for the sake of short-term profits and sales. In my operational role, far from the speculation of the day traders and hedge fund managers, I had to make difficult decisions based on measurement tools and sound, structured problem-solving practices, understanding the longer-term aftereffects. On my mind were Deming's insights that link the consumer to the production process, with the production process a valuable part of the consumer.[26] In his discussions with American businesses in the decades following World War II, Deming railed against this capitalistic financial approach, contending that profits and management rewards should be secondary to the proper processes that ensure efficiency. To Deming, undertaking rational functions focused on the value of the consumer within the production process was the foundation for everything else, including company profit and management compensation. Today these concepts are far removed, with technology widening the rift, so we scarcely know better. Yet maybe there's hope with a new measurement of value through a great liberator of unlimited, cheap information harnessed for the public good rather than the commoditization of people, processes, and technologies to sell more goods to consumers. That is, if we choose to use it properly.

A value chain model isn't a bifurcation of consumers and producers but entrepreneurship that allows innovation to flourish, a self-organizing model of individuals and organizations in endless dynamic configurations. Moreover, this ready-made model is adaptable to the 21st-century realities of the globalization and digitization of the economy, evolving from outdated theories of structured relationships between owners of capital, technology, and labor. Price is no longer required to replace value because value is measurable using ample data and analytics tools. Instead, price is an element to value rather than vice versa. Rising levels of inequality and the impact of negative interest rates should be antithetical to the most basic tenets of a 21st-century definition of economics as a viable discipline.[27] When then Federal Reserve Chair and now Treasury Secretary Janet Yellen asked out loud whether the cutthroat competition of online retailers might be stopping goods producers from raising prices, it was a clear indication that the finance and economics industry has lost its ability to connect to an economy that is too complex for its outdated principles.[28] Leaders like Yellen need to provide justifiable answers to an increasingly alienated and enraged public who are no longer served well by US economic policy. Without a 21st-century tool to measure value, what is the potential for a 21st-century value chain supply chain? Rather than placing the onus on the institution to create value, a new model must arise, that of the individual or node to drive innovation and economic balance through a more appropriate model for the 21st century.

The Value of Free(dom)

A 21st-century definition of the supply chain, the value chain, must break free from the ancestral lineage of institutional finance and economics that has unintentionally thwarted innovation in the US economy for decades in favor of short-term growth through consumption and government spending. Whether the current financial market should be regulated or reformed is another subject for another book. My focus is on developing an alternative market model to emerge for individuals acting as nodes to express their market intentions through these nonmarket transactions, the focus of the remainder of this book. Of course, consumers will continue to purchase goods from big-box retailers, and Big Tech companies will profit through their nonmarket transactions. Day traders and hedge fund managers will stock speculate, and they should be free to do so in a competitive market environment. However, none of these should prohibit the development of public, open-source platforms for individuals and communities to create their markets and seek alternative value propositions through newly created public-private partnerships. Rather than relying solely on an institutional-based economy model that commoditizes labor, leaving citizens alienated, a new model can emerge centered around the node or individual unit as a viable alternative.

Maybe these Big Tech companies are on to something that can be replicated through a model that focuses on restoring a multiplier effect between the producer/worker and consumer. These models of *free*, a value proposition to its users, have made Meta and Amazon, two of the most valuable companies globally, leverage a new relationship based on the commoditization of something genuine—data and information. These companies understand that the data and information from the consumer are more valuable than the money they would pay for a service. This model is three steps ahead of the financial analysts, economists, and policymakers stuck in the old finance, economics, and supply chain paradigms. When economists theorized that inflation levels were too low because productivity growth was strong, Silicon Valley executives laughed it off because they have the data and information to understand better what is happening through a transformation of a new economy and supply chain system.[29] Rather than only the Big Tech companies using the power of data and information to find clever ways to peddle products and services through our data, how about using these strategies to add value within the community through our supply chains? A new approach seems to be the perfect foundation for a value chain supply chain—the use of data and information to make *free* possible not solely for us as consumers but also for us as nodes, the individual expression of a new supply chain system.

A public policy strategy based on this concept of *free* should have differences from its use in the private sector currently dominated by the Big Tech giants. Because these companies have shareholders and must satisfy their needs as their means of institutional existence, the Big Tech companies have developed this concept of *free*, monetizing data and information for profit. Akin to how corporations have stakeholders, so do governments. Likewise, governments can enable this concept of *free* on behalf of its stakeholders, the nodes, who can profit from monetizing data and information, just as is the case with Meta and Amazon. Why not set up a public-private partnership system through a community-based supply chain for its citizens and nodes to compete in the most expressive form of innovation? This could lead to a model of local self-reliance, not an abolishment of capitalism or even large, monopolistic multinational corporations but rather a platform alternative to compete—a value chain. "Local self-reliance" is a term that stands for having the right conditions put in place by a government entity to allow individual success and to have the freedom from interference from other people, such as those who have prevented segments of the population from participating in the process. Pulling oneself up by the bootstraps isn't possible if bootstraps are not provided. The government's role is not to do the pulling but rather to provide equal opportunity of the bootstraps to make it possible for any citizen to succeed. Resources must also exist through education to succeed in a technology-based economy rather than only having skills to participate as commoditized labor. Education is also an investment, and it will require taxpayers and businesses to pay for it, volunteer to support it, and perhaps even forgo some short-term benefits for a more significant long-term good. This new community-based value chain system will rely on digital technology, so it will be essential to close the growing digital divide across the country through the educational system. These actions can rebuild the trust between individuals, communities, and institutions.

During the Second Industrial Revolution, nursery schools and kindergartens were established to teach students to read as an essential skill for the future. Today there is a similar roadblock to a 21st-century supply chain transformation: the great digital divide in the United States, where an estimated 21 million Americans don't have internet access, and up to 163 million, nearly half of all Americans, don't have broadband.[30] It is no surprise that those most affected are skewed mainly in rural areas and inner cities, the same disaffected population impacted by deindustrialization decades ago. For this new economic approach to succeed, the digital divide must be eliminated to provide equal opportunity. Without addressing these shortcomings, there will only be a continuation of the lack of retraining of the blue-collar classes that lingers from the deindustrialization of the 1980s. How can a new economy build America's communities and equal opportunities within them if data and information are not widely available to nearly half of the nation's population? This effort could be America's Belt and Road Initiative, not building physical bridges and roads in other countries but digital ones in America's most disconnected communities. Today is a critical moment to consider how building a solid supply chain for the future isn't about immediate, short-term benefits but rather long-term investment in the whole nation. Think of the digital infrastructure and educational system for the 21st century as akin to the railroad that connected both coasts in the 19th century; without the railroad, the Industrial Revolution would never have taken off as it did across the nation and then around the world. The same is true for this investment that we must make into our digital infrastructure, our self-reliant Belt and Road Initiative.

A value chain model platformed by the government on behalf of its citizens or nodes is a paradigm shift in thinking about the economy but is not intended to replace the existing system ingrained into our supply chains and culture. It will take time for citizens and government policymakers to understand the potential of this concept, especially given the outdated economic measurement tools that need to be replaced. It will take time to develop the policies and train our citizens to be nodes, especially the young in those disaffected areas, to understand that today's technologies will enable them to be a part of our supply chains tomorrow. This concept of a community-based supply chain will be nodal—that is, technology will connect the individual to others around the world. A community-based model is an alternative to today's model that can compete against these systems of economies of scale, enabling all communities and nodes within it to be connected and relevant in a global model. America should let China play to win in a 20th-century supply chain model while moving forward with a 21st-century model. China's ancient culture is more suited for a traditional model, while the United States is built more on a local self-reliance platform of individualism, innovation, and an entrepreneurial spirit. America's supply chain strategy can shift to the nodal supply chain of peer-to-peer to leverage our strengths in a hypercompetitive global market model. America should play the game to win and focus on winning as a collective team of Americans, one node at a time.

The Community-Based Supply Chain

The community-based supply chain is an exciting concept: a networked, nodal, peer-to-peer model enabled by technology for the public good as well as the private sector to create a value chain as an improved balance between supply and demand to compete within an ecosystem through a privately networked and multinational corporation-concentrated model that has spiky benefits. This value chain model is a networked hub-and-spoke system that is self-organized as required rather than a highly structured and concentrated institutional model. Through a connected self-organizing marketplace, individuals as nodes have the potential to compete and coop-erate in a supply chain system rather than be limited to a job with no opportunity or value added, especially in the blue-collar roles—what cultural anthropologist David Graeber calls a "bullshit job." It was not just Marx who raised concerns about the worker in a capitalist system regarding the alienation in being treated as a tool of pro-duction. Adam Smith also wondered about the viability for workers to be only taught to follow the instructions of capitalism, making them as stupid and as ignorant as possible for a human to become.[31] A value chain model creates a model for individuals to participate in the supply chain as both producers and consumers rather than just the latter. In contrast, the demand chain model focuses on the customer experience as a means to an end (owning a product) without regard to the customer's role in the production supply chain system. A community-based model redefines the part of the individual as an integral element in a value-based process without being a conflict to technology between the role of a producer and consumer. It enables a 20th-century blue-collar worker to return to the field, albeit in a new 21st-century model.

These nodal supply chains can be built from the ground up as networking appli-cations consistent with what's happening in the media industry. Think of the model of how social media scales today, one nodal relationship at a time, versus the large mass-market multinational news corporations such as CNN, the BBC, and CBS. As a stand-alone entity, CNN has massive capabilities to cover the news, but not as great as a crowdsourced model of countless micro sources of media that can interlink across social media through applications such as Twitter, Facebook, and others. According to a Pew Research study from 2018, social media has surpassed newspapers and is gaining ground on other mediums as a source for American news media.[32] Like social media companies using a network of telecommunications that began as a public util-ity, these nodal supply chain models can innovate by using a public platform to add value to the community. Today a model of peers in a network produces news from a decentralized node versus a larger centralized source. In a similar design, the local communities would potentially create and make products. In contrast to subsidies to large corporations to build a factory in town for a business case that doesn't work, this would be akin to providing a public utility to the community, like a power grid, to allow those in the jurisdiction to build their businesses in a nodal, self-organizing manner.

This concept for a 21st-century supply chain system is ready for prime time: decentralized, peer-to-peer networked models are already emerging in other industries, such as taxis (Uber) and hotels (Airbnb), and Amazon is a portal for small producers and distributors. With global and last-mile shipping costs continuing to improve in efficiency at an accelerating, maddening rate, and as advanced, digital manufacturing technologies increase in capability and fall in price, all signs point to this community-based model to be the supply chain of the future. This type of model is the ultimate expression of the intent of capitalism, allowing capital to flow fluidly across the consumer, worker, owner/producer, citizen, and investor in a self-organized manner and with technology reducing the barriers to entry. The nodes in a peer-to-peer value chain become an intersection within the local community and global market, and a municipality can ensure the health of its community through proper levels of infrastructure and education. Rather than the large multinational corporations being the aggregators of efficiency through global supply chains, the community becomes the linchpin on behalf of their citizenry, no longer dependent on the immense global supply chains but able to connect with them. Of course, there might be many reasons why this networked community supply chain model may fail when deployed, especially in competition within a massively scaled global supply chain system. Still, there are more reasons why this model is a more sustainable, balanced model of local self-reliance, the cultural embodiment of the American spirit. Finally, and most important, this nodal supply chain can restore the viability of the American Dream to those who have been forgotten and left on the outside for decades. There is no hope in today's model, while a transformation to a nodal supply chain offers the hope and opportunities of a new American Dream.

Large multinational corporations and their supply chains won't disappear, but they will need to adapt to this new definition of competition in a model that will change the concentration of power, community by community. For example, a large soft drink manufacturer/brand, such as Diet Coke, and its supply chain, including Walmart, Amazon, and Target, will need to maintain and establish a new market position not branded nationally or even internationally but branded a community at a time, continuously. Given fewer barriers to entry, there will be more legitimate peer-to-peer startups popping up and self-organizing, community by community. As owner-operators, individuals have more freedom than in the past, when thin bands of employment opportunity limits freedom. The future possibilities might only be limited by one's imagination and work ethic if everyone has equal access to broadband, hardware, and education. Think about how influencers monetize their roles on Facebook, Snapchat, and TikTok, building careers on new platforms—this could also happen in this community-based supply chain. It is also possible that this new model can solve future supply problems of the next pandemic, which will lead to the viability of small offshoots of peer-to-peer manufacturers that can begin producing items, such as masks, that can be aggregated through these new "glocal" supply chain systems. Most importantly, a node can be defined as an element of value within a community, leading to inner cities such as Baltimore and Flint creating their community-based supply chains focused on value rather than scale and marketing. The focus of a local politician in a disenfranchised community must be to play a different game, one that the politician can win and that brings value to local citizens and the community.

Data as the "New Oil"

Recall that it was the two Os, oil and organization, that fueled the growth of the Second Industrial Revolution to the most significant period of economic growth in the history of human civilization. Oil is the super-lubricant that powered the Second Industrial Revolution, and organization was its structure. Midway through the 20th century, theorists began to raise concerns regarding the marginal utility of oil to power the economy; in 1956 geologist M. King Hubbert calculated that "Peak Oil" would occur around 2000, leading to an eventual disruption to global markets. Today there's an opposite concern for some in this conventional oil-based economy due to the trillions of dollars' worth of fossil fuel assets that remain in the ground and need to be extracted for profit before it could be banned. Although oil will remain a significant variable as the energy source of today's economy, its role as the driver in this 21st-century supply chain will diminish over time in favor of more technological factors, particularly data and information.

The replacement for oil in the 21st century will be Big Data that will power the future of the supply chain, making it more virtual than physical, a significant paradigm shift. Today's business models are awash with data, not for the betterment of this nodal entrepreneur that I propose but mainly for the benefit of the Big Tech companies and their consumers. Blockchain is the technology that can level the playing field between Big Tech and the nodal entrepreneur. This technology language will make the value chain system flow within a community-based supply chain if it achieves this purpose. One of the barriers to entry that exists today for small entrepreneurs and nodes is a restriction from entering the large, centralized, highly integrated supply chains of Walmart and Amazon. Today Amazon does have a marketplace feature that allows nodes and small businesses to conduct commerce on its platform. Still, a large institutional model limits the degrees of freedom and profit motive for the individual to act in their own best interest. A blockchain technology platform could eradicate these structured relationships using distributed electronic records if implemented as a community utility. It could also level the playing field of the competitive transactional advantages today owned by the large, highly integrated supply chains. While the internet has provided equal access, it does not offer similar integration and efficiency of transactions to draw on identical records, which happens fluently within a large corporation's enterprise resource planning tool and is relatively easy across companies through these relationships. Suppose the blockchain can seamlessly allow different parties, self-organized spontaneously, to create an in situ supply chain within a community or across communities to use the transactional records of distributed parties. In that case, these transactions developed by an infinite number of individual entrepreneurs can compete in efficiency with today's large, integrated supply chains. Transactions can occur spontaneously and on scale between producers, planners, shippers, and retailers as nodes self-organize for market creation. Having these distributed supply chain systems is the key to the entire community-based supply chain system, the future super-lubricant, just as oil and organization played this role during the Second Industrial Revolution.

A new supply chain would be the lubricant not only for the seamless flow of data and information across these self-organizing community-based systems but for the flow of payments as well. In China, the Ant Group, a transformational company focused on digital financial transactions, was started by a famous Alibaba entrepreneur who said, "if the banks don't change, we'll change the banks."[33] This model of revolutionizing how people manage their money on a digital platform, called Ant, is leading the way in the fintech industry. This microenterprise model will provide a financial infrastructure for the node, providing the value chain with the potential to compete in a peer-to-peer, frictionless model. In other countries, this is taking shape, running on the blockchain that is beginning to level the playing fields for the micro-companies that I call the future nodes.

This super-lubricant is not yet ready to transform the next evolution of the supply chain, the value chain, but it will happen sooner than we think; it is in process and needs a structural design to develop into this community-based system. In its present state of development, the blockchain is overhyped and oversold. The overhead required to shuffle data between a hypothetical unlimited source of participants makes it slower and costlier than today's centralized payment companies.[34] There are also questions of standards—who will establish them and how will a platform for standards that is flexible enough to enable such self-organizing market activity be created?. There are also concerns regarding security, as today it is used often for nefarious illegal activities without traceability. But drawbacks are typical for any transformational technology, as was the case with the internet in the late 1990s when it first became available to a broader audience. Finding answers within the blockchain to create a public highway path for nodes to compete against the big guys is perhaps the most important nut to crack for creating a value chain system. Today's supply chains rely on economies of scale transactions between partners to push and pull data and information to achieve consumer objectives, making it significantly disadvantageous for new entrants. As was evident in the US-China trade war of 2018 and 2019, supply chains sought to migrate away from Chinese production facilities, but fluidity in making supplier changes is not as easy as flipping a switch. Due to these system limitations, supply chains are not resilient in flexibility and scale.

The communication model of blockchain can revolutionize these limitations, much as oil unleashed the scale and flexibility of the early 20th century. Because blockchains are distributed ledger systems, they can centralize and decentralize data and information as required. As a result, supply chains should become liberated from their private system limitations, a challenge facing these systems from the onset. Today a distribution center orders its medical supplies from a few manufacturers who can coordinate with it from a planning standpoint. Changing suppliers on the fly is too difficult from a transactional standpoint. So much has been discussed through the pandemic of crops rotting in the fields, milk poured down the drain, and suppliers with products unable to reach the demand signals of both the private and nonprofit sectors. In a distributed ledger system, food products could more seamlessly pivot away from sources that did not demand these commodities to those who need them without herculean efforts. As transformational as today's supply chains are within a global roadmap, glaring opportunities for better coordination and less friction are missed when we are limited to the inefficient organizational structures developed in the 20th century. Blockchains can become the super-lubricant for a new 21st-century supply chain, just as important as the super-lubricant 1.0, oil. Our ancestors could not have conceived how a fossil fuel could unleash an industrial revolution capable of such remarkable achievements. Today few can imagine how the new super-lubricant—blockchain—can transform the new 21st-century supply chain, one that replaces the focus on price with that on value.

A decentralized ledger blockchain system will not entirely replace the large, global models of centralization and scale already in place. Instead, it will provide an alternative venue to this institutional model, allowing nodes and communities to fend for themselves and gain self-reliance. A conventional approach will likely exist for many large-scale, global supply chains, while peer-to-peer supply chain systems will take shape informally based on the value between the stakeholders. These micro industries will provide instant opportunities for competition and value once the structure and super-lubricant are in place for a flat playing field for all nodes to enter. Who would have thought that it was possible? It may seem like a panacea for now, but it is a potential future roadmap compared to today's outdated supply chain and economic prospects.

Revenge of the Nodes

Noted futurist Alvin Toffler aided China's ascension as a supply chain and technology superpower. Partnering alongside Chinese premier and general secretary Zhao Ziyang, Toffler assisted the Chinese in developing technology and supply chain policies during the 1980s.[35] Toffler's vision for the future was a rapidly evolving society driven by technology where citizens must be trained to avoid being left behind. His 1980 book *The Third Wave*, one of the top-selling books of all time, significantly influenced China's view of its 21st-century supply chain. Toffler's thinking was anchored on what would happen in a postindustrial society when consumption reached saturation and companies and nations could no longer achieve growth through mass-produced products. To accomplish this new economy, Toffler devised the concept of a "prosumer," a combination of producer and consumer, and the idea of mass customization. Some of what Toffler predicted has come true—notably, the impact of technology on consumers, workers, and society—but his forecasts of a prosumer proved wrong, at least for now. At the same time, globalization and mass production have continued to grow. If anything, Toffler emphasized a consumer's desire for customization, an element of a product life cycle that did not add value back to the individual. Psychologist Barry Schwartz's famous research and book *The Paradox of Choice* argues against customization, finding that too much involvement and choice can lead to anxiety and unhappiness when consumers want convenience.[36] Other than the true do-it-yourselfers, or "DIYers," who want to make their own craft beer, most consumers would instead rely on the comfort and innovation of a product in their lives, their definition of value. An individual or node only wants to be involved if that involvement has an intention, a purpose, which is an essential clue for the value chain economy.

A value chain could be the use of markets and now supply chains in some form of production processes and consumption that improve an individual's life, not necessarily as a hobby but as a way of making a living and enjoying the fruits of one's labor. In the 1970s and 1980s, when Toffler wrote his books, he could not have conceived of digital collaboration through data and information as both the catalyst and the glue of a 21st-century supply chain, a virtual system of electrons replacing conventional factories to enable peers, or nodes, as a part of the process. This is happening today only in the niche, hobby-driven DIY culture leveraging the emergence of open-source hardware and software, 3D printing, and other tools, and it is hardly a substantial future competitor to the existing supply chain system. These hubs on the internet are often called makerspaces or hackerspaces, such as Fab Labs, where this new economic model is just in its infancy. These hackerspaces will become hubs for innovation and entrepreneurship activity, both in physical and virtual settings, that have the potential to revolutionize how work (supply chains, governments, communities) and societies are self-organized. The term "self-organized" is essential because the future of the supply chain will become these informal clusters of nodes that organize, disband, and re-organize in different configurations. Through processes and tools such as blockchain and these communities, the future of the producer and consumer, manufacturing, logistics, and retail will be radically different from today. While these niche communities are exciting and evolving, a mainstream value chain platform driven by local communities, not hobbyists, needs to become the platform of this new supply chain economy, both virtual and real, which will be more of a network than a traditional supply chain. For the new supply chain economy to be in the self-interest of the node as a citizen of a community, it needs to be implemented as a public utility, like electricity and water.

The centralized feature in this new model isn't a DIY hobby enthusiast but rather a node as a function of a peer-to-peer supply chain model that can solve problems by creating supply to satisfy demand in microtransactions that link into larger scale through these blockchain networks. For example, news sources used to be defined only as mass-produced newspapers and news channels; when I grew up in Baltimore, there were only two newspapers and three major news stations. Today in my home-town the sole major newspaper is struggling to stay in business. Still, a potpourri of mass media television news options must compete with a makers' market of DIY media through podcasts, blogs, and social media posts. A value chain nodal supply chain is moving in the same direction today, being prototyped through hobbyists and STEM enthusiasts in the hacker sphere. It will ultimately become the new supply chain, a virtual one that exists in the physical world, available to all. Mass production will continue to exist, as will the mass marketing of these products, but nodes will also become their marketing arm. They will use digital marketing methods that flow seamlessly and instantaneously within these electron supply chains. Through block-chain transactional systems, nodes will instantaneously create marketing campaigns, products, services, and distribution channels.

This emerging nodal supply chain is fascinating and has the potential to transform the system from a demand chain to a value chain with one enormous challenge, bigger than the challenge of the technology itself: the growing divide between those who are anchored into this information economy and those who sit on the outside, continuing to fall further behind. Today the makers, DIYers, and collaborators are stereotypical of those with advanced education, typically niche groups in the STEM fields. At the same time, large segments of communities and whole socioeconomic classes of workers and consumers are not involved. On its current trajectory, this digital segmentation will undoubtedly increase the digital divide as this new economy and society take shape, further exacerbating existing societal ills that have plagued society for decades since the deindustrialization of the 1970s. These fractures will widen across nations in fields such as supercomputing, cloud computing, 3D printing, and artificial intelligence. Nations such as the United States, China, South Korea, Japan, and Germany will further surpass countries that are not investing in these technologies to the same extent. Likewise, within a nation and a community, this supply chain transformation could end up creating even more significant gaps between the haves and have-nots if greater investment in infrastructure and education provides only equal opportunities but does not achieve equal outcomes. Today the emergence of a STEM-based economy and supply chain overwhelmingly prefers the higher socioeconomic classes, which must be addressed. A 21st-century community-based supply chain strategy needs to unify, not further the digital and societal divides.

According to an article in the *Harvard Business Review* in 2018, the emergence of digital tools and technologies, including Big Data, cloud computing, and artificial intelligence, means the field of supply chain management risks becoming obsolete, run automatically rather than through workers; in contrast to this automation dystopia view, Toffler and I call these future workers the future nodes in a nodal supply chain.[37] It is an interesting claim: our future supply chain as a demand chain will become an automaton—a technological entity that itself doesn't need much or any human intervention—versus a community-based version as a value chain of nodes, of citizens. The nodal value chain can be one of the nearly infinite possibilities: a front-end supply chain that aggregates demand and develops a supply chain plan, linking sourcing to manufacturing to distribution delivered by technology and automation to be delivered to your doorsteps, enabled by human nodes. A model of a wholly automated supply chain system produced by machines alone is dystopian and unimaginative of how humans as nodes add value to the process rather than commoditizing the system in a 20th-century price-based model. Ironically, rather than killing the supply chain, this nodal model saves it by decentralizing it from a global model of large multinational corporations with a single focus on the short-term market and financial objectives focused on price and cost. The math is clear: A value chain approach leads to economic growth through a peer-to-peer multiplier effect that embodies the American culture in the 21st century versus competing in an outdated supply chain system that commoditizes the supply chain through technology and leads to the death of supply chain management through automation. The commoditized supply chain to be put to death is the capital of the concentrated, global corporate system. In contrast, the nodal supply chain is alive within a community to draw value to the nodes, not solely to the shareholders. Of these options, it seems reasonable to explore a value chain model as a potential best path for the American culture and its communities.

Supply chains aren't going to become obsolete because they already are obsolete;

there isn't enough oxygen in this present model for the best interests of the American people to coexist with the interests of multinational corporations, the burgeoning Chinese economy, and those of other developing nations. The goal of the US strategy should be to win the game that can be won versus the one that has been lost for decades. For the government and policymakers who have been keeping score using the wrong techniques and segmenting the population, it's time to redefine the method using the value chain model as presented here. How will government organizations respond to these new challenges and opportunities in the 21st century, and how will the public and private sectors move forward? The answer to these questions will be the key to whether America's institutions can regain lost trust. With public morale as low as it has ever been and contention and division at dangerously high levels, it is a perfect time for a pivot to head in a new direction. Suppose these institutions know their rightful place in American society as a supporting role to the communities and individuals, rather than vice versa. In that case, the long, hard journey required to solve the foundational problem of American culture can finally begin.

CHAPTER 4

21ST-CENTURY REINDUSTRIALIZATION

Win the Right Game

"We've learned a good lesson," President Donald Trump said on April 19, 2020, at the daily White House Coronavirus Task Force briefing. He was talking about America's painful dependence on overseas medical supply manufacturing and the need for reshoring as a mitigation strategy and to counter national security risks posed by, as Trump called them, the globalists who design and run these supply chains. The 2020 COVID-19 pandemic became a flashpoint for many Americans in their understanding of the inherent weaknesses in the supply chain system. Yet, as significant as those weaknesses are, they are just the latest in a string of failures defining the US supply chain over the past decades. Will this "good lesson" learned during the COVID-19 pandemic lead to sustainable, longer-term corrective actions, or will we soon forget the lesson when life returns to some form of normal? If history is our guide, these weaknesses in the global supply chain will be ignored, and the news cycle will focus on the next tragedy, scandal, or whatever. Two years since the Trump speech, with Americans out of lockdown and not required to wear masks, it seems as if these lessons learned are taking a backseat to more pressing problems, such as historic levels of inflation. The lack of a straightforward remedy to these problems has a numbing effect; as a Baltimore City councilmember sadly remarked after the riots following the death of Freddie Gray in police custody, "All the cameras have gone, but the socioeconomic plight of the community has remained."[1]

These cracks and fault lines are further widened each successive year, leading to greater hostility, frustration, and division. It is hard to divorce the lack of an industrial strategy that was the bread and butter of the middle class from these guttural rages against the machine that are growing in number and intensity. There are other variables for sure, but the lack of a viable path to a middle-class lifestyle for a large percentage of the population has had a debilitating impact that takes various shapes and forms. In the 1960s and 1970s America's policymaking institutions ignored the problem of deindustrialization while it struggled with sociocultural challenges that led to political unrest and division in society. The American people and its policymakers must move toward unity—away from partisan, divisive politics and away from a model of "fictitious capital," a term coined by Karl Marx that describes a pivot from innovation and tangible growth to government stimulus spending and market over-consumption antithetical to investment and strategy. These sociopolitical issues are inextricably linked to a lack of a 21st-century supply chain strategy.

Indeed, creating a long-term strategic direction for manufacturing is not as immediately satisfying for politicians and constituents as a stimulus check. But it would be a longer-term investment in the future, a shot in the arm for American unity, patriotism, and hope. For example, China's Made in China 2025 strategy and the Belt and Road Initiative (BRI) are manufacturing strategies to recreate the world supply chain system. The West struggles with China's top-down decision-making approach through Communist Party officials. While perhaps limited through a lack of free speech, there are some indications that the Chinese people have a sense of national pride and excitement regarding their self-reliance and growth in the advanced manufacturing global economy. As discussed in chapter 3, the Chinese public has a higher trust in its government officials than American citizens have in their leaders, despite China's repressiveness toward individual freedoms, however, this may wane through the COVID-19 lockdowns happening in China's big cities in the spring of 2022.

The global supply chain and the multinational companies seem to also be responding favorably to China's strategies. According to the Commercial Aircraft Corporation of China, American companies such as GE and Honeywell are cooperating with China by participating in projects relating to Made in China 2025 as significant suppliers of parts for Chinese-made aircraft.[2] The American government's official response to these initiatives has been partisan and procedural, much different from the seriousness of our nation's response to the Soviet's launch of a satellite in the late 1950s. On October 4, 1957, America faced its "Sputnik moment," a wake-up call to rally in the face of Russia overtaking the United States in the fields of science and technology. Rather than politics and procedural plotting, America developed a serious space strategy, executed it efficiently between the public and private sectors, and became the first nation to land a man on the moon in 1969. Many technological innovations came from this initiative, including the World Wide Web, the basis of today's e-commerce platform. The elapsed time between the Sputnik moment and the landing of a man on the moon was twelve years, a testament to the nation's willingness to invest time and money in a long-term strategy. STEM educational programs have provided a foundation to develop students for working and competing in related fields in business and research. As a K–12 student in the 1970s and 1980s, I remember the shift toward math and science and the encouragement from the public education system to become a scientist to solve America's challenges. Today America faces a similar challenge from the Chinese with its two massive and aspirational initiatives to strengthen its industrial base for the future and for self-reliance from its adversaries.

Over sixty years after the Sputnik moment, it is a different world. America is no longer the world's sole economic superpower. The American public is divided and no longer confident in the United States' response to such challenges. The nation has shifted from the STEM fields and lacks an effective supply chain strategy. Short-term financial models and quick fixes will not be successful; we need sacrifice and a commitment to restore our place as an industrial superpower focused on the 21st century.

Making America Smart Again

In 2016, after Donald Trump was elected the president of the United States, renowned scientist Neil deGrasse Tyson was a guest on *The Late Show*, hosted by Stephen Colbert. A meme was born that night when Colbert asked Tyson how he plans to deal with having "a president who doesn't believe in science." Tyson, who strongly advocates for a greater focus on STEM in the K–12 system, responded that he would be on a four-year mission "to make America smart again."[3] His quip became an inadvertent dividing line between the blue-collar and white-collar, college-educated workers. Statements such as "Make America smart again" and "Make America great again" reveal painful ideological divides that fracture people into camps rather than create social norms as a rallying cause.

America needs a focused STEM education strategy to compete for the future of science, technology, engineering, math, and, yes, the supply chain. However, the plan needs to unify, not divide, in achieving the goal. Unfortunately, a digital and STEM divide exist in American society, often tied to ideology and income inequality. These divisions have persisted ever since the famous Sputnik moment. During the 1950s the nation united in competition arising from the success of the Soviet satellite, but the plan was not effective across socioeconomic segments, with students from white-collar backgrounds taking part and the marginalized sectors, the inner cities, and the rural communities left out. This divide in the American educational system goes back even further. At the beginning of the 19th century, education focused on literacy and other remedial skills required for factory work, but by the late 19th century, "high school was an elite enterprise," with less than 7 percent of high-school-age youths enrolled and with a math-centric curriculum.[4] A more significant percentage of the population slowly trickled into high school education, reaching three-quarters of the school-age population by World War II. The Sputnik moment led to an emphasis on math and science and then fell backward again until the next perceived threat when Japan became an industrial competitor. It has seesawed back again, now in response to competition from China. It has been a pattern of urgency and complacency, hardly sufficient for a national strategy.

Beyond teaching students the basic life coping skills of reading, writing, and arithmetic, what is needed most as a crucial dimension for success in a digital, global supply chain system is structured problem solving and critical thinking skills. But even many of today's college students struggle with understanding the difference between *how to think* versus *what to think*. Unfortunately, much of today's education pedagogy is focused on teaching content and testing for memorization rather than providing the information and requiring the student to answer "what the data/information is telling you?" Because a student today can google any question and in a matter of a few seconds can retrieve information content, a pedagogy based on memorization is pointless compared to when I was in college, when it was important. Innovation and entrepreneurship begins by establishing the problem statement, gathering the data, analyzing the data, and developing recommendations by thinking outside the box and challenging conventional wisdom. America must teach critical thinking and structured problem solving widely across the spectrum of the population. America's educational system is outdated to the realities of data, information, and 21st-century problem-solving.

In many US school systems, especially those in inner cities and rural towns, children are dispassionately trained for marginalized roles, or "shit jobs" and "bullshit jobs," as David Graeber called them. Graeber said shit jobs are compliant, dull, and robotic and won't lead to any sense of life security, and bullshit jobs are ones in which the workers are adequately or even well paid but the jobs have little meaning, with even the workers secretly believing the jobs shouldn't exist.[5] Policymakers must not perpetuate a divided nation, with blue collars burdened with shit jobs and white collars working in bullshit jobs. A 21st-century supply chain and manufacturing system that enables the individual as a node can provide degrees of freedom to think and succeed, but it will require our educational systems to teach students digital and critical thinking skills. Can the public school system train our children for these jobs that do not yet exist? The answer is that it must by no longer training our students for jobs of the past and by focusing on, to paraphrase Wayne Gretsky, skating "where the puck is going to be." This will require a paradigm shift in America's public education system.

A complete reengineering of the educational system to meet the needs of a 21st-century economy is required as soon as possible. Today only a fraction of the population is trained for the STEM jobs of the future. This digital and STEM divide is one of the most devastating economic problems today, with the gap widening at an accelerating rate. If these apparent problems continue to be ignored, progress toward this new economic model of the value chain will be limited and unequal, furthering the culture and economic divide in the nation and impacting economic growth. Reengineering our societal values through education must be founded on trust, common goals, and equal opportunities across all social class sectors rather than just the college educated. The future of a balanced production- and consumption-based economy through a value chain is perhaps the most significant challenge in education that America has ever faced, a challenge to educate everyone within this rapidly emerging digital future. It must become a covenant of sorts through a business case that demonstrates the substantial return on investment—beyond business—that it can achieve. Rather than the blue-collar jobs of the past, a 21st-century approach to manufacturing needs jobs relating to science; jobs for electrical, mechanical, civil, industrial, and chemical engineers; and jobs for support, administrative, and hands-on roles.

The digital divide is not just a technical problem but a proverbial canary in the coal mine of civil discourse that grows in intensity and can only be fixed through education. The lack of attention to this harbinger of many problems demonstrates that America's institutions are failing to recognize the root cause of the problems and instead are focusing on a culture of increasing consumption and short-termism. In politics and public conversation today, it is easier to choose a side and blame others for issues rather than focusing on these painful and complex challenges, especially in a political and financial system that focuses on short-term benefits.

To be competitive in the future, America must not just win the proverbial "brain game" against China; it must disperse the benefits of education across the general population more than it has previously. Today American universities such as MIT are still known as the top research institutions for math and computing, but some experts suggest that in a matter of five years top-flight universities in China, such as Tsinghua University, may surpass them.[6] America's education needs to win across all segments rather than a primary focus on the top 5–10 percent of students. This becomes the real Sputnik moment for America's future. Improving America's capabilities within the STEM fields across communities and for all individuals must be at the heart of its strategy for supply chain and manufacturing success. But it must focus beyond the genius kids who go to MIT and Stanford to include the small-town kids in Kentucky and inner-city kids of Baltimore. This doesn't mean everyone needs to be a STEM genius; instead, the country needs to create training and development programs centered around a STEM economy. Rather than an unrealistic goal for everyone to go to Stanford or MIT, there needs to be a post-secondary-education plan for every young adult in society. For some this will mean going to an elite university while others will study at a university that focuses on different aspects of the 21st-century manufacturing and supply-chain-based economy. Trade schools and community colleges must become more of a focus for newly minted high school–educated graduates to participate more effectively in this new economy.

A commitment to investment in the next generation of Americans to enter the workforce will lead to a wide range of possibilities to grow the economy through this value chained, peer-to-peer supply chain and manufacturing system. New roles within a new economy across the supply chain include product design, sourcing, planning, manufacturing, logistics, and sustainability. Through investment in education and community infrastructure, local, state, and national policymakers now have a new canvas to create economic enterprise zones rather than force-fitting multinational corporations into beleaguered communities for more mindless low-paying jobs. A 21st-century supply chain strategy opens many opportunities for municipalities and constituency groups to determine areas of focus, as China does with its provinces to develop strategies. For example, a national strategy could be to invest in enterprise zones based on various state and local strategies and to provide an overall direction on a base curriculum for every American student in the K–12 system related to STEM, critical thinking, and collaboration. This strategy centers on attracting more of America's top talent to the educational sector, focusing on the most vital role in society—the training and development of the next generation. The world is entering a new type of brain game that America must win through a commitment to these practices, but it requires a paradigm shift toward the long term versus pandering to short-term interests. Can the American public and its institutions that are locked in on meeting short-term interests pivot to a new long-term, sustainable future? The answer is yes, if we can see the value of a shared vision that brings us together, not divides us.

An American Silk Road

China's BRI scale is genuinely breathtaking, with its imagination to recreate a supply chain from the legendary ancient trade routes from China to Rome. Nearly ten years ago a professor at Beijing University urged China to reopen commercial routes to the West through three silk roads: one through Southeast Asia, one through South Asia, and the third through central Asia.[7] Less than a year after this research, President Xi Jinping announced a ten-year, $2.5 trillion strategy linking China and its neighbors in the BRI. An initiative of this scale is unprecedented in history, involving countries responsible for 55 percent of the world's gross national product, 70 percent of its population, and 75 percent of the known energy reserves.[8] Moreover, China's strategy will not just modify the scope and path of the entire global supply chain and its commerce patterns; it will develop a land bridge for central Asia that has been a veritable no-man's land for centuries. The challenges associated with creating a multimodal, multinational supply chain will be enormous, as this world region is often thought of as the backwater channels of the defunct communist system of the old Soviet bloc.[9] Such a strategy, while ambitious, puts China in the driver's seat as a world leader, with the vision to do the impossible in bringing some of the most remote areas of the world together into the global supply chain.

China's strategy is by far the most ambitious, but other nations have plans as well. India has a "Connect Central Asia" policy, and practically every other major player in the region, such as Turkey, Iran, and Russia, is seeking to insert their influence in the development of the future supply chain system. In addition, eastern nations of the European Union, such as Estonia, Poland, Hungary, Bulgaria, and Romania, are ready to be connected to a modernized 21st-century digital commerce system.

China's so-called land bridge across central Asia is analogous to America's flyover states, a phrase often used pejoratively to explain those states between the populous East and West Coasts. A comparison between the Kyrgyz Republic and Kansas is not entirely reasonable, but it does provide a general perspective regarding development, educational, and political differences in the nation. Not just the flyover states in the United States—Kansas, Oklahoma, Alabama, and West Virginia, to name a few—but areas within large US cities are "drive-around" places that have been largely ignored since the deindustrialization of the 1970s and 1980s, and residents of these areas have higher distrust in institutions such as government and business. A strategic focus on the white-collar knowledge economy without a strategy for employing the displaced American blue-collar worker was a result of the lack of an institutional strategy following deindustrialization. This is analogous to the Soviets for decades of failing to develop central Asia, which was considered a region of instability due to ethnic conflicts. In contrast to China's land bridge, America needs to build a virtual bridge across its flyover states and drive-around areas, connecting its white-collar and blue-collar economies through a 21st-century manufacturing strategy.

America's 21st-century manufacturing needs to reengineer its school systems to teach its students in the fields of STEM and digital, to teach them *how to think* rather than *what to think*, and to move away from the outdated model for a factory worker of the 20th century coming from a farm. First, a transformative approach to education must become table stakes for every student to become proficient in the STEM field and exercise critical thinking and collaboration skills. Second, broadband capacity and availability must become a public utility, regulated and accessible to all to ensure that every American has world-class access to the internet, which will become the platform for the next supply chain. Third, students must be trained in using the internet for equal participation in this new economy. Finally, there must become an effective model of public-private partnerships to balance the needs of each element in their functional roles in the economy and society. Rather than the autocratic, state-run business model of China, America's model needs to be the driver of innovation to address the widely known problems of today that cannot be solved without both entities working together. It must be a public-private partnership that starts with the individual, extends to the community, and expands across institutions. In this model, the public and private institutions are in place to support individuals in communities as a 21st-century model of capitalism and supply chain and to enable private enterprise, not displace it.

An American Silk Road as a manufacturing strategy links Rust Belt cities back into the US economy through digital and advanced manufacturing. Like China's Silk Road, America will require a substantial financial investment, not to build ocean ports in faraway lands but rather to create networks in our communities. Imagine how this strategy, focusing on red-state flyover towns and blue-state inner cities, could become a rallying cry to counter the current state of chaos and tribalism that defines American politics. Sixty years ago, President John Kennedy challenged the nation to put a man on the moon before the end of the decade, an audacious target to galvanize the country. Let's set a similarly bold target to build this American Silk Road by the end of the 2020s. Rather than hubs for advanced manufacturing being only in Silicon Valley, California; Austin, Texas; or Boston, Massachusetts (the usual high-tech suspects), why not go bold and rebuild manufacturing where it started and later was abandoned?

The future of manufacturing is often discussed related to the technologies, such as additive manufacturing and 3D printing, but should begin with a focus on people and processes to effectively enable these tools if the goals are for wider-reaching public benefit. While advances in technologies will take shape in private industry in the United States perhaps more quickly than we can imagine, the digital divide and lack of STEM skills could inhibit that progress for the broader societal benefit. For decades, advances in automation led to improvements for higher-skilled workers, such as engineers, and had a negative impact on the medium- and lower-skilled workers.[10] In their insightful 2011 book *Race Against the Machine*, Erik Brynjolfsson and Andrew McAfee raise this concern with substantial evidence that advancing technology improves the production process but at a high labor cost, leading to growing wealth inequality in society. To address this problem, Brynjolfsson and McAfee propose government funding and investment in entrepreneurship and infrastructure.[11] Nearly ten years after the publication of their book, technologies continue to advance but societal problems continue to worsen.

What are the alternatives to this model of a 21st-century American Silk Road built on a foundational platform of ubiquitous broadband and bridging the digital and STEM divide in education? Is the continuation of the status quo a viable option? Or can efforts to bring 20th-century manufacturing back to the United States solve our supply chain problem? Political efforts to save manufacturing in the United States through policy rather than sound business financials within a global supply chain system have been suboptimal. In 2017 the Taiwanese electronics manufacturer Foxconn announced its partnership with Wisconsin to build a $10 billion factory to produce flat-screen televisions and LCD panels, proclaiming that America had entered the mass-scale consumer electronics business. This was one of the most significant cases of corporate welfare in US history, with Foxconn receiving close to $5 billion in subsidies for its plan to employ 3,000 employees initially and eventually up to 13,000. According to some estimates, this subsidy was predicted to cost the state $231,000 per job created, but the cost was even higher given that the number of actual jobs was much lower.[12] In June 2018 President Trump visited the facility, calling it "the eighth wonder of the world," but by 2019 the plans were already changing. The initial plans to produce LCD screens were scrapped due to high manufacturing labor costs in the United States—as if this should have been a surprise. With hopes of factory production dwindling compared to its original intention, the number of employees eventually hired was less than half of the initial numbers, reaching only approximately 1,300, and most of them were engineers and researchers rather than factory workers. In April 2020 the factory shifted gears, partnering with Medtronic to manufacture respirators, but that relationship ended seven months later, in November 2020. Finally, in April 2021 the partnership entered into a hollowed-out agreement that lowered Foxconn's investment in the facility, the available tax credits, and the number of employees, with no specific requirement of the factory's intended use. Rather than corporate welfare handouts to prop up unfavorable business cases, public sector investments should be made to enable individual entrepreneurs and communities.

It has become a popular political talking point that we should reshore manufacturing from global supply chains back to America. In 2016 candidate Trump promised to make America the manufacturing hub again. Likewise, candidate Joe Biden campaigned on a "made in America" platform four years later. These feel-good proposals warrant attention from voters, especially after shortages in the health care sector related to COVID-19 that led to deaths and devastation. However, they are merely campaign slogans without detailed substance for change, as I advocate for in my community-based supply chain model. It takes only basic math to invalidate the idea that we can return to manufacturing as we knew it, as should have been apparent with this Foxconn/Wisconsin deal before it ever was enacted and public funds dispersed.

21st-Century Manufacturing

The plan for an American Silk Road is different from the campaign promises of the past because it is a public-private investment in American citizens and their communities, not giveaways to multinational corporations; it builds the technological infrastructure of the future, not the past. Public expenditures for manufacturing and supply chain should bet on the individual entrepreneur, not the giant multinational corporation with interests primarily focused on its shareholders. In Wisconsin, gamesmanship and wishful thinking led to the Foxconn initiative that promised to bring forth 13,000 high-paying jobs through subsidization to create $20-an-hour American manufacturing jobs with benefits. The numbers for this project didn't work, even with subsidization, and the operation ultimately netted fewer workers and more automation but with an enormous outlay of taxpayer public funding. The project had a negative return on investment because it was a political gimmick rather than a solid business case fostered on industrial engineering principles. It is not a gimmick to seek manufacturing jobs back in Wisconsin, but it must be a forward-looking investment focused on innovation and technology. This approach to manufacturing has a positive return on investment when all stakeholders are factored into the equation.

A 21st-century manufacturing model of the future must be a digital model and, therefore, must first invest in broadband technology. According to a study by the consultancy firm CTC Technology and Energy, it would cost between $13 billion and $19 billion to deploy high-speed broadband fiber for the remaining areas of need in the United States, a relatively small investment into the future of the US economy compared with trillions of dollars in stimulus money distributed to businesses and individuals during the COVID-19 pandemic.[13] A broadband internet system across the United States to connect every community would be the impetus for states and communities to build public square entrepreneurial zones for nodes to set up shop in a new peer-to-peer model. This model would center on advanced digital manufacturing as the ultimate game changer for nodal, personal production using a public technology backbone. Think of this as less of a public works program of the past and more of a publicly financed backbone, just like building a highway or an ocean port. Each community can focus on its own areas of expertise, such as health care if it is close to a highly regarded university or clinic, and could attract aspiring peer-to-peer nodes in this field and ancillary service providers. This could also lead to the democratization of advanced manufacturing for health care to incentivize entrepreneurs in game-changing solutions such as medical devices and pharmaceuticals. This community-based approach allows the value of the work to be owned by the community itself, a 21st-century proper proliferation of innovation and free enterprise. Today investments in community are focused on critical projects, such as schools and roads, that are important but do not enable direct economic growth for that locality. Given the interconnectivity of even local communities to the world through the internet, these investments should be made.

This democracy of manufacturing at a community level would arise through a public utility purchase of advanced manufacturing technology for public use. Like cattle ranchers leasing federal land, peer-to-peer manufacturers would contract the use of technology, not receiving a subsidy or a handout but a viable public-private partnership. Today the largest supply chain companies in the world invest in cutting-edge technology capital projects and leverage low-cost labor and tax locations, being the decision-makers in who produces what, when, and where and in how innovation and entrepreneurship is introduced. With a viable network infrastructure across the United States, the local community can claim greater control of its destiny through investments in advanced manufacturing equipment for individual producers or nodes who will pay a fee (excise tax, use fee, property taxes, etc.) for its use. This wouldn't be a state-run enterprise like exists in China but rather the state would incentivize the individual entrepreneur to create innovation. The start-up costs for localized manufacturing could be funded through community fees or grants from the state or federal government. The community is healthier when industrial activity resides within its borders and user fees are a business enterprise function. Unlike socialism, where the state operates production, the state's involvement in this model is to enable economic growth through infrastructure, much like investments in water, electricity, and roads. In contrast, the Foxconn factory in Wisconsin is corporate- and state-sponsored socialism through public subsidies. Taxpayer- and user-funded investments to enable innovation would create a multiplier effect using the technologies of the 21st century. Because the communities and individuals pay taxes to fund the governments, they will be investing in themselves as an institution. This is an ultimate expression of capitalism through a public-private partnership.

Through a technology infrastructure in place via broadband to allow every community in the United States to participate, and with the cost of advanced manufacturing technology continuing to decline, the barriers to small manufacturing will fall, providing an incentive for communities to invest in these technologies to attract nodal manufacturing to gain a tax revenue base—and healthy citizens. This was the case during the early years of the twentieth century, when immigrants and farmers flocked to the factories to create a better way of life. But in today's long-tailed manufacturing and supply chains, local governments are essentially powerless to create enterprise zones to do the same. In the future, with a robust broadband network in place courtesy of a federal or state investment, a municipality can develop a sound business case to purchase advanced manufacturing or 3D printing to establish a production hub for the community. It may seem as farfetched, but it is true that these municipality communities can compete against clothing manufacturers, pharmaceutical companies, and even Amazon through lower inventory costs and greater consumer loyalty, the one factor most important to Amazon founder Jeff Bezos. The community wins through geography rather than loses because of it, as it does today. This model will win not because it is state-sponsored but rather because it yields the greatest value to the community and the individual.

Let's face facts: a large global manufacturer like Foxconn will never choose a community in Baltimore or Flint to start a new operation even if they are practically bribed to do so. Moreover, in 2002, Flint was placed in a state of financial emergency because it accrued $30 million in debt due to falling tax revenues. Without a tax base, a city like Flint cannot fund necessary public programs as it spins out of control with crime, drugs, unemployment, and other problems. Inner cities and rural communities need a tax base through commerce, not public welfare. With advanced manufacturing and production capabilities through these emerging technologies of 3D printing and the blockchain, a smaller structural footprint and the initial capital spend could be conducive to starting these inner-city and rural town enterprise zones. In a 20th-century free-market model, an individual entrepreneur could not afford to invest in these technologies and in depressed communities, but in the 21st century they won't have to—they will just pay a utility cost.

Why not an American version of the Silk Road in the 21st century? There were numerous reasons why America would not be able to get a man on the moon in the 1960s—but it did in 1969. However, as a solution for the future, an American Silk Road checks all the boxes: it focuses on both red and blue states, on the most depressed areas. It is a manufacturing strategy that resonates with the voters, with increased production adding health and resiliency to the economy. It is a focus on technology and innovation of the future, not the manufacturing of the past. It leverages America's strengths rather than its weaknesses in competing globally. The individual and the community drive this strategy, it is financially viable, and the role of government is to enable these stakeholders rather than overtake the private sector. The design empowers the individual or the node to escape a dead-end $15 an hour service job to become a nodal entrepreneur in the 21st century supply chain, reestablishing the American Dream. In this model, community colleges and trade schools are reimagined to cater to the new blue-collar roles of the future, focused on digitization with many different paths presented to our youth when they graduate from K–12 education. Finally, this strategy has the potential to bring Americans together rather than further dividing us. There may be concerns about this initiative, like any transformation. Still, the alternatives of wishing to restore the past or relying solely on the existing global supply chain offer little hope.

Critics of this model will note that the technology of 3D printing for additive manufacturing is not quite ready for prime time, but if the strategy is to act only when technology is ready for widespread applications, it will be too late for communities and individuals to participate when it is ready. It will take time to sell and weave this concept across the national, state, and local public and private entities and to educate citizens to participate in this model. A public enterprise model must compete against multinational supply chains investing today for the future. The vision of a networked, community-based manufacturing hub that can self-organize from community to community, state to state, and across the planet through digital tools that enable the individual—the node—is a paradigm shift from today's model. This new model will need to be designed, and the public will need to be taught how it will work and how they can get involved.

A digitally networked supply chain can work as follows: the product's design is created by a node or a team, and it may be an open-source design already available for all to use in a nodal supply chain strategy model. The product can be sourced within its local community or anywhere else in the world. The design can be sold by the designer or provided in a commercial or noncommercial form. Others will self-organize in the sourcing and planning of the supply chain before the design goes to production. These supply chain partners can connect seamlessly and dynamically through peer-to-peer transactions (blockchain) and organize based on their specialization. One node may specialize in the sourcing of a specific type of material. Others can be responsible for the forecasting, planning, and network modeling of the product through the supply chain. At each of the advanced 3D manufacturing centers, nodes will be responsible for the production planning element of the process, such as coordinating work orders, developing efficient production schedules, managing the plan of inbound materials, and scheduling the cleaning and maintenance breaks for the equipment. Yet each of these roles is nodal, meaning there isn't a large multinational corporation that owns the overall process but rather an expression of individual entrepreneurship. The goal in this model isn't to reduce the supply chain processes into as much automation as possible because the roles in the process are a part of a value chain, bringing value to the individual and the community. The goal is not solely to create shareholder wealth for an owner because the platform is a public utility with a plan to multiply economic growth across all stakeholders. In comparison to any other option, this model of a 21st century supply chain best embodies the concept of a multiplier effect across various stakeholders.

Once the work order is scheduled and the production process occurs, the back-end fulfillment cycle occurs, with nodes responsible for distributing the product to the end consumer. In this back-end execution process, the node may choose to market the product themselves or use third-party distribution and fulfillment centers, such as Amazon's role in the market today. In addition, the node can decide to make products for customers on demand or make the product in advance and develop an inventory strategy with other node third parties. As mentioned in the last chapter, the transactions of a pure peer-to-peer model must be executable over a distributed private electronic ledger system built on a blockchain that can enable seamless transactions, including payment. The degrees of freedom expressed in supply chain stakeholders can be near infinite: today the potential opportunities for flexible manufacturing are limited by the required scale, both in capital and in information technology investments. A combination of mature technology applications in advanced 3D printing and blockchain can be revolutionized in the future. It does not become a replacement for the existing large-scale, centralized global supply chain system but an alternative to it. The future of the supply chain will be one of glocalization, a hybrid between global and local. Systems will seamlessly flow between large centralized, global supply chains and many decentralized local ones run through these new technologies.

Blockchain and 3D printing technologies are not sufficiently mature for this model but will change sooner than we think, and there is much work to be done to develop this strategy in the meantime. Therefore, the policymakers cannot wait for the technologies to mature to begin the strategic design so a window of economic growth can move forward as soon as possible and replace the current market model of spiky globalization that leaves so many individuals and communities behind. There are so many business opportunities to leverage before these technologies take shape, and that can be happening today through the vision and adoption of a 21st-century supply chain strategy. The financial cost-benefit will invert the utility model from the technology owner to the worker or node as an alternative to being solely at the investor's benefit.

Critics may raise concerns regarding the public sector funding for broadband infrastructure, education transformation, and advanced manufacturing hardware. It has already been mentioned that corporate welfare schemes have not been successful in a 21st-century approach to manufacturing for America, so we must shift our thinking toward forward-thinking approaches, as is advocated in this chapter. It should be also noted that regardless of America's manufacturing strategy of the future, other nations are investing in this infrastructure as well. For example, China's Vision 2035 is to have a global blockchain standard by that year, a blockchain service network to change the nature of supply chain transactions. In industries such as finance, banking, health care, government, and supply chain, China is an early adopter in using the blockchain framework for business in the 21st century. So even if this model of the future is perceived by some as too forward-thinking, it should be understood that in other nations such as China, it is moving ahead. There is not much time for America to develop its strategy to compete.

In contrast, America's policymakers are embroiled in meaningless political tropes without substance. Of course, there is no shortage of short-term, immediate focus areas for the government, such as climate change, global conflicts, virus pandemics, homelessness, drug addiction, and racial and income inequality, among others. Asking our leaders to focus on something longer term may seem unreasonable except when it is understood that a 21st-century supply chain strategy is an investment for a new future that can directly address some of these short-term challenges, especially related to the economy. A virtual bridge tying the white- and blue-collar workers of America, enabled by an improved educational system, is the winning formula for a nation that has always been known for its innovation. There is a rational business case for this new model when all the factors are included, and none are considered externalities in the calculation. Are Americans ready for this change, or do they wish for things to remain the same? It's time to look in the mirror and toward the future.

Getting Started

The United States is on the right track for this future strategy, starting with an investment in the nation's telecommunication infrastructure. President Biden's $2 trillion infrastructure bill, signed into law in November 2021, includes a $65 billion investment in broadband, with $42.5 billion focused on the estimated 14.5 million Americans who do not have access to the internet.[14] Hopefully, quick deployment of the telecommunications infrastructure can address these access issues. Next is to escalate STEM and digital education funding for K–12 schools across the United States. According to the US Department of Education, spending to emphasize the STEM fields in the public education system has been rising, with an expenditure of close to $600 million in 2020 and grant funding expected to increase.[15] However, unlike broadband infrastructure spending, which is more clear-cut relative to funding utilization, the federal government's role in the education system is complicated. Education is essentially a state and local responsibility in the United States. As a result, a small portion of funding, perhaps as high as 10 percent, is received by local jurisdictions from the federal government, often in grants that are less strategic direction than case-by-case initiatives.

China's Ministry of Education governs that country's education system, ensuring the implementation of a national strategic directive. However, due to America's federalist system of states' rights and local community school boards, establishing a national platform to transform classroom curricula is challenging, especially in today's divided political environment. Local school boards determine students' competency expectations as well as teachers' hardware and software requirements. Like the challenges of a Congress where elected officials are required to run for election every two years, school board members must also focus on short-term interests to be elected and re-elected into office. This short-term focus of those who run America's education system often leads to funding objectives that are not as focused on the longer-term "difficult in" strategies. Improving America's inner city, rural, and even many suburban school districts for STEM education is often too heavy a lift for school boards and their community members when so many pressing short-term needs exist, including insufficient textbooks and other materials. Given America's toxic political system, it may seem like an impossible task to address a national standard of STEM education across the countless number of local school boards for a nation as large as the United States. Still, it is a measure that we must address for our national future. Perhaps a national strategy that unifies both blue- and white-collar workers can lead to guidelines that connect it to our local municipalities.

With technological infrastructure moving in the right direction, a real focus must shift to nationwide educational reforms, implemented community by community. With effort, these transformations can be in flight in time for the United States to build its platform through advanced manufacturing and blockchain, the two most important technologies for the future of manufacturing. However, even before these future technologies are ready for prime time in communities, K–12 students must be trained in these concepts and their applications. Students must also be trained in this concept of a community-based system to understand that *they*, not a corporate manager or some other leader, will be directing their future careers. Leadership skills and structured problem solving will be essential. Once the technology infrastructure is in place and the education system is reformed to graduate students who are proficient in the 21st-century system, it will be time for policymakers to fund these advanced manufacturing hubs in local communities. Governments will need to partner with communities to balance funding, grants, and professional support to get these operations and their practices up and running.

Providing proper education, technological infrastructure, and micro incentives for the individual prosumer can lead to a healthier manufacturing strategy that includes a more significant percentage of the communities and their populations. China is spreading its seeds across Central and Southern Asia, Africa, and other areas through its BRI and Made in China 2025 strategy. America's strategy is more ambitious and game-changing because it is building a public-private partnership of entrepreneurship and innovation that does not and cannot exist in China's model.

And it's not just China that is planning for technology advancement on behalf of a new supply chain system. Industrial symbiosis has taken shape on a smaller scale in Europe as a network of disparate business operations that cohabitate in an enterprise zone to improve efficiency and reduce waste through connected processes. For example, the Kalundborg Eco-Industrial Park in Denmark is an enterprise zone that links a power plant, fish farm, manufacturer, and oil refinery. By creating this industrial park, the Danish government established the infrastructure and strategy for private sector companies to be entrepreneurial and environmentally friendly to achieve more significant objectives. Rather than replicating this, which is more of a 20th-century supply chain, a prototype for its 21st-century model would be an enterprise zone for advanced manufacturing in a US community, as discussed in this chapter. While some nations such as China may be ahead of the United States today relative to these newer technologies to advance a digital supply chain, there is no country with an environment as suitable for innovation and entrepreneurship than America. The nation just needs the will and focus to make it happen as soon as possible. The time to start moving forward is now.

This new approach to reindustrialization must happen as quickly as possible, and as rationally and collectively as possible. However, these strategies must be better thought out than the big corporate welfare-funded giveaways, such as the Foxconn project in Wisconsin, which was doomed from the start. As a creative approach to a value chain, an initial prototype should be undertaken in a community in need of investment, such as Baltimore, Flint, or a rural town in West Virginia. Because the advanced manufacturing and blockchain applications are just at their initial stages, investments in these technologies would have to be updated and iterative, which could be viable given their small-scale model. According to experts in 3D print-ing and advanced manufacturing, the most significant barriers to their applications are supply chain-related: the current supply chain system discourages innovations.[16] Therefore, the sooner we can deploy some model prototypes, the sooner we can learn how these community-based supply chains can compete against today's large-scale, outdated, 20th-century manufacturing and supply chain models. If this is a matter of the chicken and the egg, and if we don't transform our supply chains soon enough, America will exempt itself (once again) from the next phase of manufacturing and supply chain, enabling global competitors to gain advantages by being the first to market.

Funding for an enterprise zone prototype should commence immediately: choose a location, such as Baltimore or Flint; design the public-private partnership of this nodal, community-based system, including investments in technology infrastructure and education; and commence the implementation of new technologies around a supply chain with an advanced manufacturing printer and blockchain system to sup-port it. This will be the next era of the worker in the supply chain system: first, the craftsman made the product by hand, one by one, but without a modern-day supply chain system. Next came the production line worker in America, a part of a process that multiplied economic growth through a balance in supply and demand and an early-onset supply chain system. Then America lost its manufacturing and supply chain leadership to a spiky global supply chain model built on low-cost labor, ad-vanced technology, and logistics. Due to this metamorphism, the connection between the worker and production was lost, leading to the dissonance that exists today, driven by the economies of scale of large multinational corporations that alone can afford the capital investments. It is time to bring the worker, owner, and citizen together as a node in the supply chain system, leading to a new model of markets and capitalism that applies benefit to all stakeholders.

Good technology must start with good manufacturing practices. According to W. Edwards Deming, the father of good manufacturing practices, new machinery and gadgets are not the answer and cannot be successful without good people and processes.[17] The natural response to these supply chain challenges is not manufactur-ing itself but how superior methods enable advanced manufacturing. With good people, processes, and technology, 3D printing will begin to enter the mainstream of manufacturing, no longer just a tool for prototyping and remedial components. According to a 2019 study by the French company Sculpteo, which specializes in 3D printing, 80 percent of companies say 3D printing enables them to innovate faster, and 51 percent use 3D printing in production.[18] The growth of 3D printing is mainly in the production of parts for industry, medicine, and automobiles, with large manu-facturers using this process in large-scale production. Most uses of 3D printing are straightforward designs using uniform polymers that are more easily melted and ex-truded than other materials like metals, which require higher temperatures and more complex manufacturing processes such as lasers and electron beams to fuse materials into shapes. Suppose the sophistication of materials and manufacturing continues to advance, as is expected. Why would a manufacturing site be limited to a particular product, such as one location producing automobiles while another makes medical ventilators? Some experts believe that one day it will be possible to build products based on their locational needs rather than one product manufactured at this factory and the other at a factory somewhere far away. This could lead to a consolidated manufacturing facility of abbreviated supply chains and lower inventory levels and cycle times, leading to higher efficiency, profitability, and even sustainability.[19] As a result, the cost of innovation in the product life-cycle process will be reduced because the company will no longer need to reach a particular scale volume. After all, the cost of printing will not vary from Unit 1 to Unit 1 million. Finally, and most importantly, the value of production will be restored to where consumption occurs.

Certain thresholds need to be met for advanced manufacturing to surpass mass production. According to Peter Diamandis, entrepreneur and chair of the nonprofit XPRIZE, 3D printers will increase in speed by 50 to 100 times and will become more usable, and other materials currently in use in 3D printing (more than 250 types) will overtake plastics as the primary feedstock, including composites. In addition, 3D printers will grow in more mainstream uses, such as food production. For example, 3D printing can print meat using plant-based proteins rather than animal-based feed-stock, which is expensive and bad for the environment. Other mainstream products such as a 3D-printed garment, shoes, phone cases, machine parts, and jewelry could become mainstream in the next five years, depending on the supply chain system.[20]

The possibilities for how 3D printing can revolutionize manufacturing appear almost endless, including improvements in our food system, not just in the produc-tion of more sustainable foods from plant protein but also in the distribution of food by creating products that can be sent to poorer communities made from recipes of simple ingredients. Suppose nutritious foods could be made into powders of suitable organic molecules with a shelf life of years, if not decades. A powder form of food that could be 3D printed on demand may not hold all the romance associated with fresh food related to culture or leisure, but it can serve as a stabilizing force in regions where starvation and malnourishment run rampant. Likewise, 3D printing can make pharmaceuticals since the materials and the active pharmaceutical ingredients can be stored as powders and printed on demand. This could significantly improve the supply chain for how nations and communities can manage existing drug problems like the opioid epidemic and America's reliance on pharmaceutical manufacturing in sometimes hostile foreign countries. Through blockchain and 3D printing, the control over these substances can be drastically improved and managed by a community. There should not be circumstances like what happened in the United States, where large masses of opioids were sent to communities far out of proportion to the number of residents. Likewise, critical drugs for the US population could be better managed for cost, flexibility, and resiliency if 3D printing were possible, leading to shorter, more controlled supply chain systems. The American health professional and the health care supply chain would not have to choose between managing cost and enabling supply when needed: both would be controlled effectively in this new supply chain system.

The health care sector should focus on this community-based advanced manufacturing and supply chain system. Hopefully, as President Trump noted, America learned a good lesson during the COVID-19 pandemic. The key challenges that we faced in this global pandemic were in the availability and production of surgical and N95 masks and ventilators. To meet the global demand for masks, China, which makes most of the masks for the world, increased production almost instantaneously from 20 million a day to 110 million a day, with a unit cost that started at about 6.5 cents and then swung wildly after that, with accusations that games were being played on the market, including hoarding. A mask is a relatively simple product to make, but in today's production model, factories are designed for specific products, so production increases require retooling and reshaping the overall production line. This meant producers of similar products outside of China could not immediately begin producing masks to meet the new demand.

In contrast, 3D printing does not require such changes but instead needs scaling capacity to produce many such items in such a rapid period. This is not possible by relying on a few large producers, but many community manufacturing centers could shift production to this product and provide greater production capacity for each machine and the corresponding supply chain system. Of course, it will take time for this type of supply chain network to come online, but it is possible; meanwhile, it can be implemented as a supplement to the existing large global manufacturers.

The same transformation will eventually be possible for more sophisticated health care products, like ventilators, but done differently. Rather than the supply chain focusing tens of thousands of local community-based 3D printers on mask production, a linked national supply chain of 3D printers can have roles in the parts and components of ventilators, including overseas manufacturers. During the global pandemic, 3D printers made face shields, a process that isn't yet as efficient as a mass producer in China, but it is a start. Today a smartphone is sourced from more than forty-five nations and assembled in China and Taiwan. The 21st-century 3D-model of production could be a similar but glocalized design. 3D production schedulers can design a network based on logistics and the capability of 3D printers to develop parts and components for a ventilator that can be sourced most efficiently and then sent to local manufacturing sites where these products can be assembled quickly for use or even placed in inventory in case of an emergency. The supply chain will be nodal, so the capacity and capability of a community's 3D printer will be known, scheduled, and networked accordingly, with nodes involved as those who own the designs of specific parts required to produce the ventilator. There are plenty of jobs available for designers, planners, distributors, and shippers in this model. These new manufacturing models would also enable today's ridiculously inefficient and dangerous health care supply chains to be rationalized, from the manufacturers to the distributors to the hospital systems themselves. This problem became apparent through the COVID-19 pandemic when we needed it to be most efficient. 3D-printed materials can be developed on the fly at hospitals and customized to a patient's need, enabling surgeons to make more effective decisions rather than being hamstrung by supply availability and cost. For example, a 3D scan of a patient can lead to personalized prosthetics and even a model of pharmaceuticals that becomes a modern-day apothecary model of the patient getting customized prescriptions rather than mass-produced drugs from large firms.

Win the Right Game

Government policies incentivizing or even requiring multinational firms to move production to the United States will lead to the next round of Band-Aid solutions that don't solve the problem of a relevant supply chain system for the 21st century. Multinational corporations have goals that are often different from and sometimes contradictory to that of a specific country and the local community. To some extent, this is the nature of capitalism. Suppose our nation has learned a good lesson, as President Trump said. In that case, we should understand it is essential to balance the public and private interests within our supply chains and understand what is in our collective self-interest at the community and individual levels. China has developed breathtaking strategies for the 21st century that, if successfully enacted, will enable them to be leaders in the future global economy, despite its draconian approach to public-private partnerships. What about the United States and other nations? Today America is losing by playing the wrong game, whether it is a trade war against China or seeking to pressure the multinational corporations within a global supply chain who are focused on their own objectives, which are different from any country's goals. The United States should focus on what makes the nation great—its people—and it should create a manufacturing system to enable the strength of the American people through its local communities.

America needs to play the right game with the right balance of people, processes, and technologies to win. What is in the best interest of the American people—citizens, customers, workers, and owners—through market-based solutions? It certainly isn't to do an about-face away from capitalism because the American citizen no longer trusts multinational corporations that do not act in the population's best interest. And yet some of the strategies that have been attempted in US states, such as subsidizing large corporations, should not be classified as free-market capitalism but rather state-funded corporate welfare. Compared to any nation, especially China, America is unique for its individualism and innovation, so why not enable a 21st-century version of capitalism and a supply chain that allows this competitive advantage? Ironically, the conventional wisdom of the supply chain is that capitalism is expressed through economies of scale through significant capital investment by substantial multinational corporations when, in fact, public investment in infrastructure to enable an individual entrepreneur could genuinely be the most significant expression of capitalism as well as a multiplier of future growth. This does not mean that large private companies cannot compete and even try to dominate the market, but there should be fewer barriers to competition from an open-source, nodal alternative in the supply chain. This is winning at the right game.

Another element of winning the right game is including more American citizens back into the manufacturing and supply chain process. A national strategy could take many steps forward and then as many steps back if a large percentage of the population is excluded from the process, as has been the case for five decades or more in the United States. Those who live in rural and inner-city communities without a proper STEM education have been prevented from participating, intentionally or unintentionally. The problem has become so great that many in these communities have given up hope and are resentful of the so-called college-educated elites who have created the myth of a meritocracy, blaming the failure of the disenfranchised on themselves for a game they can't win. Winning the right game doesn't mean an equal outcome but rather an equal chance. We need to recognize that few multinational corporations are willing to invest in Flint and Baltimore and the tens of thousands of small, unknown, and forgotten towns. Today we can face the challenges that our country has faced for decades, such as the ignored cores of rural towns and inner cities and the emerging critical matters of a global health care pandemic, through the same approach. America needs to stop blaming international competitors, large corporations, and even our citizens; we need to look in the mirror, dust ourselves off, and build an exciting model for the future. America needs to win the right game, and the financials for these business cases show that we can, so let's get started!

CHAPTER 5

VIRTUAL LOGISTICS

Enabling Community-Based Supply Chains

The unofficial kickoff to a "new normal" may have happened in April 2020 when Dr. Anthony Fauci warned Americans that they should never shake hands again, not that they shouldn't until the vaccine is administered or after herd immunity is achieved, but *never*.[1] These "never lists" have grown in number to include the possibility of never again blowing out the candles on a birthday cake, never letting your kid jump in a ball pit at a McDonalds or Chucky Cheese, never bumping into strangers while dancing at a crowded bar, or even never hugging or kissing a friend on the cheek.[2] Never is a long time, and it's complicated to accept terms like "never" and "always" in any situation, even the aftermath of a black swan event like the COVID-19 pandemic. But, for sure, the world will never be the same after COVID-19. Millions have and will continue to die worldwide, tens of millions in the developing world who were pulled out of poverty will fall back in, and fifty million Americans are now facing food insecurity, according to Feeding America, the nation's largest hunger-relief organization.[3] It will take a good deal of time for America to recover from the pandemic, and what will come next is unsure. Still, one thing is clear: for some Americans the US economy was not so normal before the pandemic either. The nation's wealth is as concentrated as it has ever been in history: in 2020, 55 percent of Americans owned stock, but the top 1 percent owned 51.4 percent, and 87.2 percent of stocks were controlled by the top 10 percent of wealthy Americans.[4] The United States has the highest income inequality of the G7 nations, and the wealth gap in the United States doubled from 1989 to 2016.[5] Today's level of inequality is unimaginable, as high as it was during the Great Depression of the 1930s. Indeed, these are extraordinary times requiring transformational change. This chapter addresses the importance of a community-based supply chain and the replacement of a primarily physical, oil-based economy with a virtual, electron-based digital economy. Actions must be taken not to get back to some definition of normal from the past but to get to a new, more appropriate model for the future.

Energy has played a significant role in developing and distributing wealth and growth since the Industrial Revolution. Seismic shifts began in the oil industry in 2008, when oil prices rose to over $145 a barrel and stayed there for over a decade.[6] Earlier in the 21st century there was concern that the world was about to hit "peak oil," the beginning of the end of cheap energy sources and potentially significant disruption to the global supply chain. These concerns have shaken the supply chain as logistics is its primary driver and oil is the super-lubricant of its transactions. Back in 2008 I remember developing a strategy for my logistics operation of alternatives if and when energy prices rose too high or oil became unavailable, planning for disruptions in my company's ability to get products to market. But shortly after the scare of 2008, innovations in the discovery and processing/distribution of natural gas in North America led to game-changing improvements in the detection of and production of natural gas reserves—increasing over 70 percent—and, voilà, there was no longer an oil crisis. In the early stage of the COVID-19 pandemic, oil prices fell below $10 a barrel before stabilizing to around $60–$70 a barrel and then ballooning to $130 in March 2022. As such, what will be the future of oil in the supply chain? Will an emergence of digitization/virtualization and the threat of climate change impact our view of oil and the physical supply chain? In November 2020, when oil prices were at some of their lowest levels, the largest renewable energy project in US history was announced to produce 1.5 gigawatts of renewable energy capacity, enough to power 300,000 homes.[7] As the world has learned from the price shocks resulting from Russia's invasion of Ukraine, oil is not going away anytime soon, but strong transformation signals emerge from a nodal supply chain of data and information driven by the blockchain and analytics. A frictionless supply chain fostered from data and information, a community-based, digital, and virtual model will take over from the conventional, physical, long-tailed model of spiky globalization built from oil. Will America's supply chain shift to a "new normal" or remain within the current state of "old abnormal"? And what will this bring to an increasingly disgruntled American population thirsty for change? A new normal needs to take shape, driven by a new type of logistics.

Transformation must be driven by a new form of logistics: virtual logistics. After all, if the future of the supply chain is to be more virtual than physical, driven by data and information rather than oil and traditional industrial assets, the engine of the supply chain system—logistics—needs to be digitized. Since its origin, the field of logistics has been one of innovation, starting back in the earliest days of civilizations through the trade routes of the Silk Road that spanned across Asia, starting in China and traversing into Europe to Rome. There are many historical accounts of logistics innovation: the Appian Way in Rome, the Lewis and Clark expedition across North America, the D-Day invasion to liberate Europe, and even the future of central Asia through the Belt and Road Initiative. So what will be the big event, the significant logistical innovation of the 21st century?

After decades of avoiding the field of supply chain management in my career, given the bad taste in my mouth from the deindustrialization of my hometown of Baltimore, I began to gravitate toward the career field of supply chain logistics. Despite the fate of my relatives who lost their jobs in the deindustrialization of the 1970s, I began to see the field in a new light based on these structured problem-solving methods that I have learned in my profession. I accepted the opportunity to run logistics for the world's largest brewery in Golden, Colorado. This experience led me to appreciate supply chain and logistics in a field where almost anything is possible and gave me the ability to think bigger scale and innovate to accomplish great things in consumer markets and beyond. My team set shipping and production records worldwide. However, I also began to understand how innovations could unintentionally disregard communities in the process. I struggled to understand that the fantastic, structured problem-solving techniques that I learned in the industry, such as Six Sigma, Lean Manufacturing, and Total Quality Management, could also lead to unintended consequences with disastrous impacts on the economy, society, and environment.

I began to connect the dots by studying how supply chains should solve economic, societal, and environmental problems. My study has revealed future possibilities through research and industry projects related to the environment, society, and specific needs under pressure, such as the health care sector. Today I am convinced that it isn't the techniques that do not work but rather their misapplication within an outdated economic system run by incapable institutions: rather than being focused on ways to improve the overall plight of the economy and its citizens, workers, and consumers, these so-called optimization techniques are primarily focused on customers and investors. As a result, the problem shouldn't be fixed by asking the wrong questions and using the wrong tools and methods: it's only through asking the right questions and using the right tools and techniques that the game can be won.

21st-Century Globalization

One of China's goals is to create a supply chain strategy that balances itself through "dual circulation," which means keeping its economy open to the world when it is in China's best interest to do so as well as pulling back from globalization to reinforce its domestic markets for stabilization. The concept is an intentionally vague term and does not seem to be clearly articulated in any detail in official Chinese government economic plans but is a foundational strategy of the nation since it entered the World Trade Organization at the beginning of the 21st century. It is sometimes described as "capitalism wih Chinese characteristics." Yet the WTO's rationale for allowing China's entry into the WTO trading community in 2001 was the expectation that this policy would lead to the liberalization of Chinese markets for both production and consumption and would transform this outdated Communist form of government closer to a neoliberal version of the West, something that has not and never will happen. Many in the West were surprised when China did not follow this path—and it was surprising to China that the West expected it to do so. Rather than the global economy becoming a monolithic Western model, the design is becoming bimodal through the influence of the world's most populated nation and second-largest economy—the People's Republic of China. China's connection to the world economy and its supply chains is best described as "shallow integration," an exuberant yet cautious approach to globalization sprinkled with various tariffs and other barriers protecting its local interests. A government researcher named Wang Jian uses the term "international circulation" and proposes that China's economy needs to grow through exports without losing control of its supply chains to an unbridled liberal market environment.[8] While a semi-closed approach to capitalism has inherent weaknesses, particularly related to innovation, it is a strategy that aspires toward greater economic self-reliance and exporting leverage that has been on full display to the world during the COVID-19 pandemic and beyond. Rather than a blatant repudiation of Western-style globalization, China seeks to fly below the radar of the West's ire and is unapologetic for what it calls "capitalism with Chinese characteristics." China's successes are not limited to the lifting of hundreds of millions of its citizens out of poverty; its gleaming, modern city landscapes; or even its role as the world's factory. China has also succeeded in sustaining its model to display Chinese characteristics rather than submitting to disadvantageous practices that favor the West, in China's opinion. A Chinese strategy of dual circulation makes sense under a Chinese planned economy integrated with market capitalism, but it will show its limitations to take advantage of the changing nature of a future, dynamic 21st-century supply chain as described in this book. A Chinese version of balanced globalization that controls its national self-interest may be viable in the short-term but not the long-term due to the potential for rising labor rates and the disconnection from innovation engines for growth. In comparison, a new logistics model in the United States built on virtualization and communities could jumpstart localized and resilient production, which has been lacking for decades. America would gain a competitive advantage over China in its own (new) version of dual circulation. China—a nation with nearly 20 percent of the world's population—has different challenges, and the United States can become the world's innovator through logistics with a balanced, technology-driven approach.

To compete in this 21st-century model of globalization, the United States needs to develop its version of dual circulation with American characteristics by creating an individual- and community-based system not through viewing capitalism and supply chains as large, monolithic structures and institutions but rather by focusing on the value chain, a nodal supply chain strategy that better balances supply and demand. This would be not just the creation of an enterprise innovation model that takes advantage of the strengths of the American culture but would also be a reindustrialization strategy to develop an American Silk Road of sorts, a networked collection of micro-manufacturing hubs at the community level using broadband infrastructure, advanced manufacturing, and a modernized approach to American education. This model leverages both America's innovation engine and the emerging 21st-century technologies. The creation of these community-based supply chain systems will enable America's expertise in logistics to resonate internally first and then project outward to the world, from localization to globalization, to create a glocal model. Compared to China's approach of dual circulation, which controls a balancing of supply and demand through a centralized governmental system in which all roads lead back to Beijing, this American system would work through individualized producer and consumer channels using American innovation. Rather than wasting time on political spats to banter over trade disputes through antiquated, incapable governmental bodies such as the WTO, the goal should be to reform markets through people, process, and technology, not bureaucracy and policy tactics. And rather than competing against the Chinese and others through a monolithic 20th-century supply chain model that cannot work in the 21st century, the focus should be forward-looking, focusing on technology and innovation.

The pathway to a 21st-century supply chain model through a community-based, nodal, or individual approach is logical. The Chinese have wisely realized that a 20th century, Western-style model of globalization is not in the best interests of its citizens, and it has adopted a model of dual circulation that has been to its benefit, albeit with longer-term negative ramifications. An American version of a new model is a publicly invested technology for a community-based system of a version of dual circulation between the public and private sectors. Through this supply chain infrastructure built as a virtual, peer-to-peer model, the public interest achieves self-reliance in a manner different from the China model. China's policy is focused on a tightly woven relationship between Big Business and government as well as collectivization and control over the public. America's model should be for the public sector to incentivize nodal self-reliance, allowing the individual to express himself or herself through the market, which couldn't be more different from the Chinese approach. A new form of virtual logistics is a paradigm shift from large-scale global multinational corporations achieving economies of scale, often enabled by large institutions. A 21st-century strategy allows giant multinational corporations and small, individualized enterprises to compete on an even playing field with less governmental intervention.

China has accepted the limitations and detriments of today's global supply chains and financial markets from their cultural perspective. In contrast, the United States has not accepted these realities, which has led to an anticapitalist sentiment among a substantial, younger population considering a dangerous alternative—socialism. Even mentioning the possibility of a community-based supply chain enabled by public sector investment would raise shouts from critics, as if today's large institutional financial market firms and multinational corporations are what Adam Smith conceived capitalism to be more than two hundred years ago. Jamie Gamble, a retired longtime partner for the law firm Simpson Thacher & Bartlett, a blue-chip firm that counts nearly all the major US companies as clients, has concluded that corporate executives who used to be his clients "are legally obligated to act like sociopaths." According to Gamble, corporations must only think about themselves and must "define what is good as what makes it more money."[9] A Chinese model of dual circulation is itself corrupted because it must obey Communist Party principles that include cronyism and self-interest, but it is not sociopathic by definition. In today's capitalist system, corporate leaders are aware of a similar loyalty pledge to the stockholder and corporate self-interest without much regard for externalities, defined as anything that does not make more profit or lead to corporate bonuses.

In contrast, communities can and should advocate for their citizens through innovation and enterprise in a model as American as apple pie. Jurisdictions gaining self-reliance for economic growth and prosperity, enabled—not mandated—by federal and state governments, would cause the right incentives, multiplying self-reliance from self-interest. An investment in community-based infrastructures such as 3D printing and logistics centers can put back on the map communities that have been excluded for over half a century. Creating local entrepreneurs can lead to an enterprise zone that multiplies additional investment and confidence for the education system. An entire glocalized supply chain can be constructed both to and for the community, networked across the planet. A networked supply chain connected to the next town over, to an Asian corporation, to a seaport, or to a municipality worldwide offers unlimited possibilities, all within its own control rather than dependent on big government or business. Think of this community-based system as one that mirrors the internet, a decentralized array of clusters, constantly changing, always connected. Its logistics are virtual algorithms rather than physical routes and destinations. To some extent, this reflects the villages of the Middle Ages, a decentralized collection of clusters creating alliances and partnerships based on self-organization and interest. This model starts virtual and then is physical, with logistics fulfillment. Logistics is moving from point A to point B; in this new model, this is done virtually as much as possible before transitioning to traditional logistical forms such as warehousing, distribution, transportation, and retail.

Logistics is the tool that connects the dots between nodes, making enterprise zones viable just as logistics allowed the proliferation of global shipping and distribution. Rather than thinking of an enterprise zone as a model to eliminate, regulate, and displace large companies such as Amazon and Walmart, think of them as their future competitors. Once the community-based system is on the network and ready to produce, the logistics system will connect the dots between supply and demand to enable innovation in the most unrestricted sense. Logistics optimization will happen through virtual algorithms fluidly transacted by a centralized, decentralized transactional blockchain system. The connecting of the dots is *many to many*, rather than *fewer to fewer*, as exists today in the enormous physical economies of scale model.

Take, for example, West Baltimore, a crumbling community plagued by drug dealing and limited to remedial employment opportunities, such as retail food service at minimum wage. With an upgraded broadband infrastructure, an open-source blockchain system to enable transactions, and an advanced manufacturing center to promote production, West Baltimore students can be taught to act as nodes within the community supply chain system. They can be trained to follow a structured problem-solving routine focused on data and analytics to develop and solve markets. A virtual logistics system would not only link them together through this community-based system but would network across communities through the internet. The planning, sourcing, and distribution of materials and services could be transacted through the blockchain and then manufactured into products and distributed and retailed within a peer-to-peer model. Physical supply chains have flown over and around communities like West Baltimore; digital systems can reintroduce a communal and global approach or glocal virtual logistics.

A proposed glocal model is antithetical to what logistics professionals have been taught for decades, that optimization is a physical point A to B primarily focused on cheap labor markets and technology. In this new model, let's call it Logistics 2.0, optimization is beyond *price* to consider *value* across all stakeholders, reducing the number of variables that today are defined as externalities. Logistics 2.0, just like Economics 2.0, should be built on a near-infinite data and analytics model that allows us to calculate the value rather than using price as a substitution. Both Logistics 1.0 and Economics 1.0 were critical factors in America losing its supply chain dominance, and Logistics 2.0 and Economics 2.0 will be instrumental in bringing it back. The good news is that the benefits of Logistics 1.0 will remain intact as necessary for the new 21st-century model, such as the FedEx business model of overnight shipping, the containerization of imports through twenty thousand standard shipping containers loaded on an ocean freighter, and Amazon next-day shipping. Logistics 2.0 is a model of spatial optimization from a different point of view because supply chains will become more virtual than physical in a 21st-century globalization model. Rather than optimizing from point A to point B to enable price innovations for consumers and producers, a digital supply chain system can eliminate these spatial challenges by eliminating these physical limitations and defining a value proposition of who is a customer and who is a producer. Consumers and producers can be anyone, living anywhere, so as long as they are networked to do so. Rather than only seeking to achieve economies of scale over large, long-tailed supply chains where it is beneficial to make a majority of the masks in one location, the objective is to achieve an economy of the network and then effectively link these community networks across the planet. The Economies of Scale 1.0 model are beneficial to consumers but only to a few producers. In contrast, an Economy of the Network 2.0 is advantageous to each community and, therefore, to any part of the world involved in the system. This new logistics model solves the age-old problem of economics in needing to substitute the variable price for value due to data, measurement, and theoretical limitations.

In today's pharmaceutical supply chain model, drugs are initially manufactured in nations where research and development are optimal and there is a viable health care system, ensuring the viability and profitability of the model. As a result, developing nations are often left out of the process until the drugs are no longer patent-protected, meaning that lifesaving medicines can sometimes be withheld from much of the market for long periods. When drugs become available as generic, their production is often migrated for production to these developing nations, which liberates supply to those countries. This is the profit motive that drives the supply chain spatially, enabled by Logistics 1.0. Now think about the financial calculus of logistics of the same pharmaceutical supply chain driven by Logistics 2.0. Rather than the supply chain system as a long-tailed, global system seeking to achieve economies of scale to ensure profit as a function of one variable or another, a digital formula of a drug can be produced locally within a networked community providing both profit and effective health policy. Using an economy of network model plus an open-source value chain design, blockchain and additive manufacturing technology, and a virtually connected logistics system from community to community, this Logistics 2.0 model can be cost effective and community resilient. In times of crisis, the primary goal should be to avoid putting patients at risk through the current long-tailed supply chains. A model of dual circulation can be enabled through American-styled logistics that bring it together and, in the process, provide the nation with a much more secure health care supply chain system. Of course, the one drawback of this model is its impact on the profitability of large pharmaceutical companies. Still, protectionism on behalf of Big Business should not be a vanguard of capitalism. Cracking this nut for the future of the 21st-century supply chain in America will be as important as it was for Wang Jian to develop the idea of dual circulation for China over thirty years ago.

The Future: Virtual Logistics

Logistics 2.0 could enable community-based supply chains and support for challenges the world may face through a future pandemic relative to an effective vaccine distribution plan. With 7.8 billion people on the planet and 75 percent of the population required to be vaccinated to reach herd immunity, 5.85 billion people would need access to the vaccine. Let's assume that these 5.85 billion people will need two vaccine shots each within three months, totaling 11.7 billion vaccine doses. This objective is infeasible within today's Logistics 1.0 long-tailed global manufacturing and distribution. The problem is not just the distribution of the vaccine but the raw materials for the vaccine, the glass vials, the latex gloves, and the needles as well as a redefinition of something called cold chain logistics, the logistics of below ambient temperatures. If the vaccines require the cold chain, a lack of a cold chain structure in some locations can impact achieving herd immunity across the planet. A cold chain for frozen foods is usually a little above or below freezing (32 degrees Fahrenheit or 0 degrees Celsius). For COVID-19 vaccines, in particular, the cold chain is between -20 degrees and -70 degrees Celsius, a condition and scale that is outside of the standards in the field. In much of the developed world today, particularly in large cities with sufficient infrastructure, this logistics system in a 2.0 model would be complicated but not impossible. However, it would be difficult if not nearly impossible for the less developed countries of the world, where more than two-thirds of the 11.7 billion doses would be administered.[10] To be effective, this logistics model doesn't just focus on transportation from the factory to the distribution center but must also include retail points, such as a clinic, pharmacy, hospital, or even a remote field location. Even in the United States, some rural communities would be a challenge. Medical technology and innovation will open the door, but supply chain logistics must make it possible. As we have seen, today's Logistics 1.0 model is ineffective in dealing with a worldwide pandemic.

Think about how a community-based supply chain delivered by Logistics 2.0 could have changed the nature of the vaccine distribution challenge we faced during the COVID-19 pandemic. A networked array of localized 3D printing manufacturing could have developed a much more streamlined approach to every stage of the pharmaceutical supply chain. Even if the start-up of the vaccine manufacturing had commenced at a few facilities, the community-based system could have planned, distributed, retailed, and administered health care in a much more rational manner rather than the arbitrary, political, and wasteful approach that impacted citizen confidence rather than built on it. An open-source platform for drug research must be followed with an open-sourced, community-based supply chain system through virtual logistics from a different value proposition model from existing capitalism.

A national platform to kick off a community-based supply chain network would commence through incentives and subsidies for the public broadband infrastructure and public education reform for the entire community. With this platform in place, digital infrastructure would network each community in the nation and around the world, similar to how a national railroad system helped to create the physical network of the US supply chain over a century ago. Then each state and local municipality could determine its separate economic development plan, perhaps through the seeding of business case funding for local communities to begin justifying their models. For example, the US government could fund the infrastructure and educational strategy, and Maryland could fund the feasibility study and proof of concept of a community-based supply chain based in the city of Baltimore. If the feasibility study is justified, the federal and state governments could offer further incentives or subsidies for local communities to purchase additional equipment for the community system, such as 3D printers, information technology equipment, and so on. Through this model, local entrepreneurs—or nodes—are funded in an innovation-based approach, but one with lower barriers to entry than exist today, such as limits based on significant capital funding requirements, making entrepreneurship a high-risk, entry-restricted endeavor. Building this 21st-century model of innovation, entrepreneurship, and supply chain through a community-based network model will take time and will require commitment. It will require iteration as the public and private sectors, as well as the nodes and existing businesses, learn how to compete against existing large multinational corporations. This is the real competitive advantage of this system compared to China's state-owned enterprises.

Once the proof of concept is validated and there is public and private interest in the model that is designed, it will lead to the creation of a new ecosystem that will attract innovators/investors and nodes of all types; a multipurpose advanced manufacturing center, enabled by logistics, could be a central point for entrepreneurs to launch products and services. This would include product designers and product developers, material sourcing, planning and coordination, and logistics, all completed through peer-to-peer relationships over the blockchain. The community-based system can focus on a specific product segment, such as pharmaceuticals or automotive components, as a starting point to achieve profitability. For example, a community-based hub in Baltimore might focus on medical devices or pharmaceuticals since the city is home to one of the top medical institutions in the world, Johns Hopkins University Medical Center. In Michigan, Detroit and Flint might focus on automotive components, given that state's history and expertise. A business case for the proof of concept may have a specific or general scope based on the knowledge and viability within the community where it is being developed. It would also enable a microfinance market model that could lead to changes in the financial markets as well.

Suppose 21st-century technology, such as 3D printers, Big Data, and sophisticated virtual networks, is deployed only in today's large private, global institutional model. This would only widen the gap between educated, networked people and people who are not educated and networked, leading to growing inequality. Furthermore, a financialized global supply chain has led to the concentration of supply production and distribution through economies of scale rather than enabling innovation through individualized entrepreneurship, resulting in a corporatist model of long-tailed supply chains that lead to spiky benefits. The alternative model is an entrepreneurial, short-tailed supply chain with a focus on aggregate stakeholder (not shareholder) value. Digital and advanced manufacturing tools allow product designers to design, product developers to develop, manufacturers to manufacture, distributors to distribute, salespeople to sell, and numerous other tasks, with fewer barriers. It also allows for other functions limited only by the community's imagination. How can economic value for this system be defined to determine its viability in this micro-based supply chain system? That will be the challenge of executing the concept, but it must become the goal. Imagine an open-sourced version of an Amazon platform covering the entire local supply chain system networked to other communities worldwide. In this new model, capital investment for the entrepreneur can be both a public and private utility rather than a private company investment. The intention of the community-based supply chain model should not be static and predetermined to end in economies of scale but rather should be a dynamic, self-organizing model for individual nodes in a supply chain system. The seeds need to sprout in non–market transactions first, just as was the case with the Big Tech firms, which are some of the largest companies in the world. While I seek through this book to explain how this system can be implemented, the real solutions will likely be beyond our imaginations if we allow the concept to sprout. Virtual logistics via a community-based supply chain is an innovation platform, not a predetermined supply chain solution.

Beginning with a proof of concept of this community-based system as a microsystem within a fully digital supply chain, all phases of the process (design, sourcing, planning, manufacturing, distribution, sustainability) are connected through the blockchain to enable peer-to-peer, seamless transactions across individual nodes within a networked group of communities. Members of the community can self-organize as appropriate for any single product launch; for example, if the open-source community develops a specific medical device or component produced across the supply chain, a band of individuals inside and outside the community can self-organize to create their supply chain system. There won't be any specific rules of responsibility, other than equal access within the community; it is entirely peer-to-peer and without defined roles of design and implementation of the product specification. Based on the capabilities of the manufacturing function, an individual can create a design and each step of the supply chain can be fulfilled within the single community system or networked with other locations as appropriate. Once additional proofs of concept are achieved and there are numerous networked communities across a state, nation, or even the world, the fluidity of the self-organization of the supply chain will grow in sophistication. Over time some community-based systems will have more advanced manufacturing centers than others or will print using specific materials that other sites cannot. A 3D/additive manufacturing technology that is sophisticated enough to print or produce products that meet the needs of industry will lead to direct competition and to the existing, more mature, and scaled global supply chain. It is not just electronic components that are sophisticated but also single material items with certain qualities, as simple as protective clothing for health care applications that require air filtration and fluid barriers of cheap throwaway or cleanable/reusable products. Products such as these are designed to meet technical specifications, which is possible today through computer-aided design but will soon be able to be produced in an additive manufacturing process. By 2030 systems should be sophisticated enough to produce some materials at this level of specification and at scale, but other products will continue to make sense within the existing conventional supply chain. Rather than relying on a few factories worldwide for a large percentage of mass-produced products, the new model envisions the world as a physical and virtual network with significant degrees of freedom of efficiency and resiliency. A networked distribution center for hundreds of thousands, if not millions, of community-based supply chains will meet the demand for any product that meets the required design specification, a printer or manufacturing site will achieve the specification, and a supply chain system will deliver the product. It is entirely possible that a community-based system could be focused on a variety of demands one month and then convert to crisis mode and dedicate much of its capacity to a specific need, such as hospital masks, the next month. Production capacity will not be limited to a discrete product as it is today. This is a 21st-century definition of innovative logistics through being virtual, not physical. This model will take time and patience to build, but it will lead to a sustainable balance between technology, capitalism, innovation, and all stakeholders for the future.

Today the world has more production capacity than consumer demand, and production is concentrated in low-cost labor markets enabled by logistics innovation that has made shipping practically free. And consumption is often concentrated away from production. A community-based model of logistically linked networks could balance these levels if capital costs are no longer a barrier due to a public-private partnership possible through sophisticated, affordable manufacturing technology. While physical logistics has become superefficient in today's global model, virtual logistics will become even more efficient due to the decrease in the shipping of physical commodities/products in favor of electrons. Reducing the barriers to investment, natural resources, and labor to a more virtual supply chain will increase the odds of alienated cities and towns rejoining the supply chain. Rather than using advanced technology networks to automate all supply chain activities, as is predicted too often for the future, the economic model will change to enable individual benefit through a nodal model. Suppose one hundred thousand networked, community-based supply chains are on the grid. Each facility provides its production capacity, availability, and product capabilities. Nodes can determine how to get their design to market by choosing a 3D printing facility and other critical supply chains, such as planners, forecasters, sourcing, transportation, distribution, and retailing, to name a few. Individuals can become nodes by playing roles within this process as a stand-alone entity with expertise in certain areas or by forming companies, but this will require enough education in the digital supply chain for individuals to become a part of it; individuals who don't have that instruction will be further left behind. In this model, the worker-citizen becomes the glue for the technology rather than being disaggregated by the large corporation and its use of it. This doesn't mean large multinational corporations cannot compete in this market model, just that they won't control the process and system to the extent as they do today. It also doesn't mean that a model to automate the entire supply chain and reduce or even eliminate the benefits of worker involvement won't sometimes happen. From this model come degrees of freedom provided by municipalities to their constituents. No more corporate welfare programs that end up buying jobs: a new, nodal-based competition model will emerge. This model leads to a new calculus of financial activity, just as Big Tech has done in its transformation of free applications.

With a nodal-based model, the term "individual entrepreneur" regains viability and relevance within the economy, no longer limited to large institutions: once an individual has an idea, it can be prototyped very quickly using computer-aided design and without significant barriers to entry; the individual entrepreneur can then either proceed to production or file for an intellectual property patent. Entry costs in this model are significantly lower, meaning that the playing field for innovation is leveled. The sourcing process changes with a product prototype; an entrepreneur can go online to develop an appropriate supply chain system design, including planning, sourcing, production, and distribution. Designs are virtually reviewed to determine the end-to-end supply chain, including its business case viability. In the current model, the entrepreneur is often tethered to the supply chain of the overseas manufacturer, for better or worse—and it's often for worse. A start-up company is burdened by the complex process of finding an affordable yet sufficiently qualified overseas manufacturer, often using intermediaries to find a manufacturing facility and requiring a high volume of production scale and then going through customs brokers and other logistics parties, who each take a piece of the profit to complete the supply chain. Then the entrepreneur needs to find a retailer to sell and promote the product; these transactions often render the effort infeasible or too inflexible. A networked community-based supply chain can significantly simplify and rationalize this process, leading to a quicker and more financially viable method of entrepreneurship and allowing individual nodes to become innovators. This model of free enterprise offers a level playing field because capital technology costs are no longer a barrier. Much has to be determined related to its implementation, but there is no doubt that it is a more sustainable model compared to the present state.

The health care industry is a prime sector to begin in this experiment. As we know, the failures of the health care sector during the opening weeks and months of the COVID-19 pandemic were extraordinary. The global supply chain broke down when we needed it the most. Items as simple as personal protective equipment to protect health care professionals were in short supply or unavailable because the supply chain wasn't sufficiently resilient to meet the pandemic—and isn't designed to be so; current supply chains are designed to be lean, just-in-time inventory models to reduce costs. Yet, for an actual just-in-time model with supply volatility, two variables must be present: enough capacity and supply chain postponement, the ability to make products in as short of a cycle as possible. Today neither of these conditions are present in our health care supply chain because the products are produced in a few factories in distant regions of the world. Today's health care supply chain is built on a theoretical Lean Manufacturing and Distribution model, which intends for a predictable balance of supply and demand and lacks resiliency when faced with unpredictable events like the pandemic. In the new 21st-century supply chain model of a networked, community-based system, both resiliency and capacity exist because the supply chain is both local and networked; it becomes a localized model of Lean Manufacturing. Let's say that under normal circumstances, the demand for hospital masks is one million masks a day; with the new model in place, this demand can be met through the conventional long-tailed supply chain *and* the networked community-based system. Each health care distributor and hospital can determine the mix between local and global manufacturing because now there is a choice. And each networked, community-based system has an option: to accept orders for the masks versus orders for other products determined by its supply chain capability and capacity. These community-based systems do not have to be product-specific because their design is digital versus today's physical model. They can quickly pivot to new products if they have the capability and capacity within their facility and network to do so. As a result, manufacturing and supply chains can quickly shift from less urgent products, which is not possible in today's discrete manufacturing model. Finally, a networked global/local, or glocal, community can rationalize supply to demand in a time of crisis and prevent profiteers and scam artists from taking advantage of difficult situations.

For health care products such as a ventilator, which requires multiple components, the supply chain can connect community-based systems that can manufacture specific parts for the process that will be delivered to another location for final assembly. In times of emergency, rather than mandating large manufacturers with inadequate and discrete capabilities to produce a needed product, such as ordering Ford and General Motors to produce ventilators, networked community-based supply chains can be self-organized quickly and efficiently when demand surges occur around the world. Countless commodity products are required to run a hospital, such as IV tubes, gauze, syringes, catheters, cups, and devices, to name a few. In the next ten years, most of these products could be made in a community-based supply chain as well as by global manufacturers, therefore improving the resiliency of these systems.

Another opportunity in the future for these local supply chains is the printing of customized materials for patients, such as prosthetics. This production and consumption is good for the local community and the overall global supply chain system.

The most exciting opportunity in health care is in the field of pharmaceuticals, a global supply chain that was broken during the opioid and COVID-19 crises. The use of 3D printing in the pharmaceutical industry offers many advantages, especially within a community-based supply chain model, as was mentioned above related to vaccine distribution (and potential production). Locally creating medicines in smaller batches and at price points similar to those for sizable global production runs can better control drug supplies, in contrast to the oversupply of opioids when enormous quantities of prescription drugs flowed into small towns because of criminal fraud. A local node could also operate a modern-day apothecary to customize medication for patients by dose, shape, size, and release characteristics.[11] 3D printing in pharmaceuticals could lead to more precise medicines tailored to a patient's pharmacogenetic profile and other characteristics like age, race, and other factors.[12] A patient's required medication could also be customized in one integrated tablet rather than multiple medications prescribed without knowledge of one medication's impact on the others.

Can a local community-based model produce and distribute simple items like those purchased from Target and Walmart as an alternative to those made in Asia? Imagine a model for how 3D printers rapidly evolve on a technology continuum. For example, a community-based system may focus on a specific type of product class based on the capability and capacity of its printers and may seek to upgrade to a newer piece of equipment. Rather than discarding or even landfilling the older equipment, the operation can choose to redeploy this equipment for commodity-based products, especially given that the capital cost associated with production is practically zero. In a model of low to zero capital and shipping costs, the price of the commodity product, such as a plastic water cup, can be a combination of the production and material cost, plus the profit/wages of the nodal producer, and no capital costs since they are fully depreciated. As a result there could potentially be millions of items such as household and office supplies that provide opportunities for community production that wasn't possible before. Especially when the externalities are brought back into the economic equation to compare the public costs associated with high levels of unemployment and underemployment within America's inner cities, these community-based systems can be effective financial supply chain models for the 21st century.

Sustainability 2.0

The conventional definition of the term "sustainability," focusing primarily on the environment, can sometimes encourage methods that aren't economically viable. Of course, this is understandable since today's outdated 20th-century supply chain system practically forces the consumer to choose sides between a purchase that is good for the environment but costs too much and a selection that is economical but harms the planet, such as single-use plastic. From this false narrative and given the demand chain economy, most consumers effectively choose not to factor the environment into their purchases. During the pandemic, the problem has only gotten worse: imagine telling a restaurant owner who is struggling to stay in business during the pandemic that they should not use single-use takeout containers because it is harmful to the environment. Or consider the plight of the poorest citizens on the planet who may not have clean water or food if it weren't for these materials that are bad for the environment. Consumers cannot consider sustainability objectives in this present system, given the built-in false narrative that what's good for the economy isn't good for the environment and vice versa. This timely example proves how today's supply chain systems are broken.

In a 21st-century community-based supply chain, a balance between economic and environmental sustainability will finally become reality—an equilibrium not solely focused on saving the planet but one that saves the planet by focusing on the local community. Sustainability 2.0 needs to be a model of self-reliance and efficacy for all stakeholders, including citizens, workers, owners, investors, and the environment. This is a model of economic growth and environmental sustainability, not one or the other. A model of free enterprise capitalism can work for both the community and the environment because in a community-based supply chain model, the goals are centered around a locality, meaning that capitalism and environmentalism go hand in hand versus today's large-scale global system where the product is produced in one location and consumed in another. In this community-based model, soft drink production happens within the locality, with the packaging and the product planned, sourced, produced, and distributed for the community's benefit. As a result, the community profits economically from the enterprise, transportation distances are shortened if not eliminated, and the used packaging materials are recycled and reused in a community-based closed-loop system. Today container material is often plastic, and this nonrenewable material could become sustainable in the future if it is sourced locally, formed, bottled, and then reused within the same cycle rather than sending the plastic waste somewhere far away, where it loses its economic value. This model could also become a hub idea for areas without natural resources, as plastic waste could become a material to enable economic growth. For example, a poorer neighborhood in the city of Baltimore could become the central point for a recycling program for the state of Maryland rather than shipping plastic to Asia or some hub in the United States. And since the supply chain system is predominately a community-based model, less energy is required to ship products produced and consumed locally. The model is a cluster of digitally networked communities that can transport or teleport a design across the world to be fulfilled at a local printer rather than made on one continent and consumed on the other. Global sustainability challenges can be solved, but only at a community level.

This Sustainability 2.0 model can achieve economic balance through higher nodal incentives (benefits in terms of wages or revenue) and lower or zero capital investments due to community investment in the costs of printers and other technical requirements as well as lower material costs through recycling in the closed-loop. Compared to today's recycling policies and systems, it would not be a forced model to reuse materials that aren't economically viable but rather a financial model that optimizes both the economy and the environment. Today consumers purchase a lot of their products through large manufacturers' wasteful, linear supply chain systems with single-use trash packaging. Over time, these community-based systems will self-correct through a balanced value chain model. Changes will occur, but not through regulations and mandates that have not succeeded. Citizen-consumers will opt for the more sustainable model when sustainability is defined as what's best for the economy and environment, often driven by the localized value propositions. While some environmental activists prioritize the global challenges that must be addressed, such as six million tons of plastic spilling into the oceans annually, most citizens are more concerned with local self-reliance challenges, such as the lack of clean drinking water within Flint, Michigan, a community of one hundred thousand people. Global sustainability issues will never be addressed as an international matter but rather as a networked collection of localities that balance the economy and environment. In this model, a digital supply chain system can be self-correcting. Suppose a particular material is too expensive to recycle. In that case, it would be redesigned through computer-aided/material genome (or even AI) technology that would use parameters to find material compositions that could be fulfilled. In this model, plastic would either become sustainable or be replaced, and harmful chemicals used in the plastic production process would be reduced. Sustainability must be solved as it can only be solved—locally, on a community-by-community basis.

Supply Chains in Balance

The American economy is facing a crisis, distracted and out of balance, and the growing weakness of these fault lines is causing more significant strains within its local communities. These problems are emblematic of a more considerable root cause of imbalance in supply chains. The term "imbalance" can be defined in many dimensions—economic, social, environmental, and others. We shouldn't assume that the protests, riots, gang violence, drug overdoses, and suicides are not correlated with the current outdated supply chains. A supply chain and logistics discussion should address more than inventory and transportation. Much work needs to be fleshed out in this 21st-century logistics model of a community-based supply chain system. But rather than debate these details at the start, it must be considered that there are no better alternatives (that I know of) presented than this model for the reasons articulated in this chapter and the book. In my roles in industry and academia, I have seen many different proposals. Few have focused on the individual and the community, possibly from a concern that focusing on the individual and community is considered socialist or managed by the government rather than the private sector. Almost no one believes that the current approach is working or that America should adopt a Chinese approach to the economy and society. A Chinese model of state-sponsored capitalism and its approach to society is not the best strategy forward for 21st-century America. Still, considerations within a dual circulation strategy can provide a lesson for the new realities of the future. An American model of innovation and entrepreneurship will beat a Chinese model of collectivism and a mix between capitalism and communism if America understands the toxicity of its present corporatist model of a private sector supply chain predominately defined in terms of multinational corporations. Why not open the model up for competition driven by our communities and individuals? Let's start with a few proofs of concept and give it a chance. What do we have to lose?

The United States' outdated supply chain system drives our economy away from balance and into more consumption that increasingly places our national security at risk, such as when shortages of essential medical and protective equipment during the pandemic led to increased loss of American lives. It may feel good when the politicians blame the Chinese for the pandemic and tariffs are applied, but those feelings of grandeur accomplish nothing for the blue-collar workers of America who once belonged to the middle class. Today's version of market capitalism has been unsustainable for decades and is a form of market dystopia with such perverse incentives that it no longer solves problems but creates them; it is akin to the phenomenon of firefighter arson, the roughly one hundred US firefighters every year who start fires for the thrill of putting them out. Whether intentionally or unintentionally, those in corporate leadership roles are financially rewarded for putting out one fire while creating another. They reasonably assert that it is their job to do so, and if they don't do it, someone else would, but this is only due to the rules of the economic game where company shareholders are the only stakeholders who matter.

This new model of a community-based supply chain system, networked with hundreds of thousands of others across the world, will take time, investment, and sacrifice. But it can radically reform the existing model of global supply chains without tearing apart the whole system, as we hear calls from the critics of capitalism. No model is perfect, and there will be challenges in creating a model of greater fairness and equality while being a competitive innovation engine. Still, we know where to start, as I have laid out in the last few chapters. Future design cannot happen overnight, and the American culture is not known for its patience. Moving forward and finding a more dynamic model for the supply chain model will lead to success over time but will require more of an inward look at ourselves than a projection outward toward the world. This should not be viewed as isolationist; as the saying goes, charity starts at home but doesn't end there. Seeding the communities will create nodal entrepreneurs from those who had been left on the outside; now they will be on the inside, able to landscape a new reality. Advanced manufacturing tools can balance supply and demand within a community through quality and productivity, the goals that Deming brought forth in the beginnings of supply chain management. A networked, community-based supply chain model becomes a glocalized model that blurs the line between local and global. Imagine how a networked world community can solve the next global pandemic in a more fluid, self-organizing, open-source fashion rather than the closed systems that are less effective and inequitable. Today the world isn't flat, as Thomas Friedman led us to believe over two decades ago, but rather it is spiky; imagine when the world becomes networked and communities are empowered and smoothened out, and when global activity is no longer synonymous with entire communities being left behind. In this model sustainability becomes more than a moral imperative; it becomes an actualized result not because we choose to save the natural world as a sole objective but because it's what's best for the economy and environment, one community at a time.

For a supply chain focused on problem solving, the consumer needs to be a rational actor, not an endless source of purchasing, a happiness machine, as the primary vehicle of economic growth. There is something perverse about a supply chain that is driven by pushing people to buy things they don't need, leading to a shallow, materialist economy and society. The perception that our economy and society have become a material world isn't subject to much debate, as evidenced by the prevalence of social media influencers. There may not be a lot of good that comes from the "Great Lockdown" of 2020, but one significant benefit has been the opportunity to rebalance our lives between the physical items we crave and buy and the emotional and spiritual connections that we need as humans to interact with our families and communities differently. When sitting down and doing a puzzle with my family during the 2020 lockdown, I reminisced of similar interactions when I was a kid because we didn't have a constant stream of personal digital media. We connected differently during the lockdown, and it was fulfilling beyond how we would have spent our time otherwise. Much good can come from a supply chain model that seeks growth through balance as well as balance in how transactions flow across the world and how we see our lives beyond commerce. This, as a wake-up call, would be a real gift stemming from the pandemic.

CHAPTER **6**

PEER-TO-PEER RETAIL

The Storeless Store

When I was a kid, I would spend most Saturdays in Baltimore with my grandmother. She lived in a Polish neighborhood in Southeast Baltimore, an area not-so-quaintly called Butcher's Hill, where my grandfather once slaughtered and butchered pigs at the Esskay meatpacking plant. Much of the neighborhood's history was intact then, such as the Catholic church that still held services in Polish and the famously immaculate white marble stoops that lined the sidewalks leading to formstone and brick rowhouses. We would walk to the local bodega called Ronnie's, where the proprietor greeted me as if I were family, asked me about school and my football team, and knew what snacks I liked, telling me whether they were in stock or not. Another place my grandmother took me was the famous Broadway Market, one of the oldest public marketplaces in the United States, opening in the late 18th century. Farmers and watermen would send their goods up the Patapsco River from the Chesapeake Bay to market. Some things change while others remain the same: the Broadway Market—a charming open-air market in the days of cookie-cutter, big-box retail—remains a Baltimore landmark on the original site, albeit modernized, while Ronnie's has been closed for decades, unable to be profitable against larger retailers with greater selection and better pricing.

Mom-and-pop stores remain, but only in the neighborhoods where big-boxers have not taken root or in chic, upper-class areas where local flare and higher prices are worn as a badge. Whether mom-and-pop or big-box, retailers have been the stitches in the fabric of Americana, the storefront of the supply chain system. In nearly any urban neighborhood in the United States, local coffee shops and Starbucks are adjacent to one another; these small independents are sometimes hanging on by a thread but are always present. It's the same story with the craft breweries that flourish in neighborhoods while the mega-breweries such as MolsonCoors and Anheuser Busch rule the roost.

For over a century, retail and supply chains have been tightly symbiotic, leading to the demand chain model of today. Before the railroad system cemented this relationship, local farmers, fishermen, and artisans distributed products to local markets through waterways, horse-drawn carriages, and other less efficient modes that limited product distribution to consumers. These stories were the basis of retail life in a city: the small corner store and large open-air market, with the more prominent outlets in the middle of the city or near the water. Not until the introduction of the railroad were large manufacturers able to grow through economies of scale in production and distribution through selling harvests and finished goods beyond their vicinities. With the railroad network, fresh produce could extend into nonagriculture areas and durable goods could be shipped more widely than before. Today the symbiotic relationship between manufacturing and distribution is similar, with economies of scale distribution taking over the world.

It's not by coincidence that the first grand department stores originated in the largest US cities, such as Chicago, New York, and Philadelphia. Marshall Field's on State Street in Chicago is often considered the department store innovator, which makes sense given the city's important role in the nation's burgeoning national railroad system of the 19th century. Chicago was then—and still is—the central hub of the US railroad system, providing a logistical advantage to a department store in the dry goods supplies that benefited its customers. Because Marshall Field's was on the main rail line in Chicago, this enabled scale and complexity in its product supply. It became an innovator for how Chicagoans shopped, offering high-end service through free shopping assistants for all customers. Other innovations of this department store were escalators, the ability to buy on credit, and products displayed in store windows to draw customers off the street. Similar department stores such as Macy's, Bloomingdale's, and Sears, Roebuck & Company were opening in large US cities through logistics innovation, leaving the city bodegas behind due to their limited supply chains. As these large department stores evolved, they would eventually use logistics to reach rural folks through a mail-order system. These mail-order systems lasted into the 1970s, as I remember thumbing through the Sears Christmas catalog to put together my list for Santa.

This was the beginning of a multiplier effect in logistics using an efficient supply chain system to bring together producers, wholesalers, logistics providers (mainly railroads), retail, and consumers. This model of an economy of scale led to winners and losers through superior logistics. For example, a local shoe cobbler in Chicago in the 1900s could no longer stay in business because Marshall Field's had a purchasing contract with a factory in Kansas City that could make shoes cheaper and ship them to Chicago on a railcar. The local cobbler offered personalized service and superior craftsmanship, but the Kansas City mass manufacturer eventually closed the gap. Through efficiencies in railroad logistics, the landed cost of the shoe in Chicago was still much cheaper than a handmade shoe, and the mass-produced shoe likely came in a wider variety of options. More consumers would purchase the mass-produced shoe shipped over the rail line at a lower price and acceptable quality—quality that would eventually surpass that of the local craftsman through structured manufacturing processes. Eventually, the department store stopped carrying the locally crafted shoe and the proprietor went out of business. Today's global supply chain is just a continuation of this path of retail, manufacturing, and logistics that has been in place for over a century. As a result of higher demand through the efficiency of national logistics, manufacturing became more sophisticated, enabling more significant capital funding to grow in scale and efficiency. However, in the cutthroat retail business, the benefits seldom trickled down to the retail worker, a notoriously low-paid job. And eventually the local producers could not compete with the regionals, the regionals could not compete with the nationals, and the nationals could not compete with the globals.

Financial credit in retail was also an essential ingredient in the secret sauce that enabled the supply chain system. Department stores were able to grow through the superior logistics of the US railroad system, offering greater variety and a range of product prices and attracting a more diverse customer base that broadened the market beyond the upper classes. One limitation to this market growth was customers who could not afford to purchase a product with discretionary cash on the spot. Without loosening the terms for how a customer could buy a product, market demand was constrained, which limited the growth of the supply chain since production and distribution was more significant than demand. There was no viable financial model to create payment terms for customers to purchase on credit, limiting an expanded sales market, especially for higher-cost products. In the 1920s credit cards—or, as they were called back then, "charge cards"—were offered only within the department store, such as a Macy's card, but eventually would evolve into a bank-issued card in 1958, when Bank of America first offered a charge card. Thus, retail credit developed from informal "tabs," to revolving credit with the shop owner, to a store-issued charge card, and to a bank-issued credit card. The average American today has four credit cards as supply chains and retailers have changed the consumer purchase dynamic.[1] Nonsecure credit is not just a vehicle for growth today for retail, it's an independent business in its own right, a driving factor of the American problem of consumerism, with Americans possessing over a trillion dollars of credit card debt and with the credit business so profitable that major card companies can write off 5 percent of their receivables annually, approximately $50 billion of what consumers purchase.

I have discussed the demand chain system in earlier chapters—the model of overconsumption to drive economic growth to such an extent that massive consumer debt and charge-offs that consumers cannot pay are an acceptable cost of doing business. In the supply chain model, the retail operation is the focal point. Legendary 20th-century Philadelphia retailer John Wanamaker described his stores as "beautiful fields of necessities, America's answer to European cathedrals."[2] Beyond the beautifully ornate architecture and window displays, these cathedrals to the demand chain were (and are) a competitive and brutal business within the supply chain system. From back then to now, from the big city department store to what it is today, omnichanneled and everywhere, the retail-driven supply chain requires a hypercompetitive combination of customer service and razor-thin margins due to the high demands from the American model of consumerism. Retail is a blood sport due to the efficacy of the supply chain system with a trail of extinct department stores and other retailers losing the battle to the dual behemoths of Walmart and Amazon. To win in this arena, retailers must be in complete integration with their customers and their supply chains in a manner that's never been seen before: they must predict what the consumer wants to buy before the consumer knows it and then must induce the consumer to purchase. Whether the consumer can afford to pay for the product or not is partially irrelevant. This secret sauce of an integrated supply chain, alongside a near frictionless credit system model, has created a demand chain as hypercompetitive as it is excessive and unsustainable for the individual consumer and the overall economy.

Relentless Execution, Omnichannel, and Pandemics

Perhaps there is no better story of the American Dream and the retail supply chain than that of Sam Walton. Starting in retail as a management trainee in an Iowa JC Penney store in 1940, Walton gained the experience he would need to open his first store in 1945, a Ben Franklin five-and-dime in Newport, Arkansas, that he bought for $20,000.[3] He turned around this unprofitable operation but lost his lease on the building and was forced to start over at another site in Bentonville, Arkansas, now the global headquarters for Walmart Inc., the largest retailer in the world. Walton graduated from the University of Missouri in 1940 with an economics degree. Still, he didn't consider himself a genius, just a practical man who understood people, and he focused on what the customer wanted rather than fancy marketing and advertising schemes or designing a retail store to look like a cathedral. Plain and straightforward, Walton's focus was to achieve the lowest prices possible for his customers through its store operations, logistics, and supply chain system, enabling it to grow to 38 locations and $44 million in annual sales by 1970 and 276 stores and $1 billion in sales by 1980.[4] Walmart ended 2021 at $559 billion in sales and is still growing, with 11,500 stores worldwide.[5] Walmart changed the nature of retail through everyday low prices (with no sale pricing) and a large selection of over 100,000 unique items in massive 100,000-plus square foot supercenters. Most importantly, Walmart's sophisticated integration with its supply chain is unrivaled, including its connection with overseas manufacturers directly rather than through wholesalers.

Many competitive advantages can be attributed to the Walmart model, but the one that is most relevant today concerns its use of data. Early on, Walmart understood customer and supplier data through demand integration across the supply chain to reduce cost and increase sales with superior inventory management. One legendary story recounts how one of Walmart's largest suppliers, Proctor & Gamble, improved its profitability dramatically in the 1980s through the improved data integration between the two companies.[6] But successful use of data is not just understanding the data on behalf of the customer but also advocating for the customer with suppliers. I witnessed this well-known corporate strategy myself while working for a Walmart supplier and seeing firsthand the uncompromising and demanding approach of its supplier relationship model. Walmart intentionally takes this customer-centric approach to maintain its edge in a fiercely competitive retail environment. Walmart uses a practice known as vendor-managed inventory, or VMI, which provides the supplier with real-time access to Walmart's information systems to access stock-level information across its network and stores. Based on this data, the supplier decides what volume of stock to send and when to send it, with these activities closely measured and managed by Walmart employees. This process ensures the lowest cost possible as well as effective customer service and variety.

The moral of the story is that Walmart is a ruthless competitor in a hypercompetitive business that is willing to go to extreme lengths to win the favor of the customer, including through complete transparency with its suppliers regarding its inventory levels and data. Walmart believes that, to win, all stakeholders involved in the demand chain model must focus on customers in the same manner. As a result, poor performers in their supply chain are replaced, whether they are manufacturers, transportation carriers, or even employees. All agents involved in Walmart's supply chain are flawlessly integrated through data and collaboration to execute its objective to provide the lowest prices always to its customers. Practically since its inception, Walmart's competitors have been playing catch-up to its Big Data strategy of collaboration and focused execution, including paying their workforce new wage levels, with Amazon, Target, and Best Buy among those who have raised minimum wage to $15 an hour, the full-time equivalent of $30,000 a year, not including overtime.[7] Low wages in retail are commonplace, but Walmart has taken it to another level, with over two million associates worldwide.

Compared to the owner-operated corner store or the department store that could sometimes sell service at an incremental cost, Walmart's (and now Amazon's) model has built itself on the "voice of the customer" to achieve higher volumes and greater efficiencies through cost management across the supply chain, including cost efficiencies in the wages of its workforce. Despite calls for higher wages from advocates who stand up for workers, the customer's voice—demanding the lowest prices—always prevails, ironically, even when the customer is sometimes also the worker. The disconnect between the worker and the customer in retail is another example of cognitive dissonance emanating from the supply chain to the public policy forum, including the classification of Walmart itself as the villain in the story. In contrast, retail sales continue to soar higher. In the 2005 documentary *Walmart: The High Cost of Low Prices*, director Robert Greenwald exposes the economic impact of what Walmart has done to workers and communities. Labor unions and nongovernmental organization advocacy groups have made themselves heard, leading Walmart to set up a public relations campaign to offset these accusations impacting the workforce. In November 2021, with a balance of power shifting toward the workers, employees of a North Carolina Walmart store walked off the job during Black Friday in the hope of securing higher wages and better working conditions.[8] Nevertheless, the company is doing exactly what the consumer is asking it to do—keep prices low, even if that means low wages too. As citizens, we sympathize with workers who require a "living wage"; as consumers, we are always looking for a bargain.

Sam Walton was right when he suggested that the minute his company took its eye off the ball, the next competitor would be primed to overtake the company as the darling in the consumer's mind. Walmart kept focused; even so, a new contender emerged in the competitive world of retail: e-commerce via the internet. As the internet matured, a hedge fund vice president named Jeff Bezos saw the potential. Upon hearing reports that the e-commerce grew annually by over 2,000 percent a year, Bezos borrowed $300,000 from his parents to start an online bookstore—Amazon—and began selling books online in 1994. Despite his enthusiasm for the business model, he still warned his early investors that it was probable that the model would fail. Nevertheless, by 1997 Amazon was already provoking the bookstore market by calling itself "the world's largest bookstore," a claim that Barnes and Noble disputed—not that Amazon wasn't the largest seller of books but rather that Amazon considered itself a bookstore rather than a "book broker." Eventually the company began to sell other products. Today Amazon accounts for over 40 percent of all e-commerce traffic, the largest and fastest-growing market channel in retail. But the 12 million products that Amazon sells through its distribution centers are just a part of its story. Its Amazon Marketplace offers approximately 350 million more products for sale through its website as a new model of e-commerce that is the real future of where retail is heading.

Amazon has redefined the customer shopper through this new concept called e-commerce. At the same time, Walmart has been steadfast and focused on its market, not taking its eye off the ball and continually improving its data and inventory management integration practices across the supply chain. Amazon designed its e-commerce platform on data and integration within a more extensive supply chain system to meet the customer's needs through its transformational fulfillment model. Amazon and Walmart had equally obsessive focuses on the customer in different business models that sped the development of information technology systems and physical distribution center models to support their growth. In collecting an enormous amount of data about the customer, Amazon's strategy today is a multilayered model of inventory that categorizes product velocity at its distribution centers, with millions of products able to be shipped the same or the next day, as well as third-party market-place items managed in collaboration with independent suppliers through Amazon's service. Amazon's mammoth facilities take in and ship tens of thousands of packages a day. Amazon also has cross-docking centers where packages shift from sellers (often overseas sellers) to Amazon, sortation centers for last-mile deliveries, and Amazon Prime hubs where customers can pick up their packages. Units are tracked as an integrated system across suppliers, the virtual marketplace, logistics shipping providers, and retailers to customers. The combination of customer orientation, convenience, ease of use, price, and availability has led to a model of growth that has far surpassed every online retailer and is taking aim at Walmart, leading to these two behemoths battling it out in the market, with everyone else falling far behind. Today Amazon is not resting on its laurels but is pushing the model to become more convenient and efficient, thus growing its market share. The company is even investing in its own dedicated transportation network to include ocean ships and railcars.

These two giants have inevitably begun to tread on each other's turf in this hy-percompetitive blood sport of retailing. What is evolving today is an uber-customer-focused model called an omnichannel, which allows customers to shop how they want—physically or virtually—and to have their order fulfilled to whatever location they want and as quickly as they want. In 2016 Walmart felt the pressure of Amazon's e-commerce growth and purchased the online retailer Jet.com for $3.3 billion, the largest acquisition of an e-commerce retailer in history. At the time Amazon's e-com-merce sales were significantly higher than Walmart's ($62 billion versus $13.6 billion, respectively, in a $373 billion market).[9] The acquisition of Jet.com, while significant, wasn't anticipated as a remedy to match Amazon's rocket ship, just a platform to help Walmart begin to catch up, a strategy that ultimately wasn't successful.[10] Since the acquisition, Walmart's e-commerce division has been constantly changing as it has tried numerous techniques to compete against Amazon, without gaining much trac-tion. With brick-and-mortar physical retailing as its bread and butter, Walmart has stayed focused on this model, leading the development of a multichannel model that has separated bricks and clicks while Amazon has steered toward omnichannel, the integration of different methods of selling and distributing as one seamless approach. Not used to losing, Walmart eventually realized in early 2020 that leadership and strategic changes were required. It began to consolidate its different channels into a unified strategy, leading to the dissolution of its Jet.com e-commerce platform. Only in such a battle of the titans could a company like Walmart—with 37 percent growth in e-commerce in 2019 and a year-over-year growth in Q2 of 2020 of 97 percent and growing twice as fast as Amazon in this space—be forced to take such a significant restructuring due to its outdated business model.[11] Walmart was growing its e-commerce business but losing money, something that its company culture was not accustomed to doing.[12]

If anything, the pandemic has been a signal to retailers that they must become omnichannel or die, with growth in e-commerce showing strong evidence that consumers are willing to shop much differently than in the past, and this trend will continue even after the virus has been contained. The e-commerce retail landscape has been changing rapidly even before the pandemic, and the acceleration of that change driven by the lockdown has continued. This news may seem what Amazon wants to happen, but this might not be the case upon closer inspection since it has awoken Walmart to compete more directly in this omnichannel model. Amazon is Amazon because it keeps pushing retail and the connected supply chain closer to the edge of the impossible. With Walmart's increased focus and competition, this hypercompetitive model is reaching a new level, with Amazon's leadership position now in play. Despite Amazon's ability to manage an overall e-commerce supply chain superior to any of its competitors (Walmart included), the service of free shipping isn't free, with Amazon forecasted to spend $11 billion on shipping in one quarter of 2020 alone— the same price it paid in an entire year just four years earlier; on an average order of $8.32, it costs $10.59 to ship for next-day shipping, a model of losing money that isn't sustainable.[13]

While Amazon's distribution center footprint continues to grow in the United States, with up to 175 US sites covering 150 million square feet by 2020, Walmart has 150 distribution centers equaling Amazon's 150 million square feet *and* has close to five thousand retail stores in all fifty states (and Supercenters in forty-nine states); indeed, 90 percent of Americans live within ten miles of a Walmart store.[14] Do the logistics math, and you'll find that even Amazon's large and growing footprint cannot keep up such a frantic pace to improve shipping service levels for more extensive geography and volume of products. In contrast, Walmart's massive retail infrastructure may be a checkmate to Amazon if it uses its physical platform advantage in an omnichannel setting, a game that Amazon cannot compete against regardless of its growing distribution center footprint. When big-box retailers learned that they could use their physical stores as distribution centers for online fulfillment during the pandemic, a new model was born. With many shoppers in closer proximity to retail stores than distribution centers, Amazon's Achilles' heel became visible in this new retail battle. Today there are no signs of turning back from what Amazon started, and there's a possibility—if not a probability—for Amazon to be "Amazoned." With shipping costs the most significant expense in e-commerce and growing steadily due to customer expectations, the shortage of drivers, and rising gas prices, Walmart may be able to head right to the edge of the cliff and stop while Amazon tumbles over. This clash of the titans will be an all-out battle, with lesser but significant retailers like Kroger and Target under immense pressure to keep up.

Revenge of the Nodes, Part II: The Storeless Store

Imagine being alive when dinosaurs ruled the earth. These beasts had no viable competitors on the planet and led by sheer size and ferocity, winning any battle without challenge for hundreds of millions of years. But 65 million years ago, a threat came from the outside, not another species but a crude rock from beyond the planet. Not *just* a rock, mind you, but one six miles long that would hit what is now the Yucatan Peninsula of Mexico and end approximately 75 percent of the plant and animal life on the planet. Few species were able to survive this event, including the dinosaurs. Without constant threat from a food chain that had the dinosaurs at the top, the smaller mammals who survived were able to thrive and evolve. This analogy shows what may happen moving forward in today's hypercompetitive retail landscape. Nobody can compete against the ferocious giants, Walmart and Amazon, and it seems that they are left to rip each other apart in this hypercompetitive landscape. But an unexplained, unexpected, and surprising force from the outside may strike, taking these two behemoths down (whatever that means). At the same time, the tiny little critters—nodes—have a chance to survive, thrive, and evolve into something more sustainable.

Could this unexplained, unexpected, and surprising event be the blockchain system, the super-lubricant of the new peer-to-peer, community-based supply chain system? Here is the potential scenario: Walmart and Amazon keep fighting each other, taking hypercompetition to unsurmountable levels, including partial or complete automation of retailing itself and the omnichannel supply chain costing practically nothing—the concept of the value of nothing, as I discuss in chapter 3. Concurrently, Amazon doubles down in its Amazon Marketplace, which today equals about 40 percent of its transactional volume; seeing this as the future of retailing, Walmart follows suit. The battle of the behemoths moves to the marketplace platform, a hybrid model of large retailers using an online presence of small producers and suppliers to offer products in the tens or even hundreds of millions to build greater capacity for their logistics network. From this comes improvements in economies of scale as well as a virtual platform using blockchain to reach the same efficiency levels as the mass scale, conventional supply chains, networking planning, production, inventory, ordering, and payment processes. Imagine these transactions' dynamic, fluid nature compared to Walmart's massive, structured, monolithic partnerships, such as Proctor & Gamble. The blockchain decentralized ledger system improves its ease of doing business, thus establishing the lingua franca of small ball, enabling other retailers to compete—even with Walmart and Amazon—such as the community-based supply chain system proposed in this book. Virtual retail is taken to the local level to create value chains to change the nature of the 21st-century supply chain. This transformation becomes the retail fluidity of the peer-to-peer blockchain network, or "Revenge of the Nodes, Part 2." Inadvertently, this could begin the decentralization of retail and the current supply chain as well as the empowerment of the node in the community.

Is it possible for Amazon to be "Amazoned" by Walmart, to beat it at its own game of next-day (or even same-day) free shipping due to Walmart's more extensive physical footprint, and is it then possible for both Amazon and Walmart to be threatened by a nodal, small-ball game of the community-based supply chain of storeless stores? At first blush, it doesn't seem possible. Still, in this supply chain system of hyper-competition, it is possible that a peer-to-peer system of micro and nano producers and retailers can arise from this environment enabled by the 21st-century lubricant of blockchain set off by the giants in competition with one another. With Walmart now posing a growing threat to Amazon's e-commerce platform for the first time in its twenty-five-year history, this fight will need to move to a different battleground, and I believe that it will be the small-ball marketplaces, the brokered model of nodal suppliers similar to the Alibaba model (discussed below). Walmart and Amazon will continue to compete for market share through large suppliers and shipping immediacy, but there are limits to how much more growth can come from this model. All that's left is to no longer go larger and more immediate but instead to go smaller and local, with these nodal supply chains enabled by blockchain. But the price for Amazon to pay for battle and victory is to expose its own supply chain model, both in dominance and in weaknesses.

When can we expect this transformation to occur? As the post–COVID-19 economy begins to emerge, societal and economic changes will result, not just in social distancing and omnichannel but supply chain resiliency as well; what is more resilient than returning to the local craftsman or mom-and-pop? Moreover, given the lessons learned from the devastation to the economy in 2020, more customers may wish to shop local to support small businesses impacted by the pandemic. Moving toward local retail could be the first step toward a more extensive peer-to-peer economic model, with individuals working as a node. With Walmart and Amazon now fighting the battle of data and information, the fight may escalate to include models like those from the East, Alibaba. According to a study conducted by an intellectual property consulting firm, Alibaba is the world's largest holder of blockchain patents, ten times the number of IBM, its nearest rival.[15] The firm is already offering "blockchain as a service," and you can bet those large US retailers will need to catch up to its online Chinese competitor as soon as possible. Concurrently, Walmart and Amazon will tamp down on their distribution centers and retail outlets to reduce costs and improve efficiencies. The competitive battle between these two giants will further exacerbate the downward pressure on wages, further hampering the digital divide and the economy's overall health, leading to more significant calls for financial reform, either within a capitalist or socialist model. This may seem antithetical today, especially as Amazon faces the pressure of unionization, but the retail market has been notorious for wage pressures on its employees. The greater divide between the haves and the have-nots will lead to greater disruption, prompting calls for nonmarket policies. At the same time, an effort to reform markets will move toward a more equitable approach—as I call it, the nodal or peer-to-peer economy and supply chain. I predict if a blockchain platform is under way, the challenge to the large-scale big-box retailers is in play, with upstart competitors to Amazon and Walmart for retail (platform) competition in 2025 and market share losses sometime between 2025 and 2030.[16]

Another impact on the future of retail is China's influence on the model. For nearly a decade China has been the leader in e-commerce, a $2 trillion market worth more than America's and Europe's e-commerce markets combined, a model that makes sense since China is more densely populated than the West and lacks conventional physical retail space and even traditional merchandising culture to sell its goods.[16] Alibaba's public offering in 2014 was the most extensive initial public offering in history, and new competitors such as JD.com, Meituan, and Pinduoduo have fueled a continuous model of growth and innovation. Today Alibaba is more of a digital platform than a retailer but much different; some define Alibaba as a bit of Amazon, e-Bay, PayPal, and Google wrapped into one, a $500 billion middleman with over 700 million users worldwide but mainly in China.[17] Unlike Amazon and Walmart, Alibaba does not control orders or inventory or own warehouses but rather is a digital marketplace. Still, it dominates Chinese e-commerce retail, having a higher share in its nation than Amazon (58.2 percent versus 39 percent, respectively).[18] These signals point away from a conventional definition of retail and more toward an Alibaba-style platform through a network of suppliers loosely coupled to connect and disconnect fluidly on the blockchain. According to most retail experts, the future of e-commerce lives in China as a bottom-up "consumer-centric" vibrant model versus the West's more top-down approach focusing on technology.[19] However, this Chinese approach to e-commerce is concentrated through a few top retailers, with the three leading firms (Alibaba, JD.com, Pinduoduo) owning 90 percent of sales versus the top three firms in the United States (Amazon, Shopify, e-Bay) possessing less than 50 percent.[20]

The future of e-commerce in China is similar to the idea proposed in this book of a community-based supply chain system, but with "Chinese characteristics." Some would call this Chinese model of e-commerce to be more social commerce than e-commerce, given the video streaming, social networking, and other elements that allow the consumer to do almost anything on their phones. Will this ubiquitous mobile phone–use model in China running platforms for everything within the same application become the next phase of e-commerce development in the United States and the West? It seems unlikely given the cultural differences between China and the United States regarding privacy and individualism versus collectivism. In contrast, a more viable model for the West is the one proposed in this book, an e-commerce platform focused on a better balance between supply and demand enabled as the technologies of 3D printing and blockchain advance to allow a peer-to-peer supply chain that focuses on community development and individual entrepreneurship. It is unlikely that the best replacement for the demand chain in the West is the social commerce platform that is rising in the East. Rather than a large network platform controlling all aspects of a consumer's experience, whether Amazon or Alibaba, what should emerge is a networked community system connected to other networks and clusters of communities centered on bringing value to the communities and the nodes within it. Today the retail model is entirely defined by private sector intentions for shareholders and investors, but this doesn't need to remain only in this model. The new retail model and, as a result, balanced consumerism can usher in a value chain to balance supply and demand within communities, networked as a 21st-century supply chain system.

Is it possible for a value chained, community-based, and networked supply chain system to be built on a model of nodes and enabled by blockchain technology to usher in a new era of consumerism that is more rational than the model that exists today? Not only is it possible, it is required if we wish to achieve a balance between supply and demand. As an alternative, not as a replacement, a nano or micro model of capitalism can improve the flow of its excess capital surplus deployed across a broader expanse of the population rather than today's neomercantilist model of a concentration of wealth to fewer. At its best, capitalism should enable the flow of excess surplus to the best value opportunity, not just for short-term, immediate gratification and wealth concentration but for longer-term, sustainable societal good. A solid business case can and should proceed in this direction to steer the flow of capital toward the many communities that have been starved of investment in the past. It is good public and private practice. An initial proof of concept in a city would be a step in the right direction, eventually leading to the networking of the community-based supply chain across the nation.

The concept of a nodal storeless store could be the catalyst to the supply chain that modifies markets from hollow centers of consumer growth to ones that solve problems in a relationship-based model. In this community-based model, the individual could be a node within the community that achieves a multiplier effect for wealth to remain in the jurisdiction rather than flowing out in a consumption-based model. A healthy ecosystem in nature is balanced, and a community should also be balanced— having a balance of supply and demand for a healthy environment. In the next chapter, I lay out a brief road map of how this can happen enabled by new technologies such as 3D printing, automation, digitization, and blockchain. However, technology alone will not solve the problem. There must be a shift away from a supply chain that is in place for consumption alone. This model won't necessarily regulate investment and consumption away from the big players such as Amazon and Walmart, especially at the onset. Still, it will naturally steer the flow of capital toward the smaller entities or nodes that better represent a value chain model. A Chinese model of e-commerce will not be helpful because it only becomes Demand Chain 2.0, the next generation in an obsession with consumers and nothing else. As Walmart and Amazon look to the future, they may be myopically obsessing for consumer favor and be primed to lose market share. They may not anticipate a six-mile-wide boulder hurtling toward the earth that is raring to change not just the future of retail and e-commerce but supply chains, economies, society, and the environment as well. Their obsessive focus on the consumer might become their undoing.

You do not need to be an expert in economics or mathematics to understand that an economy built on excessive consumerism and debt is unsustainable. Supply chain professionals are in place to drive this demand chain model to the edge of the cliff, as is happening today at Walmart, Amazon, and Alibaba. At the same time, these professionals are problem solvers. If we provide these problem solvers with a broader definition of growth, they can reduce the collateral damage to individuals, communities, and the environment. Suppose my numbers are correct and they can—and should—be proven through local proofs of concepts. In that case, communities should start moving in this direction for a new economy of the future versus the continuation of their hollowing out through these large global retail models.

On the other hand, suppose these large multinational corporations continue to drive a supply chain system based on overconsumption and consumer debt. In that case, they will choose their fates once outsiders transform a market toward balance, ushering sustainable economic growth through a model of nodes. Taking our lessons from the COVID-19 pandemic that serve as an inflection point for us to inspect our outdated systems, it's time to move on and begin transitioning to this new retail and supply chain model, away from the obsolete model built after World War II, which saved us from the Depression but ultimately delivered us where we are today. If economics is a science, a social science, and its goal is optimization as the best and only possibility, then any rational evaluation technique that provides affirmation to an unbalanced, outdated approach should be replaced; this new model is a much more favorable one for growth in a 21st-century economy.

Googling "future of retail" generates typical results; instead, the future needs something more imaginative than a bunch of high-tech storefronts and virtual reality displays that are nothing more than modern-day "beautiful fields of necessities," as John Wanamaker called it over a century ago. Virtual storerooms, virtual closets, virtual reality customer experiences, and so forth fixate on a consumer-based supply chain blindly attentive to our current marketing model without realizing how broken the current model is, no longer a reality for the future. Shopping and retailing play a significant role in our culture, leading to the price of everything and the value of nothing, a valueless high-tech chain of self-destruction. Sterile storefronts cannot replace the intended role of markets as problem solvers in human civilization. If anything, retail storefronts have brought us dystopia, not utopia, when we look deeply at a broken supply chain that few of us understand. Consumers were bunkered in their homes during the COVID-19 crisis, leading to a new retail reality even more distinct from a locality. The concept of a storeless store takes the focus away from the location (physical or virtual) and moves it back to us; problems should be solved not in the buying and selling of a product or service but in the transactions among individuals, networking up from an individual to a community, state, nation, and world. And it brings markets back as experiences that carry more value than a price.

Rather than walking around a massive, sterile Walmart or browsing the world's largest e-commerce site, Amazon, wouldn't it be an improvement in the buyer-seller relationship to have a supply chain that can be dimensionalized in small ways, large ways, or a combination to offer efficiency, resiliency, and experience? Today it's a long shot to expect retail to offer much more than this streamlined view of the supply chain that is so hypercompetitive that it has stripped away the individual, including the dignity of an associate who works in a facility under enormous pressure and for low wages. So much has been lost in the effort to gain the innovations that compose a supply chain system that does so many miracles behind the scenes but has unintended consequences in plain sight.

I miss the days of my childhood retail experiences, walking to the corner five-and-dime and Broadway Market, each with its unique character, but I miss much more than that. I think back to my grandmother, who was in her midseventies, walking three young children many blocks away to the Broadway Market rather than the closer supermarket, and how that experience taught us that it was more than just about "the buy"; today it seems the means and end are all that matter, with boxes showing up on your doorstep magically and for no extra cost after simply clicking the "order" button the day before. Convenient and cost-effective, yes, but not free, at least for society. Someone has paid for your free shipping in their wages and their ability to earn a living in this outdated supply chain system, and you may have spent a bit for it in a loss of experience. How we view transactions today is different from how our ancestors viewed them, and the imbalance in the system should give us reason to pause as it has reached an unsustainable level that is permeating our communities. Perhaps a step forward isn't to hit the "order" button and get another box the same day or the next day, and a step forward isn't about getting logistics for free when we know there is still a cost associated. Maybe the step forward is a community and supply chain in balance—supply and demand, value and worth—versus the optimization of consumption and minimization of price. When retail is fixed, the supply chain will also be fixed, enabling this 21st-century value chain that I propose in this book. How to get there is discussed in the final chapter.

CHAPTER 7

THE PLATFORM FOR TRANSFORMATION

2025 and Beyond

Before the pandemic few people were concerned with supply chains and how they work, and now there is great interest. The central theme in this newfound interest in supply chains is their importance in our daily lives, even when we don't notice. Americans must better understand these supply chain systems to address the systemic problems that they now understand as a relationship to them. Today's supply chain system has been fantastic for us as consumers and investors but not as good for us as workers or even as citizens. This book makes a case for change in the supply chain system and in public policy, marketing, technology, environmentalism, and financial markets. I believe the solutions proposed in this book are correct, but whether you agree with them is less critical than whether you walk away with a clear understanding of the problem and its root causes—and that something must be done soon.

Today what Americans need more than anything is unity and hope for the future. My grandmother told me that despite how bad things were during the Great Depression, among the people she knew, there was never a loss of hope; instead, there was optimism that things would get better, and soon. Unfortunately, as is evident in surveys by Gallup and others, much of America has been painfully divided and without hope for many years, even before the pandemic's devastation. Contrary to popular belief, Americans have not lost hope because they expect the government or business to solve our collective and individual challenges. Instead, we want an environment in which we can overcome these challenges ourselves as individuals and communities. Today's debate is distracted by whether government and business should do more or less for us, leading to impossible answers to inappropriate questions. Help from these institutions must come not by providing us with the answers but rather by enabling us to find solutions for ourselves and for each other. This book is not a prescription for how to address these problems but rather a platform to enable the American public to do so. Unfortunately, neither the public nor the private sector is doing a very good job of this, especially in our most deeply affected communities.

Describing a system as "community-based" may raise suspicion as code for a government takeover of a private enterprise. However, after reading this book you should understand that this is not the intention. Instead, a community-based system moves away from an overreliance on large institutions, especially those with interests different from American stakeholders. A community-based supply chain is just a concept today, but it could lead to a new season of optimism that is so desperately needed in this nation. A reinvention of America's inner cities and towns through its youth, infrastructure, education, and technology could be just what is needed to end the disenfranchisement that permeates much of the nation today. Serving up the function of supply chains, 21st-century style, through a digital platform offers great hope with fewer barriers to entrepreneurs who lack capital. By liberating technology from its traditional association with capital, America can address one of its most significant challenges today: how to bridge the digital divide across society to reduce inequality in all its forms. If left unaddressed, an increasingly digital supply chain will lead to a continuation of insecurity and imbalance. Conversely, an intentional focus on liberating the supply chain by mitigating this digital divide could positively impact our communities and their citizens.

Having a supply chain balanced between supply and demand is a shared common cause, excluding no one. A shared vision cannot occur when some communities do not have equal access to the tools of education and infrastructure. Do not mistake this proposal of a shared vision for a well-worn ideological competition between the virtues of large corporate institutions (favoring big business and unbridled capitalism) and the benefits of big government and socialism. I am not advocating a Chinese-style approach of large institutional reliance on a centralized Communist Party intertwined with business. Yet from the Chinese concept of dual circulation, Americans can gain an understanding of the practicality that economic growth can be good for the worker and citizen as well as the consumer and investor in a capitalist model. Any fancy footwork that conflates balancing what's good for the citizen and the company with a Chinese Communist Party model is a distortion and a distraction from the problems of a spiky global model that the United States is facing.

Data and information must be the drivers for a value chain system in the 21st century, enabled by the lingua franca of the blockchain acting as the super-lubricant, leveling the playing field with the global multinational corporations that currently dominate through capital, scale, connectivity, and integration. At first, the blockchain will be implemented solely by private corporations, but the public sector needs to be involved as well for the benefit of the individual and community. Investing in infrastructure and education will provide an open-source start-up model at the grass roots. Blockchain can be that game-changing transactional process to enable peers to connect more fluidly in both information and finances, providing a 21st-century platform for markets. Still, it can only be optimized in a balanced manner through an open-source and public-enabled platform. It must be a digital, open-sourced, and customized approach to design, sourcing, planning, manufacturing, distribution, transportation, retailing, and sustainability, including leveraging advanced 3D printing technologies. Today manufacturing in America is capital, not labor-intensive, which restricts entry, limiting opportunities for past blue-collar workers in today's workforce. Broadband- and blockchain-enabled open-source platforms would minimize entry barriers for citizens acting as nodes to return to the manufacturing sector or any supply chain–related field in a peer-to-peer, nodal supply chain model beyond a smaller niche "maker" economy. It will be more difficult for the blue-collar working class of the past to engage in this process without training to do so because the maker economy will require them to be digital entrepreneurs rather than traditional industrial workers. Success is not guaranteed in this model, and while everyone should expect equal opportunity, outcomes should not be equal. Rather than projecting our supply chain outward, as China is exploring through its Belt and Road Initiative, America's plan should be a reindustrialization plan to invest within the nation and fix the hollowed-out economy as the best expression of the country to the world. The plan requires a game-changing approach to economic growth and rejuvenation through a broader strategy across all segments of the US population, not just contained within the higher-skilled engineering community.

Nations, states, communities, and individuals must win by playing the right game, the game it can win, and the data is clear that the playing field should also reside in America's inner cities and rural communities through a community-networked supply chain that progresses outward to compete against today's long-tailed global supply chains. The competition must begin with a strategy, something that has been missing in the United States over the past fifty years. We have seen that deindustrialization without viable alternatives is no plan; likewise, reindustrialization must begin with a game plan. There's an increasing number of workers who have been displaced to dead-end service jobs or illegal street activity. If there has been a moral to the story over the past fifty years, and I think there is, it's how China has succeeded beyond expectations because it has had a longer-term and strategic game plan for its supply chain and overall economy, while America hasn't succeeded because it hasn't had a strategy. It's time to address this problem by moving forward with a strategic action plan. American leaders must be willing to lead, and citizens must sacrifice their reliance on overconsumption and instant gratification to bring forth a better future.

Five Pillars of the New Supply Chain

We're now at the beginning of the third decade of the 21st century. Rather than more conversations, task forces, and debates, the goal should be to put forth a plan as soon as possible to take the necessary steps that have been discussed in this book. The following five pillars lay the groundwork for the new supply chain.

Pillar 1: Expand Broadband Infrastructure and Availability

For America to have a digitally based, peer-to-peer nodal supply chain, every citizen in the United States must have full and equal access to broadband internet as a public utility, as with electricity and water. Unfortunately, millions of Americans, often in rural communities, don't have broadband access. Building the network itself isn't enough—broadband access needs to be affordable for all. According to a 2019 Microsoft study, approximately 162 million Americans do not have adequate (i.e., broadband speed) internet access, while 21 million to 42 million Americans do not have any access.[1] However, a 2019 Pew Research Study is more optimistic, finding that 90 percent of US adults use the internet, 73 percent have broadband access at home, and 17 percent of American adults do not have broadband access at home but own smartphones.[2] The good news is that this problem has the attention of American lawmakers: the 2020 Heroes Act has invested money to expand the nation's broadband network and provide subsidies to lower-income Americans for access, and the 2021 Infrastructure Investment and Jobs Act has allocated $65 billion to this problem. Nevertheless, a digital divide in the United States extends beyond infrastructure. Lower-income Americans need to have the same access to broadband and mobility. A consistent, growing focus on this problem will be a critical first step.

For America to be a leader in the future state supply chain, it must have the proper infrastructure for success beyond broadband. Numerous studies have been conducted regarding the weaknesses in America's physical infrastructure, with a D+ grade given by the American Society of Civil Engineers. Therefore, our nation's primary focus needs to be on the physical and virtual paths of commerce for world-class infrastructure of the 21st century. Just as we need to view manufacturing and the supply chain differently, we need to expand our definition of infrastructure to include people, processes, and technologies. Progress toward this first pillar seems to be moving in the right direction, but more is needed and faster.

Pillar 2: Invest in K-12 Digital and STEM Education

The digital divide related to broadband may soon be shrinking, but this progress is not being made regarding digital and STEM K–12 education. If anything, the divide is growing between socioeconomic classes; by recent estimates, 70 percent of future jobs will require a STEM and or digital-focused education.[3] According to the 2017 Programme for International Student Assessment, which compares the national academic achievement of fifteen-year-old students, the United States ranks thirty-eighth out of seventy-one countries for student literacy in math and twenty-fourth in science, a mediocre performance, at best, for the world's largest economy. Among the members of the Organization for Economic Cooperation and Development, the developed nations that are America's top competitors in the global economy, the

United States ranked thirtieth out of thirty-five in math and nineteenth in science, a dismal result.[4]

The data set of these scores was not segmented across socioeconomic groups; however, other studies have shown significant variation in testing scores between the classes, which is consistent with America's growing income inequality.[5] America remains one of the wealthiest nations in the world, with world-class capabilities in research and development in many of the STEM areas, but it is also one of the worst among the world's developed nations regarding its overall education system, suggesting a disproportionate strategy and allocation of its education resources. This profile seems more akin to a rising developing nation than a world-class developed one, showing a weakness that has plagued the United States for decades. If the United States wishes to install a modern, 21st-century supply chain system that is nodal and community-based, this significant vulnerability needs to be addressed soon. But with the number of competing legislative agenda items, all more immediate and short term, a paradigm shift is required in the collective American thinking to invest in K–12 STEM education to succeed in the 21st century. Focusing on Pillar 2 versus these competing agendas would demonstrate a prioritization toward the longer-term and more strategic future versus the tactical and more immediate gratification. However, the American voter must be willing to sacrifice appropriately for the policymakers to shift their agenda.

PILLAR 3: RESEARCH AND DEVELOP BLOCKCHAIN TECHNOLOGY AS PEER-TO-PEER OPERATING SYSTEM

To build the new economy of the future, we must create information highways for nodal transactions at the micro and nano levels. As discussed in the previous chapters, the blockchain centralized decentralized ledger system will become the lingua franca for this new open-sourced, nodal, peer-to-peer, community-based supply chain system. The Federal Aid Highway Act of 1956 built forty thousand miles of road to link American cities to communities of over fifty thousand people. Similar action needs to happen with the internet to create the transactional highways for this new supply chain system. Today some superhighways link the global supply chain, but these are private virtual roads—controlled by Alibaba, Walmart, Amazon, and other private companies—plans for large, structured supply chains to transact business, not for public community traffic. The node can participate on these private virtual roads but not on a level playing field, with larger entities having an advantage on these pathways. A public highway for blockchain transactions built by the community would provide everyone free, open-source access, taking down the barriers to competition in a free market. To ensure a level playing field, the public sector needs to get in the business of blockchain development.

Blockchain technology is still in its infancy. We need to invest in the technology and the logical infrastructure needed for these virtual and self-organizing supply chains to begin sprouting. Just as the Federal Aid Highway Act of 1956 led to commerce growth through a physically networked America, something like a Federal Aid Blockchain Act would do the same to lay out a virtual highway for a new supply chain to take shape. The federal government would build the virtual roads and ensure the activity and development to guarantee free travel, as the federal Department of Transportation does with physical roads. The goal is for fair travel via market and nonmarket transactions to be available to anyone, not concentrated on only those with scale and capital, as exists today. This would be a public-private partnership that invests in the future economic growth of a new economy. The public and private sectors in China are investing in this infrastructure and the United States must step forward to compete in the future of supply chain.

PILLAR 4: ADVANCED MANUFACTURING AND 3D PRINTER RESEARCH AND DEVELOPMENT

With the broadband internet infrastructure and accessibility in place, a national program to improve digital and STEM education for all Americans, and a blockchain transactional system that enables free and fair travel, the system is ready for nodal entrepreneurs to innovate through a focus on nodal manufacturing, distribution, and retailing (a storeless store). The process must begin with manufacturing, the anchor of the supply chain system. Advanced manufacturing benefits from various institutes' and universities' research and development labs, but so far it has not benefited as much from government-funded innovation labs, in part because the federal government lacks a coherent strategy for advanced manufacturing. Just as with the development of the US space program in the late 1950s after the Soviet launch of its Sputnik satellite, the same should happen in the United States regarding manufacturing. Advanced manufacturing should become a new strategic emphasis through a reindustrialization program. Innovations such as 3D printing and other advanced manufacturing elements must achieve a more significant role in America's economic strategy. This strategy should include public-private partnerships, with significant levels of investment from both sectors.

What better way to link America's past to the future than through an educated workforce that restores a legacy of its manufacturing past into the future?

PILLAR 5: CREATE A PUBLIC-PRIVATE PARTNERSHIP MODEL THROUGH MARKET INCENTIVES

Today federal, state, and local governments provide market incentives to industries that are important to the US economy. Conservative estimates put US direct subsidies to the fossil fuel industry at roughly $20 billion per year, with 20 percent currently allocated to coal and 80 percent to natural gas and crude oil.[6] To stabilize the farming industry, which composes a little more than 5 percent of the total economy, the government granted $370 billion in subsidies between 1995 and 2017.[7] Subsidies for these industries may be necessary, but are subsidies not also warranted for a broader population segment that has been left on the outside for decades? The term "public-private partnership" seems to be a dirty word in some applications but acceptable in others. It has been more of a political strategy than an efficient and practical approach to economic development. A nodal, peer-to-peer, community-based supply chain has the potential for more significant economic growth and local self-reliance than the farming and fossil fuel industries and would provide the foundation for a value chain approach for a 21st-century economy. Imagine the investment and production benefit to the US GDP of thousands of peer-to-peer, nodal supply chains across the nation—self-organizing and generating wages/revenue, jobs, a tax base for citizen nodes, and fewer environmental and social externalities. Moving forward in an information-based economy, an investment of our tax dollars in the individual—the node—is more American than anything else. This seems like the perfect opportunity for a burgeoning public-private partnership. Rather than a political and ideological version of turning this idea off and on, the United States should look at how China and other nations have used this model to lead to breathtaking economic growth in its own ways. The same transformational strategy should be used in America to support the individual and community rather than enable large institutions. In studying the best practices of other nations, America should learn how the public and private sectors can work better together on behalf of citizens and communities.

Building the Network

For the strategy to be successful, America must first commit to it over the long term and not take divergent, partisan paths based on the political process and election cycles. Rather than economic advisers waxing poetic over bringing manufacturing back to the United States from China, a promise that is often made and never kept despite the best of intentions, the goal of this model is to build the foundation from which a value chain will naturally emerge, without threats and trade wars. Second, a reindustrialization strategy is a movement toward the future, not the past, and it requires a level of individual commitment that Americans are not used to. Third, reindustrialization requires an apolitical approach that does not reset priorities every two years of an election cycle or segment the population into groups for electoral gain. Finally, long-term planning should not be restricted to autocracies. Democracies such as the United States should be able to take a rational, empirical approach to implement long-term strategies based on supply chain and STEM, and to move quicker toward them. Suppose the American government, through its people, commits to the five pillars outlined above for a 21st-century approach to supply chains. In that case, the possibilities could be even more breathtaking than what's happening in China today since America's approach would focus on communities and individuals, not on the aims of a centralized government. For this to happen, there needs to be a level of leadership, strategy, vision, and sacrifice that has been absent in America for decades.

After the five pillars are in place, it is time to start building out the network, community by community, through a public-private partnership model that self-organizes based on priorities and capabilities. With the federal government investing in broadband infrastructure and K–12 education, research and development into the key areas of blockchain and advanced manufacturing, and public-private partnering, then states and local communities should proceed through incentives and strategic plans to determine how to move their communities forward, including the communities' educational systems. Upon finding viable strategic focus areas, such as health care, recycling, sustainability, pharmaceuticals, automotive, electronics, food production, and so forth, a healthy capitalistic model can take shape, leading to investments in states and communities through 3D printing, predictive analytics tools, automation, and other advanced technologies on behalf of the citizen nodes.

It is critical for private sector companies to accept that an economic model exists for healthy participation with their communities in mutual agreement without squeezing out the individual, the node. It will not be possible to win by sucking all the oxygen from the competition through multinational corporations, scale, and capital investments. Instead, large corporations, such as those in the logistics and planning spaces, could assist in the networking, both physical and logical, of goods and services from one community to another, leading to connected commerce across a distributed, decentralized network. In these activities, government institutions will advocate for their communities and citizens rather than picking favorites and enabling the welfare state that creates dependency rather than empowerment. There should not be a defined expectation for how these networked communities will self-organize, interact, collaborate, and even compete in a balanced approach between the interests of the public and private sectors, enabled by individuals; that would be against the concept of how self-organizing individuals and communities can succeed. Municipal governments shouldn't call balls and strikes but should ensure that this new supply chain system streamlines fluidity and fairness. This is important: for this model to work, it cannot allow the big multinational players to exert influence through capital and political connections; the localities and states need to ensure that the public infrastructure stays public to ensure a level playing field that doesn't concentrate wealth, leading to the exclusion of those who are least able to afford to be on the outside. If this new model can happen, a 21st-century value chain can emerge that embodies a free-flow model of capitalism as imagined over the centuries.

A US Supply Chain Revival?

After decades of losing in the global competition for manufacturing and supply chain leadership, the United States could tilt the scale in a matter of a decade in favor of an American model built on the individual and community driving innovation and growth rather than the model from China with large, structured institutions as the drivers. China's vision of its public-private enterprise strategy is for the government to assign private sector leadership (and sometimes take away that leadership) for initiatives to e-commerce companies such as Alibaba; to artificial intelligence companies such as Baidu and Megvii; to semiconductor companies such as Huawei, SMIC, and Fujian Jinhua Integrated Circuit; and to pharmaceutical companies such as Sinopharm, among others. In this national strategy, China's centralized federal government controls the relationship between the public and private institutions, including the national government's investment in a 5G network to create smart cities that can be considered a threat to the citizens' liberties rather than a community-based system that could empower them. Therefore, rather than a reactionary or even a potential surveillance capitalism approach modeled after China, and rather than focusing on trade disputes and crying foul, America needs to learn from China as a competitor and develop its own strategy on behalf of its stakeholders, the American people, through liberal democratic principles.

A new model to achieve self-reliance and an American revival in manufacturing and supply chain can be supported through a nonprotectionist model without concern for what China does with its Made in China 2025 policy and Belt and Road Initiative. Suppose the American strategy is to focus on our current hollowed-out economy and build outward to the globalized world without being distracted by what's happening in China. In that case, the United States can achieve its objectives for its people, driving a feeling of hope that is missing today. The goal should be to have networked communities as manufacturing and logistics centers for the new economy in place as soon as possible. How long will it take for these technologies to mature sufficiently to reach the goals set forth in this book? We will learn the answer only through strategy, proofs of concept, true public-private partnerships, and investing. Imagine the American landscape filled with peer-to-peer manufacturing hubs across the nation, with an entire ecosystem emerging to support them—a winning strategy by investing, not consuming away, the resources of the world's largest economy. Likewise, a revival of its balanced supply chain principles will lead to a resurgence in the US economic system and begin to address the symptoms that ail us relating to societal inequities and the growing imbalance between the haves and have-nots. Rather than obsessing over the Chinese, Americans need to sacrifice, understand a longer-term vision, and work together toward the nation's aims for the common good.

Back to the Future

This book looks back to tell the story of an American supply chain system that once led the world and—looking into the future—can do so again in a 21st-century posture. Looking back to the American supply chain–driven economy of the past shows how supply chains have enabled the American Dream. Still, it does so today for consumers, but not in a balanced manner that allows everyone a chance to succeed as a stakeholder. Now is the time to proceed with a 21st-century model, not one of the 19th or even the 20th century. To the doubters of the viability of the model for the future explained in this book, I ask once more: what are the better alternatives? For those who believe that America can be made great again by restoring the manufacturing of the past, such ideological pandering will never restore the industrial steel mills on the Patapsco River in Baltimore, the automotive plants in Flint, Michigan, the textile mills of the rural South, or the coal mines in West Virginia and western Pennsylvania. Those days are gone and will never return. It is understandable why we reminisce because those jobs and lifestyles were never replaced. But there's hope for the future, and we can move forward together with a new model. Not only does the government need to invest in the future for Americans, but it also needs to establish a vision of the future, a new American Dream. Not everyone achieved their own American Dream as my grandmother did, but that dream represents hope for a more inclusive and more balanced future if we choose to make it happen. As the nation learns to deal with its present-day socioeconomic and cultural challenges, a new dream of what is possible for the 21st century can be established when new intentions from the government and private sectors take steps to put in place the new model, and citizens will see how the dream can be achieved and will aspire toward it.

Today there is skepticism regarding the efficacy of America's public and private institutions, and rightfully so. Much of the distrust has to do with the role of these institutions in society; should they be the drivers or the enablers of change and growth? This question is the crux of the policy position that America and every other nation must answer. When the public and private sectors show they make and keep promises, new trust in societal institutions will be slowly reinforced. Not even a few years ago, the solutions I propose would have been viewed as nothing more than a concept. Today's supply chains and technology are advancing to the point that not only is it entirely possible that my solution is viable, it is also optimally the right strategy. Getting from the current state to the future will take time, patience, and sacrifice. The biggest question is whether we will elect politicians who are strong enough to lead us and if we will be willing to sacrifice for the future. If the answer is no, then nothing will change, and the chaos, instability, and moroseness will only grow, boiling over again and again. However, if we succeed in reestablishing trust and implementing a long-term strategy together as a nation, there is hope for a new supply chain for the 21st century. There's no better time than the present to move forward.

NOTES

Introduction

1. R. Andres Castaneda Aguilar, Aleksander Eilertsen, Tony Fujs, Christoph Lakner, Daniel Gerszon Mahler, Minh Cong Nguyen, Marta Schoch, Samuel Kofi Tetteh Baah, Martha Viveros, and Haoyu Wu, "April 2022 Global Poverty Update from the World Bank," *World Bank*, April 8, 2022, https://blogs.worldbank.org/opendata/april-2022-global-poverty -update-world-bank.
2. Todd Maiden, "How Big Is the Logistics Industry?" *Freightwaves*, January 11, 2020, https://www.freightwaves.com/news/how-big-is-the-logistics-industry.
3. "Public Top 100," alphaliner.axmarine.com, accessed April 13, 2020.
4. Knut Alicke, Richa Gupta, and Vera Trautwein, "Resetting Supply Chains for the Next Normal," *McKinsey Quarterly*, July 21, 2020, https://www.mckinsey.com/business-func tions/operations/our-insights/resetting-supply-chains-for-the-next-normal.
5. "Q4'21 Outlook: The Logistics of Seasonal Cheer," *Panjiva Research*, September 27, 2021, https://panjiva.com/research/q421-outlook-the-logistics-of-cheer/43032.
6. "Is the World Economy Recovering?" *Economist*, September 16, 2020, https://www.econ omist.com/finance-and-economics/2020/09/16/is-the-world-economy-recovering.
7. Derek Thompson, "The Richest Cities for Young People: 1980 vs. Today," *Atlantic*, February 15, 2015, https://www.theatlantic.com/business/archive/2015/02/for-great-american -cities-the-rich-dont-always-get-richer/385513/.
8. "W. Edwards Deming, Discussing the Leadership We Need in Our Organizations," interview with Bill Scherkenbach (February 1984), The Deming Institute, September 16, 2016, https://deming.org/w-edward-deming-discussing-the-leadership-we-need-in-our -organizations/.
9. Mike Patton, "U.S. Role in Global Economy Declines Nearly 50%," *Forbes*, February 29, 2020, https://www.forbes.com/sites/mikepatton/2016/02/29/u-s-role-in-global-eco nomy-declines-nearly-50/?sh=289cd66c5e9e.
10. Drew Desilver, "For Most U.S. Workers, Real Wages Have Barely Budged in Decades," Pew Research Center, August 7, 2018, https://www.pewresearch.org/fact-tank/2018/08/07 /for-most-us-workers-real-wages-have-barely-budged-for-decades/.
11. Elise Gould, "State of Working America Wages 2019," Economic Policy Institute, February 20, 2020, https://www.epi.org/publication/swa-wages-2019/.
12. Gould.

13. Drew Desilver, "U.S. Students' Academic Achievement Still Lags That of Their Peers in Many Other Countries," Pew Research Center, February 15, 2017, https://www.pewre search.org/fact-tank/2017/02/15/u-s-students-internationally-math-science/.
14. "2022 Best Global Universities," US News and World Report, https://www.usnews.com /education/best-global-universities/rankings.
15. Vijay Vaitheeswaran, "Supply Chains Are Undergoing a Dramatic Transformation," *Economist*, July 11, 2019.
16. James Pennington, "Every Minute, One Garbage Truck of Plastic Is Dumped into Our Oceans. This Has to Stop," World Economic Forum, October 27, 2016, https://www.we forum.org/agenda/2016/10/every-minute-one-garbage-truck-of-plastic-is-dumped-into -our-oceans/.
17. Laura Silver, Shannon Schumacher, and Mara Mordecai, "In U.S. and UK, Globalization Leaves Some Feeling 'Left Behind' or 'Swept Up,'" Pew Research Center, October 5, 2020, https://www.pewresearch.org/2020/10/05/in-u-s-and-uk-globalization-leaves-some-fee ling-left-behind-or-swept-up/.
18. Jessica R. Nicholson, "2015: What Is Made in America?" *ESA Issue Brief* #0-17, US Department of Commerce, March 28, 2017, https://www.commerce.gov/sites/default /files/migrated/reports/2015-what-is-made-in-america_0.pdf.
19. Andrew Allen, "P&G Warns 17,600 Products Possibly Hit by Coronavirus," *Supply Management*, February 21, 2020, https://www.cips.org/supply-management/news/2020 /february/pg-warns-17600-products-possibly-hit-by-coronavirus/.
20. "The New Order of Trade," *Economist*, October 9, 2021.
21. "Shipping Container History: Boxes to Buildings," Discover Containers, 2020, https:// www.discovercontainers.com/a-complete-history-of-the-shipping-container/.
22. Jack Buffington, *Peak Plastic: The Rise or Fall of Our Synthetic World* (Santa Barbara, CA: Praeger, 2019).
23. Sarah Kaplan, "By 2050, There Will Be More Plastic Than Fish in the World's Oceans, Study Says," *Washington Post*, January 20, 2016, https://www.washingtonpost.com/news /morning-mix/wp/2016/01/20/by-2050-there-will-be-more-plastic-than-fish-in-the -worlds-oceans-study-says/.
24. "Data from PPE Shortage Index Shows U.S. Still Has Urgent Need for PPE" (2020), accessed on April 14, 2022, https://getusppe.org/data/.
25. Robert Rapier, "How Fossil Fuels Subsidize Us," *Resilience*, May 15, 2014, https://www .resilience.org/stories/2014-05-15/how-fossil-fuels-subsidize-us/.
26. "About 7% of Fossil Fuels Are Consumed for Non-Combustion Use in the United States," US Energy Information Agency, April 6, 2018, https://www.eia.gov/todayinenergy/detail .php?id=35672.
27. Tim Worstall, "The Story of Henry Ford's $5 a Day Wages: It's Not What You Think," *Forbes*, March 4, 2012, https://www.forbes.com/sites/timworstall/2012/03/04/the-story -of-henry-fords-5-a-day-wages-its-not-what-you-think/?sh=1ca915d766d2.
28. Peter Drucker, *Post-Capitalist Society* (New York: Harper Business, 1993), 49–50.
29. Drucker, 36.
30. Matthew Pinto-Chilcott, "The History of Human Resource Management (HRM),"

LinkedIn, August 18, 2015, https://www.linkedin.com/pulse/history-human-resource-man agement-hrm-matthew-pinto-chilcott/.

Chapter 1. How America Lost Supply Chain Leadership

1. Martijn Lofvers, "D-Day Planning and Execution," *Supply Chain Movement*, no. 2 (February 2012), https://www.supplychainmovement.com/wp-content/uploads/2014/06/D -day-planning-and-Eexcution-the-Supply-Chain-of-Operation-Overlord-1944.pdf.
2. Sarah Pruitt, "How Did the Nazis Really Lose World War II?" *History*, May 3, 2017, https://www.history.com/news/how-did-the-nazis-really-lose-world-war-ii.
3. Cecil Bohanan, "Economic Recovery: Lessons from the Post-World War II Period," *Mercatus on Policy*, no. 112 (August 2012), https://www.mercatus.org/system/files/PostWWII _Recovery_Bohanon_MOP112-%281%29-copy.pdf.
4. John Galbraith, *American Capitalism: The Concept of Countervailing Power* (London: Routledge, 2017).
5. Bohanan, "Economic Recovery."
6. Gabor Steingart, *The War for Wealth* (New York: MacGraw Hill, 2008).
7. Bohanan, "Economic Recovery."
8. Steingart, *The War for Wealth*.
9. Ted Unarce, *We Are Stronger Than We Think* (New York: Page Publishing, 2018).
10. Lizabeth Cohen, "A Consumers' Republic: The Politics of Mass Consumption in Postwar America," *Journal of Consumer Research* 31, no. 1 (2004): 236–39.
11. Edna Ullmann-Margalit and Avishai Margalit, *Isaiah Berlin: A Celebration* (Chicago: University of Chicago Press, 2001).
12. Edward L. Bernays and Howard Walden Cutler, *The Engineering of Consent* (Norman: University of Oklahoma Press, 1969).
13. Lisa Held, "Psychoanalysis Shapes Consumer Culture: Or How Sigmund Freud, His Nephew and a Box of Cigars Forever Changed American Marketing," *American Psychological Association* 40, no. 11 (2009), https://www.apa.org/monitor/2009/12/consumer.
14. Edward Bernays, *Propaganda* (New York: Liveright, 1933), 71.
15. Tim Adams, "How Freud Got Under Our Skin," *Guardian*, March 10, 2002, https://www .theguardian.com/education/2002/mar/10/medicalscience.highereducation.
16. Bernard London, "Ending the Depression through Planned Obsolescence" (1932), https:// upload.wikimedia.org/wikipedia/commons/2/27/London_(1932)_Ending_the_depre ssion_through_planned_obsolescence.pdf.
17. London.
18. Lawrence Glickman, *Buying Power: A History of Consumer Activism in America* (Chicago: University of Chicago Press, 2012).
19. Victor Lebow, "Price Competition in 1955," *Journal of Retailing* (Spring 1955), https:// www.academia.edu/21551517/Price_Competition_in_1955.
20. George Packer, *The Unwinding: An Inner History of the New America* (London: Faber and Faber, 2013).
21. Milton Friedman, "A Friedman Doctrine: The Social Responsibility of Business to Increase Its Profits," *New York Times*, September 13, 1970.

22. Michael Jensen, *A Theory of the Firm: Governance, Residual Claims, and Organizational Forms* (Cambridge, MA: Harvard University Press, 2003).

23. Steve Denning, "The Origin of 'The World's Dumbest Idea': Milton Friedman," *Forbes*, June 26, 2013, https://www.forbes.com/sites/stevedenning/2013/06/26/the-origin-of-the-worlds-dumbest-idea-milton-friedman/#4166488d870e.

24. Michael Jacobs, and D. W. Mullins, *Short-Term America: The Causes and Cures of Our Business Myopia* (Cambridge, MA: Harvard Business School Press, 1991).

25. John Maynard Keynes, *The General Theory of Employment, Interest and Money* (New York: MacMillan, 1942).

26. John Bogle, *Battle for the Soul of Capitalism* (New Haven, CT: Yale University Press, 2008).

27. Govinda Bhutada, "The Share of the US Economy over Time," *Visual Capitalist*, January 14, 2021, https://www.visualcapitalist.com/u-s-share-of-global-economy-over-time/.

28. W. Edwards Deming, *Out of the Crisis* (Boston: MIT Press, 2018).

29. Jacobs and Mullins, *Short-Term America*.

30. Alvin Toffler, *The Third Wave* (New York: Bantam, 1980).

31. Peter F. Drucker, *Concept of the Corporation* (Boston: Beacon, 1960).

32. Thomas Davenport, *Thinking for a Living: How to Get Better Performance and Results from Knowledge Workers* (Boston: Harvard Business School Press, 2008).

33. Rick Wartzman, "What Peter Drucker Knew about 2020," *Harvard Business Review*, October 16, 2014, https://hbr.org/2014/10/what-peter-drucker-knew-about-2020.

34. Jack Buffington, *An Easy Out: Corporate America's Addiction to Outsourcing* (Westport, CT: Praeger, 2007).

35. Thomas Friedman, *The World Is Flat: A Brief History of the Twenty-First Century* (New York: Picador, 2005).

36. Robert E. Scott, "A Conservative Estimate of 'The Wal-Mart Effect,'" *Economic Policy Institute*, December 9, 2015, https://www.epi.org/publication/the-wal-mart-effect/.

37. Scott.

38. Marc Levinson, *The Box: How the Shipping Container Made the World Smaller and the World Economy Bigger* (Princeton, NJ: Princeton University Press, 2006).

39. Vijay Vaitheeswaran, "Supply Chains Are Undergoing a Dramatic Transformation," *Economist*, July 11, 2019.

40. Steingart, *The War for Wealth*.

41. Kishore Mahbubani, "While America Slept: How the United States Botched China's Rise," *Foreign Affairs*, February 27, 2013, https://foreignpolicy.com/2013/02/27/while-america-slept/.

42. Richard Florida, "The World Is Spiky: Globalization Has Changed the Economic Playing Field, but Hasn't Leveled It," *Atlantic* 296 (2005): 48–51.

43. Ha-Joon Chang, *Bad Samaritans: The Myth of Free Trade and the Secret History of Capitalism* (New York: Bloomsbury, 2010).

44. Julian Coman, "Interview: Michael Sandel: 'The Populist Backlash Has Been a Revolt against the Tyranny of Merit.'" *Guardian*, September 6, 2020, https://www.theguardian.com/books/2020/sep/06/michael-sandel-the-populist-backlash-has-been-a-revolt-against-the-tyranny-of-merit.

45. Peter F. Drucker, *The New Realities: In Government and Politics . . . in Economy and Business . . . in Society . . . and in World View* (New York: HarperCollins, 1994).
46. Robert Z. Lawrence, "Does Manufacturing Have the Largest 'Multiplier' for the Domestic Economy?" *Peterson Institute for International Economics*, March 22, 2017, https://www .piie.com/blogs/realtime-economic-issues-watch/does-manufacturing-have-largest-em ployment-multiplier-domestic.
47. Lee E. Ohanian, "Competition and the Decline of the Rust Belt," *Minneapolis Federal Reserve*, December 20, 2014, https://www.minneapolisfed.org/article/2014/competition -and-the-decline-of-the-rust-belt.
48. Thomas Holmes and Lee E. Ohanian, *Paychecks or Promises? Lessons from the Death Spiral of Detroit*, Economic Policy Paper 14-4 (2014), Federal Reserve Bank of Minneapolis.
49. Andrew Chatzky, James McBride, and Mohammed Aly Sergie, "NAFTA and the USMCA: Weighing the Impact of North American Trade," *Council on Foreign Relations*, July 1, 2020, https://www.cfr.org/backgrounder/naftas-economic-impact.
50. Chatzky et al.
51. "Address of Wm. McC. Martin, Jr., Chairman, Board of Governors of the Federal Reserve System, before the New York Group of the Investment Bankers Association of America," October 19, 1955, https://fraser.stlouisfed.org/title/statements-speeches-wil liam-mcchesney-martin-jr-448/address-new-york-group-investment-bankers-association- america-7800.

Chapter 2. Fallouts from Deindustrialization

1. David Ignatious, "The Rest of the World Is Taking Advantage of a Distracted America," *Washington Post*, October 2, 2020, https://www.washingtonpost.com/opinions/the-rest -of-the-world-is-taking-advantage-of-a-distracted-america/2020/10/06/fe6879d8-0801 -11eb-a166-dc429b380d10_story.html.
2. Dina Gusovsky, "Americans Consume Vast Number of the World's Opioids," *CNBC*, April 26, 2016, https://www.cnbc.com/2016/04/27/americans-consume-almost-all-of -the-global-opioid-supply.html.
3. Chris Kahn, "COVID-19 Fading as Dominant Political Issue as Americans Focus on Inflation, Economy: Reuters/Ipsos Poll," Reuters, November 4, 2021, https://www.re uters.com/world/us/covid-19-fading-dominant-political-issue-americans-focus-inflation -economy-2021-11-04/.
4. Huang Yixuan, "What Lies Ahead for China's Economy in 2022?" *Shine*, December 14, 2021, https://www.shine.cn/news/in-focus/2112149497/.
5. "Standard & Poor's 500 Index History Chart January 4, 1960 through November 19, 2021," FedPrimeRate, accessed November 19, 2021, http://www.fedprimerate.com/s -and-p-500-index-history-chart.htm.
6. "And the Poor Get Poorer," *Economist*, October 3, 2020.
7. "Millennial Socialism," *Economist*, February 14, 2019.
8. Lydia Chavez, "The Year the Bottom Fell out of Steel," *New York Times*, June 20, 1982, https://www.nytimes.com/1982/06/20/business/the-year-the-bottom-fell-out-for-steel .html?auth=link-dismiss-google1tap.

9. "The History of Baltimore," Baltimore City Department of Planning, n.d., https://plan ning.baltimorecity.gov/sites/default/files/History%20of%20Baltimore.pdf.

10. "Baltimore's Drug Problem: It's Costing Too Much Not to Spend More on It," Abell Foundation, October 1993, https://www.abell.org/sites/default/files/publications/Balti mores%20Drug%20Problem.pdf.

11. Brandon Lazovic, "The Rise and Fall of Flint, Michigan Beginning in the 1800s," *Odyssey*, February 16, 2016, https://www.theodysseyonline.com/rise-fall-flint-michigan-beginning -1800s.

12. Lazovic.

13. Lazovic.

14. Andrew Highsmith, *Demolition Means Progress: Flint, Michigan, and the Fate of the American Metropolis* (Chicago: University of Chicago Press, 2016).

15. Lazovic, "The Rise and Fall of Flint."

16. "River of Fire," *Economist*, July 21, 2018.

17. Christina Sterbenz and Erin Fuchs. "How Flint, Michigan Became the Most Dangerous City In America," *Business Insider*, June 16, 2013, https://www.businessinsider.com/why -is-flint-michigan-dangerous-2013-6.

18. "River of Fire."

19. Ryan Felton, "What General Motors Did to Flint," *Jalopnik*, April 28, 2017, https:// jalopnik.com/what-general-motors-did-to-flint-1794493131.

20. Felton.

21. Eduardo Porter, "The Hard Truths of Trying to 'Save' the Rural Economy," *New York Times*, December 14, 2018, https://www.nytimes.com/interactive/2018/12/14/opinion /rural-america-trump-decline.html.

22. "The Death Curve," *Economist*, February 23, 2019.

23. "Drug Overdose Deaths in the US Top 100,000 Annually," Centers for Disease Control and Prevention, November 17, 2021, https://www.cdc.gov/nchs/pressroom/nchs_press _releases/2021/20211117.htm.

24. Holly Hedegaard and Marianne Spencer, "Urban–Rural Differences in Drug Overdose Death Rates, 1999–2019," National Center for Health Statistics, March 2021, https:// www.cdc.gov/nchs/products/databriefs/db403.htm.

25. "Alexa, How Much Is It?," *Economist*, October 12, 2019.

26. Private corporate data provided by executives known to the author, whose identity must remain anonymous because the data has not been publicly released.

27. Alejandra Salgado, "Weber: Ocean Shipping Rates 'Four Times Historical Averages,'" *Supply Chain Dive*, March 8, 2022, https://www.supplychaindive.com/news/weber-faces -high-container-costs-sets-third-price-increase-ocean-freight/619319/.

28. Robert Lawrence and Lawrence Edwards, "US Employment Deindustrialization: Insights from History and the International Experience," Petersen Institute for International Economics, October 2013, https://www.piie.com/publications/pb/pb13-27.pdf.

29. Martin Baily and Barry Bosworth, "US Manufacturing: Understanding Its Past and Its Potential Future," *Journal of Economic Perspectives* 28, no. 1 (February 1, 2014): 3–26.

30. Robert E. Scott, "Manufacturing Job Loss: Trade, Not Productivity, Is the Culprit,"

Economic Policy Institute, August 11, 2015, https://www.epi.org/publication/manufactur
ing-job-loss-trade-not-productivity-is-the-culprit/.

31. Robert E. Scott, "The Wal-Mart Effect: Its Chinese Imports Have Displaced Nearly
200,000 US Jobs," *Economic Policy Institute*, June 25, 2007, https://www.epi.org/publica
tion/ib235/.

32. Alana Semeuls, "Free Shipping Isn't Hurting Amazon," *Atlantic*, April 27, 2018, https://
www.theatlantic.com/technology/archive/2018/04/free-shipping-isnt-hurting-ama
zon/559052/.

33. Steve Banker, "Walmart's Massive Investment in Supply Chain Transformation," *Forbes*,
April 23, 2021, https://www.forbes.com/sites/stevebanker/2021/04/23/walmarts-massive
-investment-in-a-supply-chain-transformation/?sh=79725106340e.

34. "Amazon and Alibaba Are Pacesetters of the Next Supply-Chain Revolution," *Economist*,
July 11, 2019.

35. Michael Sainato, "'I'm Not a Robot': Amazon Workers Condemn Unsafe, Grueling
Conditions at Warehouse," *Guardian*, February 5, 2020, https://www.theguardian.com
/technology/2020/feb/05/amazon-workers-protest-unsafe-grueling-conditions-warehouse.

36. Henry Curr, "The Peril and the Promise," *Economist*, October 10, 2020.

37. Kimberly Amadeo, "China's Economy and Its Effect on the US Economy: The Surprising
Ways China Affects the US Economy," *The Balance*, February 21, 2020, https://www
.thebalance.com/china-economy-facts-effect-on-us-economy-3306345.

38. "The People's Dictator," *Economist*, October 2, 2021.

39. Jonathan Woetzel, Jeongmin Seong, Nick Leung, Joe Ngai, James Manyika, Anu Madgav-
kar, Susan Lund, and Audrewy Mironenko, *China and the World: Inside the Dynamics of a
Changing Relationship*, McKinsey Institute, July 2019, https://www.mckinsey.com/~/media
/mckinsey/featured%20insights/china/china%20and%20the%20world%20inside%20
the%20dynamics%20of%20a%20changing%20relationship/mgi-china-and-the-world
-full-report-june-2019-vf.ashx.

40. Loren Thompson, "Coronavirus Highlights US Strategic Vulnerabilities Spawned by
Over-Reliance On China," *Forbes*, March 30, 2020, https://www.forbes.com/sites/loren
thompson/2020/03/30/coronavirus-highlights-us-strategic-vulnerabilities-spawned-by
-over-reliance-on-china/#467e4db369a1.

41. Lauren Thomas, "Coronavirus Wreaks Havoc on Retail Supply Chains Globally, Even
as China's Factories Come Back Online," *CNBC*, March 16, 2020, https://www.cnbc
.com/2020/03/16/coronavirus-wreaks-havoc-on-retail-supply-chains-globally.html.

42. Doug Palmer and Finbarr Bermingham, "US Policymakers Worry about China
'Weaponizing' Drug Exports," *South China Morning Post*, December 20, 2019, https://www
.politico.com/news/2019/12/20/policymakers-worry-china-drug-exports-088126.

43. Palmer and Bermingham.

44. Holly Strom and Kenneth Schell, "The Other US Prescription Drug Problem: China's
Dominance in the Production of Generic Drugs Is Part of a Greater Medical Security
Threat to the United States," *US News and World Report*, October 1, 2019, https://www
.usnews.com/news/best-countries/articles/2019-10-01/commentary-us-reliance-on-china
-for-generic-drugs-is-a-security-threat.

45. Didi Martinez, Brenda Breslauer, and Stephanie Gosk, "Tainted Drugs: Ex-FDA Inspector Warns of Dangers in US Meds Made in China, India," *NBC News*, May 10, 2019, https://www.nbcnews.com/health/health-news/tainted-drugs-ex-fda-inspector-warns-dangers-u-s-meds-n1002971.

46. Eric Palmer, "How Much Does US Rely on China for Drugs? FDA Simply Doesn't Know," *Fierce Pharma*, March 12, 2020, https://www.fiercepharma.com/manufacturing/how-much-does-u-s-rely-china-for-drugs-fda-simply-doesn-t-know.

47. John Xie, "World Depends on China for Face Masks but Can Country Deliver?," *Voice of America News*, March 19, 2020, https://www.voanews.com/science-health/coronavirus-outbreak/world-depends-china-face-masks-can-country-deliver.

48. "Politics Aside, US Relies on China Supplies to Fight COVID-19: Experts," *Channel News Asia*, April 3, 2020, https://www.channelnewsasia.com/news/asia/coronavirus-covid-19-united-states-china-trade-war-12604690.

49. Mark Maremont, Austen Hufford, and Tom McGinty, "US Pays High Prices for Masks from Unproven Vendors in Coronavirus Fight," *Wall Street Journal*, April 18, 2020, https://www.wsj.com/articles/u-s-pays-high-prices-for-masks-from-unproven-vendors-in-coronavirus-fight-11587218400.

50. Andre Månberger and Bjorn Stenqvist, "Global Metal Flows in the Renewable Energy Transition: Exploring the Effects of Substitutes, Technological Mix and Development," *Energy Policy* 119 (August 1, 2018): 226–41.

51. Jim Constantopoulos, "America's Achilles' Heel: Mineral Import Reliance on China," *Ruidoso News*, May 30, 2019, https://www.ruidosonews.com/story/opinion/columnists/2019/05/30/americas-achilles-heel-mineral-import-reliance-china/1284312001/.

52. Weilun Soon, "From Alibaba's Jack Ma to JD.com's Richard Liu: Here Are China's 'Old Guard' Tech Founders Who Have Walked Away from Leadership Roles amid Beijing's Tech Crackdown," *Business Insider*, April 12, 2022, https://www.businessinsider.in/tech/news/from-alibabaaposs-jack-ma-to-jd-comaposs-richard-liu-here-are-chinaaposs-aposold-guardapos-tech-founders-who-have-walked-away-from-leadership-roles-amid-beijing-aposs-tech-crackdown/slidelist/90798656.cms.

53. Luzi-Ann Javier and Justina Vasquez, "US Drones Scour for Rare Earths to End Reliance on China," *Bloomberg News*, February 7, 2020, https://www.bloomberg.com/news/articles/2020-02-07/u-s-scours-for-rare-earths-to-end-addiction-to-chinese-imports#:~:text=The%20U.S.%20is%20deploying%20drones,its%20dependence%20on%20Chinese%20imports.

54. Aaron Klein, "Decline in US Shipbuilding Industry: A Cautionary Tale of Foreign Subsidies Destroying US Jobs," *Eno Center for Transportation*, September 1, 2015, https://www.enotrans.org/article/decline-u-s-shipbuilding-industry-cautionary-tale-foreign-sub sidies-destroying-u-s-jobs/.

55. Thompson, "Coronavirus Highlights US."

56. Jianna Liu, "It's Time China Became Self-Reliant in Chips," *China Daily*, June 12, 2019, https://www.chinadaily.com.cn/a/201906/12/WS5d00348da3101765772309df.html.

57. "The New Order of Trade," *Economist*, October 9, 2021.

58. "The New Order of Trade."

59. Robert Z. Lawrence, "Challenges in Achieving Inclusive Growth through Manufacturing," Peterson Institute for International Economics, Policy Brief 19-11, August 2019, https://www.piie.com/publications/policy-briefs/manufacturing-and-inclusive-growth-challenges-china.
60. Jack Goodman, "Has China Lifted 100 Million out of Poverty?," *BBC*, February 28, 2021, https://www.bbc.com/news/56213271.
61. "Black Cat, White Cat, Fat Cat, Thin Cat," *Economist*, October 2, 2021.
62. "China's New Reality," *Economist*, October 2, 2021.
63. Lawrence, "Challenges in Achieving Inclusive Growth."
64. Jane Leibrock, "Measuring the American Dream: Results from Surveying Americans about What the American Dream Means to Them," *Even*, 2019, http://pages.even.com/rs/583-LJI-771/images/Even_measuring_the_american_dream.pdf.
65. Kai Ryssdal and Maria Hollenhorst. "What's Gonna Happen to the Consumer Economy?," *Marketplace*, April 6, 2020, https://www.marketplace.org/2020/04/06/whats-gonna-happen-to-the-consumer-economy/.
66. Kimberly Amadeo, "Components of GDP Explained," *Balance*, June 26, 2020, https://www.thebalance.com/components-of-gdp-explanation-formula-and-chart-3306015.
67. Elise Gould, "State of Working America's Wages 2019," *Economic Policy Institute*, February 20, 2020, https://www.epi.org/publication/swa-wages-2019/#:~:text=From%202018%20to%202019%2C%20the,%25%20at%20the%2010th%20percentile.
68. Scott Kennedy, "Made in China 2025," *Center for Strategic and International Studies*, June 1, 2015, https://www.csis.org/analysis/made-china-2025.
69. James McBride and Andrew Chatzky, "Is 'Made in China 2025' a Threat to Global Trade?," *Council for Foreign Affairs*, May 13, 2019, https://www.cfr.org/backgrounder/made-china-2025-threat-global-trade.
70. Jonathan Woetzel, Nicklas Garemo, Jan Mischke, Martin Hjerpe, and Robert Palter, "Bridging Global Infrastructure Gaps," *McKinsey & Company*, June 14, 2016, https://www.mckinsey.com/~/media/mckinsey/business%20functions/operations/our%20insights/bridging%20global%20infrastructure%20gaps/bridging-global-infrastructure-gaps-full-report-june-2016.pdf.
71. Woetzel, et al.
72. Joseph Kane and Adie Tomer, "Shifting into an Era of Repair: US Infrastructure Spending Trend," Brookings Institute, May 10, 2019, https://www.brookings.edu/research/shifting-into-an-era-of-repair-us-infrastructure-spending-trends/.
73. Kane and Tomer.
74. "State Expenditure Report," National Association of State Budget Officers (2019), https://higherlogicdownload.s3.amazonaws.com/NASBO/9d2d2db1-c943-4f1b-b750-0fca152d64c2/UploadedImages/SER%20Archive/2019_State_Expenditure_Report-S.pdf.

Chapter 3. New Economics

1. Richard Wike, Janell Fetterolf, and Mara Mordecai, "U.S. Image Plummets Internationally as Most Say Country Has Handled Coronavirus Badly," Pew Research Center, September

15, 2020, https://www.pewresearch.org/global/2020/09/15/us-image-plummets-interna
tionally-as-most-say-country-has-handled-coronavirus-badly/.

2. Matthew Lee, "Poll: Many Americans Blame Virus Crisis on Us Government," Associated Press, October 5, 2020, https://apnews.com/article/virus-outbreak-donald-trump-health -united-states-china-89f3f568802f32e6bafdbeee1c53abe2.

3. Megan Brenan, "Americans' Confidence in Major US Institutions Dips," Gallup, July 14, 2021, https://news.gallup.com/poll/352316/ameicans-confidence-major-institutions-dips .aspx.

4. "Trust in Government: 1958–2015," Pew Research Center, November 23, 2015, https:// www.pewresearch.org/politics/2015/11/23/1-trust-in-government-1958-2015/.

5. Isabel Wilkerson, *Caste: The Origin of Our Discontents* (New York: Random House, 2020).

6. David Horowitz, *The Enemy Within: How a Totalitarian Movement Is Destroying America* (Washington, DC: Regnery, 2021).

7. Julianne Hill, "Why Are US Parties So Polarized?" Northwestern School of Engineering, August 25, 2020, https://www.mccormick.northwestern.edu/news/articles/2020/08/why -are-us-parties-so-polarized.html.

8. Hill.

9. Jill Kimball, "US Is Polarizing Faster Than Other Democracies, Study Finds," Brown University, January 21, 2020, https://www.brown.edu/news/2020-01-21/polarization.

10. "Real Gross Domestic Product by Major Demand Category," Bureau of Labor Statistics, https://www.bls.gov/emp/tables/real-gdp-major-demand-category.htm.

11. Elise Gould, "State of Working America Wages 2019," Economic Policy Institute, February 20, 2020, https://www.epi.org/publication/swa-wages-2019/.

12. Gould.

13. "Real Wage Trends, 1979–2019," *Congressional Research Service*, 2019, https://fas.org/sgp /crs/misc/R45090.pdf.

14. Rakesh Kochhar, "The American Middle Class Is Stable in Size, but Losing Ground Financially to Upper-Income Families," Pew Research Center, September 6, 2018, https:// www.pewresearch.org/fact-tank/2018/09/06/the-american-middle-class-is-stable-in-size -but-losing-ground-financially-to-upper-income-families/.

15. Mark J. Perry, "The 'Decline of Manufacturing' Is an Inevitable, Global Phenomenon, and That's Something to Celebrate," American Enterprise Institute, December 16, 2012, https://www.aei.org/carpe-diem/the-decline-of-manufacturing-is-an-inevitable-global -phenomenon-and-thats-something-to-celebrate/.

16. "Ending Poverty," United Nations, n.d., https://www.un.org/en/global-issues/ending- poverty.

17. "World GDP Growth," *Economist*, March 19, 2016, https://www.economist.com/eco nomic-and-financial-indicators/2016/03/19/world-gdp.

18. "Income, Poverty and Health Insurance Coverage in the United States: 2020," US Census Bureau, September 14, 2021, https://www.census.gov/newsroom/press-releases/2021/in come-poverty-health-insurance-coverage.html.

19. "An Age of Giants," *Economist*, November 17, 2018.

20. Adil Abdela and Marshall Steinbaum, "The United States Has a Concentration Problem,"

Roosevelt Institute, September 2018, https://www.ftc.gov/system/files/documents/pub lic_comments/2018/09/ftc-2018-0074-d-0042-155544.pdf.

21. Will Oremus, "'Competition Is for Losers': How Peter Thiel Helped Facebook Embrace Monopoly," *OneZero*, December 12, 2020, https://medium.com/one-zero/competition -is-for-losers-how-peter-thiel-helped-facebook-embrace-monopoly-9a3dd2be1c20.

22. "Alexa, How Much Is It?," *Economist*, October 12, 2019.

23. "Most Valuable Companies in the World," *FXSSI*, November 3, 2020, https://fxssi.com /top-10-most-valuable-companies-in-the-world.

24. Oscar Wilde, *The Complete Illustrated Works of Oscar Wilde* (London: Bounty, 2013).

25. "Book TV," C-Span, April 16, 2008, https://www.c-span.org/person/?1028402/Jack Buffington.

26. W. Edward Deming, *Out of the Crisis* (Boston: MIT Press, 2018).

27. Mohammed El-Erian, "Economists Must Think Broader—or Risk Becoming Irrelevant," *Guardian*, March 11, 2019, https://www.theguardian.com/business/2019/mar/11/why -economics-must-get-broader-before-it-gets-better.

28. "Alexa, How Much Is It?"

29. "Alexa, How Much Is It?"

30. Joyce Winslow, "America's Digital Divide," Pew Research, July 26, 2019, https://www .pewtrusts.org/en/trust/archive/summer-2019/americas-digital-divide.

31. "Millennial Socialism," *Economist*, February 14, 2019, https://www.economist.com/lead ers/2019/02/14/millennial-socialism.

32. Elisa Shearer, "Social Media Outpaces Print Newspapers in the US as a News Source," Pew Research, December 10, 2018, https://www.pewresearch.org/fact-tank/2018/12/10 /social-media-outpaces-print-newspapers-in-the-u-s-as-a-news-source/.

33. "Queen of the Colony," *Economist*, October 10, 2020.

34. "The Promise of Blockchain Technology," *Economist*, August 30, 2018.

35. Julian Gewirtz, "The Futurists of Beijing: Alvin Toffler, Zhao Ziyang, and China's "New Technological Revolution, 1979–1991," *Journal of Asian Studies* 78, no. 1 (February 1, 2019): 115–40.

36. Barry Schwartz, *The Paradox of Choice: Why More Is Less* (New York: HarperCollins, 2003).

37. Allan Lyall, Pierre Mercier, and Stefan Gstettner, "The Death of Supply Chain Management," *Harvard Business Review*, June 15, 2018, https://hbr.org/2018/06/the-death-of-supply -chain-management.

Chapter 4. 21st-Century Reindustrialization

1. "City on the Brink," *Economist*, August 3, 2019.

2. "U.S. Urged to Grasp Made in China 2025," *China News*, April 11, 2018, http://en.people .cn/n3/2018/0411/c90000-9447733.html.

3. Matt Wilstein, "Neil deGrasse Tyson on President Trump: 'Make America Smart Again'," *Daily Beast*, April 13, 2017, https://www.thedailybeast.com/neil-degrasse-tyson-on-presi dent-trump-make-america-smart-again.

4. Sonia B. Buffington, "The Maths Wars," *Economist*, November 6, 2021.

5. David Graeber and Élise Roy, *Bullshit Jobs: A Theory* (New York: Simon and Schuster, 2018).

6. "Tsinghua University May Soon Top the World League in Science Research," *Economist*, November 17, 2018, https://www.economist.com/china/2018/11/17/tsinghua-university -may-soon-top-the-world-league-in-science-research?fsrc=scn/tw/te/bl/ed/tsinghuauni versitymaysoontoptheworldleagueinscienceresearchseizingthelaurels.

7. Antoine Bondaz, "Rebalancing China's Geopolitics," in *One Belt, One Road: China's Great Leap Outward*, edited by Agatha Kratz and Francois Godement (London: European Council on Foreign Relations, 2015).

8. Diane Cohen, "China's Second Opening," In *One Belt, One Road: China's Great Leap Outward* (London: European Council on Foreign Relations, 2015).

9. Alexander C. Pacek, Review of *Institutional Change and Political Continuity in Post-Soviet Central Asia*, by Pauline Luong, *Journal of Politics* 65, no. 2 (May 2003).

10. Georg Graetz and Guy Michaels, "Robots at Work," Centre for Economic Policy Research, March 2015, https://cep.lse.ac.uk/pubs/download/dp1335.pdf.

11. Erik Brynjolfsson and Andrew McAfee, *Race against the Machine: How the Digital Revolution Is Accelerating Innovation, Driving Productivity, and Irreversibly Transforming Employment and the Economy* (Boston: Digital Frontier, 2012).

12. Patrick Marley and Jason Stein, "Foxconn Announces $10 Billion Investment in Wisconsin and Up to 13,000 Jobs," *Milwaukee Journal Sentinel*, July 26, 2017, https://www.jsonline .com/story/news/2017/07/26/scott-walker-heads-d-c-trump-prepares-wisconsin-fox conn-announcement/512077001/.

13. Dian Schauffhauser, "Cost to Connect Rural America: $19 Billion or Less," *The Journal*, February 20, 2018, https://thejournal.com/articles/2018/02/20/cost-to-connect-rural -america-19-billion-or-less.aspx.

14. Lucy Perkins, "Doyle Says Biden's Infrastructure Plan Will Make Broadband More Accessible and Equitable," *WESA*, November 29, 2021, https://www.wesa.fm/politics -government/2021-11-29/doyle-says-bidens-infrastructure-plan-will-make-broadband -more-accessible-and-equitable.

15. "The Condition of Education 2020," U.S. Department of Education, May 2020, https:// nces.ed.gov/pubs2020/2020144.pdf.

16. Rob Spiegel, "Is 3D Printing Ready for Scaled Production?," *Design News*, January 28, 2019, https://www.designnews.com/materials-assembly/3d-printing-ready-scaled-produc tion/166630619160153.

17. W. Edwards Deming, *Out of the Crisis* (Boston: MIT Press, 2018).

18. Louis Columbus, "The State of 3-D Printing as of 2019," *Forbes,* May 27, 2019, https:// www.forbes.com/sites/louiscolumbus/2019/05/27/the-state-of-3d-printing-2019/?sh =7e53e76146c2.

19. Jason Pontin, "3-D Printing Is the Future of Factories (for Real This Time)," *Wired*, July 11, 2018, https://www.wired.com/story/ideas-jason-pontin-3d-printing/.

20. Peter Diamandis, "5 Big Breakthroughs to Anticipate in 3D Printing," *Singularity Hub*, April 8, 2019, https://singularityhub.com/2019/04/08/5-big-breakthroughs-to-anticipate -in-3d-printing/.

Chapter 5. Virtual Logistics

1. Anthony Fauci, interview with Kate Linebaugh for *The Journal*, the podcast of the *Wall Street Journal*, April 7, 2020, https://www.wsj.com/podcasts/the-journal/dr-anthony-fauci-on-how-life-returns-to-normal/d5754969-7027-431e-89fa-e12788ed9879?mod=article_inline.
2. Caitlin Gibson, "Blowing out Candles Is Basically Spitting on Your Friends' Cake," *Washington Post*, July 20, 2020.
3. Nina Strochlic, "One in Six Americans Could Go Hungry in 2020 if Pandemic Persists," *National Geographic*, November 24, 2020.
4. Bob Pisani, "Wealth Gap Grows as Rising Corporate Profits Boost Stock Holdings Controlled by the Richest Households," *CNBC*, August 27, 2020.
5. Katherine Schaeffer, "6 Facts about Income Inequality in the US," *Pew Research Center*, February 7, 2020, https://www.pewresearch.org/fact-tank/2020/02/07/6-facts-about-economic-inequality-in-the-u-s/.
6. "FACTBOX: Why Oil Prices Hit a Record High above $145," Reuters, July 3, 2008, https://www.reuters.com/article/us-oil-prices/factbox-why-oil-prices-hit-a-record-high-above-145-idUSL0322022020080703.
7. Alexandra Kelley, "Largest Solar Project in US History Announced," *The Hill*, November 24, 2020, https://thehill.com/changing-america/sustainability/energy/527402-largest-solar-project-in-us-history-announced.
8. "Circling Back," *Economist*, November 7, 2020.
9. Megha Chakrabarti, "Executives 'Are Legally Obligated to Act Like Sociopaths,' Former Corporate Lawyer Says," *WBUR*, July 31, 2019, https://www.wbur.org/onpoint/2019/07/31/executives-corporate-america-sociopaths-ethics-stakeholders.
10. In 2018 about 17 percent of the world's population lived in developed countries. Briang Wang, "Developed Country Population from 17% to over 50% of the World by 2050," *NextBigFuture*, November 19, 2018, https://www.nextbigfuture.com/2018/11/developed-country-population-from-17-to-over-50-of-world-by-2050.html.
11. Ali Assad, Usama Ahmad, and Juber Akhtar, "3D Printing in Pharmaceutical Sector: An Overview," in *Pharmaceutical Formulation Design: Recent Practices*, edited by Usama Ahmad and Juber Akhtar (London: IntechOpen, 2020), *Open Access*, https://www.intechopen.com/books/pharmaceutical-formulation-design-recent-practices/3d-printing-in-pharmaceutical-sector-an-overview.
12. Ibrahim Ozbolat and Yin Yu, "Bioprinting toward Organ Fabrication: Challenges and Future Trends," *IEEE Transactions on Biomedical Engineering* 30, no. 3 (2013): 691–99.

Chapter 6. Peer-to-Peer Retail

1. Alexandria White, "Americans Have an Average of 4 Credit Cards—Is That Too Many?" *CNBC*, August 27, 2020, https://www.cnbc.com/select/how-many-credit-cards-does-the-average-american-have/.
2. "Ode to the Shopping Mall," *Economist*, May 7, 2020, https://www.economist.com/united-states/2020/05/07/ode-to-the-shopping-mall.
3. Walmart Museum, accessed March 15, 2022, https://www.walmartmuseum.com/content/walmartmuseum/en_us/timeline/decades/1950/artifact/2343.html.

4. Alex Planes, "How Walmart Became the World's Biggest Retailer," *Motley Fool*, July 2, 2013, https://www.fool.com/investing/general/2013/07/02/how-wal-mart-became-the-worlds-biggest-retailer.aspx.

5. "Walmart Q4 FY22 Earnings Release," Walmart Corporation, February 17, 2022, https://corporate.walmart.com/media-library/document/q4-fy22-earnings-release/_proxyDocument?id=0000017f-0521-deb8-ab7f-372d1d5a0000#:~:text=Total%20revenue%20was%20%24572.8%20billion,on%20a%20two%2Dyear%20stack.

6. Matt Waller, "How Sharing Data Drives Supply Chain Innovation," *Industry Week*, August 12, 2013, https://www.industryweek.com/supply-chain/supplier-relationships/article/21960963/how-sharing-data-drives-supply-chain-innovation.

7. Nathaniel Meyersohn, "Walmart Just Boosted Pay to $15. It's Not What You Think," *CNN*, February 18, 2021, https://www.cnn.com/2021/02/18/investing/walmart-minimum-wage-retail/index.html.

8. "NC Walmart Employees Strike for Higher Wages on Black Friday," *Charlotte Observer*, November 26, 2021, https://www.charlotteobserver.com/news/business/article256140907.html.

9. "NC Walmart Employees Strike."

10. Christina Cheddar-Berk and Krystina Gustafson. "Walmart to Buy Jet.com in $3.3 Billion Deal," *CNBC*, August 8, 2016, https://www.cnbc.com/2016/08/08/wal-mart-to-by-jetcom-in-3-billion-deal.html.

11. Daniel Keyes, "Walmart's US e-Commerce Sales Hit 97% Annual Growth in Its Most Recent Quarter," *Business Insider*, August 19, 2020, https://www.businessinsider.com/walmart-ecommerce-sales-reach-sky-high-growth-in-recent-quarter-2020-8.

12. Ben Unglesbee, "Walmart Cuts Corporate Jobs as It Focuses on Omnichannel Push," *Retail Dive*, July 31, 2020, https://www.retaildive.com/news/walmart-cuts-corporate-jobs-as-it-focuses-on-omnichannel-push/582691/.

13. Stephen McBride, "Walmart Has Made a Genius Move to Beat Amazon," *ETF Trends*, January 18, 2020, https://www.etftrends.com/disruptive-technology-channel/walmart-has-made-a-genius-move-to-beat-amazon.

14. McBride.

15. Paddy Baker, "Alibaba on Track to Be the Largest Blockchain Patent Holder by End of 2020: Study," *Coindesk*, September 17, 2020, https://www.coindesk.com/alibaba-blockchain-patents.

16. "The Future of Global e-Commerce," *Economist*, January 2, 2021, 7.

17. Chris Dunne, "Amazon Versus Alibaba—Who Is Winning?" *Repriceexpress*, September 24, 2020, https://www.repricerexpress.com/amazon-vs-alibaba-winning/.

18. Dunne.

19. "The Great Mall of China," *Economist*, January 2, 2021, 47.

20. "The Great Mall of China."

Chapter 7. The Platform for Transformation

1. Gigi Sohn, "How to Make Broadband Affordable and Accessible to Everyone," CNN, September 10, 2020, https://www.cnn.com/2020/09/09/perspectives/broadband-internet-affordable-accessible/index.html.

2. "Internet/Broadband Fact Sheet," Pew Research Center, June 12, 2019, https://www.pew research.org/internet/fact-sheet/internet-broadband/.

3. Drew Desilver, "US Students' Academic Achievement Still Lags That of Their Peers in Many Other Countries," Pew Research Center, February 15, 2017, https://www.pewre search.org/fact-tank/2017/02/15/u-s-students-internationally-math-science/.

4. Desilver.

5. Matt Barnum, "The Pandemic's Toll: National Test Scores Show Progress Slowed, Gaps Widened," *Chalkbeat*, July 28, 2021, https://www.chalkbeat.org/2021/7/28/22596904 /pandemic-covid-school-learning-loss-nwea-mckinsey.

6. Amaury Laporte, "Fact Sheet: Fossil Fuel Subsidies: A Closer Look at Tax Breaks and Societal Costs," Environmental and Energy Study Institute, July 29, 2019, https://www .eesi.org/papers/view/fact-sheet-fossil-fuel-subsidies-a-closer-look-at-tax-breaks-and-soci etal-costs.

7. Kimberley Amadeo, "Farm Subsidies with Pros, Cons, and Impact," *The Balance*, June 29, 2020, https://www.thebalance.com/farm-subsidies-4173885.

SELECTED BIBLIOGRAPHY

Bogle, John. *Battle for the Soul of Capitalism*. New Haven, CT: Yale University Press, 2008.

Brynjolfsson, Erik, and Andrew McAfee. *Race against the Machine: How the Digital Revolution Is Accelerating Innovation, Driving Productivity, and Irreversibly Transforming Employment and the Economy*. Lexington, MA: Digital Frontier Press, 2012.

Buffington, Jack. *An Easy Out: Corporate America's Addiction to Outsourcing*. Westport, CT: Praeger, 2007.

Chang, Ha-Joon. *Bad Samaritans: The Myth of Free Trade and the Secret History of Capitalism*. New York: Bloomsbury, 2009.

Deming, W. Edwards. *Out of the Crisis*. 2nd ed. Boston: MIT Press, 1986.

Drucker, Peter. *Post-Capitalist Society*. New York: Harper Business, 1993.

Friedman, Thomas. *The World Is Flat: A Brief History of the 21st Century*. New York: Farrar, Straus and Giroux, 2007.

Graeber, David, and Elise Roy. *Bullshit Jobs: A Theory*. New York: Simon and Schuster, 2018.

Mahbubani, Kishore. *Can Asians Think? Understanding the Divide between East and West*. Hanover, NH: Steerforth, 2002.

Packard, Vance. *The Waste Makers*. Brooklyn: Ig Publishing, 1988.

Packer, George. *The Unwinding: Thirty Years of American Decline*. London: Vintage, 2013.

Pinker, Steven. *The Better Angels of Our Nature: Why Violence Has Declined*. New York: Penguin Books, 2012.

Sandel, Michael. *The Tyranny of Merit: What's Become of the Common Good?* New York: Farrar, Straus and Giroux, 2020.

Schwartz, Barry. *The Paradox of Choice*. New York: HarperCollins, 2003.

Steingart, Gabor. *The War for Wealth*. New York: McGraw-Hill Professional, 2008.

Taylor, Frederick Winslow. *The Principles of Scientific Management*. New York: Productivity Press, 2017. First published 1911 by Harper & Brothers.

INDEX

accessibility. *See* equal access
Alibaba, 70, 125–26, 138
Amazon, 38–40, 58–60, 65, 69: business model, 39, 58, 120; distribution, 103, 123–24; history, 121–22; predictive analytics, 6
American Dream, 13, 17–18, 35, 46, 56, 57, 68, 87, 119, 139
American Silk Road, 81–84, 87, 101
An Easy Out (Jack Buffington), 24–25, 30, 63
Ant Group, 43, 70
Apple, 58

Baltimore, Maryland, 34–35, 86–87, 91–92, 103–6, 116
Bernays, Edward, 19–21, 60. *See also* "engineering consent," marketing
Big Data, 59, 69–70, 120
Big Tech, 58–65, 69, 107
blockchain technology, 69–71, 73, 87–89, 92, 103–4, 125–27, 131–32, 134–35
blue-collar workforce, 5, 12, 23–25, 29, 38, 56–57, 67, 82, 89, 114
Bogle, John, 22
broadband technology, 59, 82, 85–86, 90, 105, 132, 133–35

capitalism, 10, 13, 17–18, 28, 56, 60, 68, 96, 104; China and, 43–44, 99–100, 114; loss of confidence in, 33–34; new model for, 82–83, 92, 112, 127. *See also* surveillance capitalism
Chang, Ha-Joon, 28
China: Belt and Road Initiative (BRI), 49–50, 81–82, 138; capitalism, 43–44, 99–101; challenges to, 45–46; deindustrialization in, 45; domestic issues, 32, 44; dual circulation, 99–101; economy, 40–45; "Made in China," 48, 77; suppliers 6–7; Vision 2035, 89; as world's factory, 27, 94
citizens, 6, 7, 65, 96: investment in, 84, 86–87, 102, 137; as nodes, 66, 74, 132; as workers vs. consumer, 54, 121
community-based supply chain; concept, 130–31; defined, 67–68; logistics, 105–12
consumer, 18–19, 37, 56, 101–4, 115, 119; -based economy, 28, 30; data and, 58–60, 65; as nodes, 65–67; prosumer, 72; sustainability and, 112; vs. worker, 39, 54, 67, 121. *See also* citizens
consumerism: advent, 17–18; economy, 16, 27, 28–29, 118–19; Packard on, 21
containerization, 26, 37, 103
COVID-19 pandemic, 8, 31, 76; assessment, 52–53; economic impacts, 2–3, 33, 125, 129; mask supply chain, 42; new normal, 97–98; vaccines, 42, 104–5
creative destruction, 38–39
credit cards, 118

data, 24, 59, 62, 98, 119–20, 131; from consumer, 60, 65; as "New Oil," 69–71. *See also* Big Data
deindustrialization, 3–6, 13, 23–25, 26, 35–38, 53, 56–57, 82; Drucker on, 29
delivery mechanisms, 2, 19
demand chain, 18–19, 28, 47, 67, 74, 118–19; Demand Chain 2.0, 128
Deming, W. Edwards, 4–5, 23–24, 50, 63, 92. *See also* Toyota Production System (TPS)
department stores, 26, 117–19
digital divide, 66, 80–85, 125, 131, 133

ABOUT THE AUTHOR

Jack Buffington is the program director and a professor of supply chain management at the University of Denver and director of supply chain and sustainability practices at First Key Consulting, the world's leading beer industry consulting firm. He has held numerous leadership positions in supply chain, operations, and information technology at Molson Coors Brewing Company, one of the largest beer manufacturers in the world. Jack was a postdoctoral researcher at the Royal Institute of Technology in Stockholm, Sweden, and Lulea University of Technology in Lulea, Sweden. He is the author of several previous books, including *The Recycling Myth: Disruptive Innovation to Improve the Environment* (2015) and *Peak Plastic: The Rise or Fall of Our Synthetic World* (2018).